Data Science Crash Course

Statistical mathematics, advanced data analysis, and computational techniques for insightful decision making

Dr. Deepti Chopra

www.bpbonline.com

First Edition 2026

ISBN: 978-93-65898-958

LIMITS OF LIABILITY AND DISCLAIMER OF WARRANTY

The information contained in this book is true and correct to the best of author's and publisher's knowledge. The author has made every effort to ensure the accuracy of these publications, but the publisher cannot be held responsible for any loss or damage arising from any information in this book.

All trademarks referred to in the book are acknowledged as properties of their respective owners but BPB Publications cannot guarantee the accuracy of this information.

Distributors:

BPB PUBLICATIONS
20, Ansari Road, Darya Ganj
New Delhi-110002
Ph: 23254990/23254991

DECCAN AGENCIES
4-3-329, Bank Street,
Hyderabad-500195
Ph: 24756967/24756400

MICRO MEDIA
Shop No. 5, Mahendra Chambers,
150 DN Rd. Next to Capital Cinema,
V.T. (C.S.T.) Station, MUMBAI-400 001
Ph: 22078296/22078297

To View Complete BPB Publications Catalogue Scan the QR Code:

Published by Manish Jain for BPB Publications, 20 Ansari Road, Darya Ganj, New Delhi-110002 and Printed by him at Repro India Ltd., Rewari.

www.bpbonline.com

Dedicated to

My family and friends

About the Author

Dr. Deepti Chopra is an accomplished academician specializing in information technology, with a primary focus on **natural language processing** (**NLP**) and **artificial intelligence** (**AI**). With over 10.5 years of experience in academia, she has made significant contributions to both research and teaching domains. Deepti's expertise lies in areas such as machine translation, named entity recognition, morphological analysis, and machine transliteration.

Deepti began her academic journey by obtaining a bachelor's degree in computer science and engineering from Rajasthan College of Engineering for Women. Throughout her undergraduate studies, she consistently excelled and secured top positions in her college. Driven by her passion for language and technology, she pursued a master's degree in computer science and engineering from Banasthali Vidyapith, where she once again showcased exceptional skills and graduated with top honors.

Motivated to delve deeper into her research interests, Deepti pursued a Ph.D. in computer science and engineering from Banasthali Vidyapith. Her doctoral research revolved around enhancing the quality of machine translation, and she achieved remarkable success in this area. Consequently, she earned a Ph.D. degree with a specialization in quality improvement of machine translation. Her doctoral work resulted in the publication of numerous research papers and the grant of an Australian patent for her innovative approach in named entity translation.

Deepti's commitment to advancing knowledge in her field is reflected in her extensive publication record. She has authored multiple books, most notably *Building Machine Learning Systems using Python* and *Flutter and Dart: Up and Running*. Additionally, her research papers have been published in reputable international conferences and journals.

Deepti's commitment and her ability to apply research findings to practical solutions solidify her position as a prominent figure in the field.

About the Reviewers

- **Peeyush Maharshi** is a technology leader and enterprise architect specializing in data modernization and AI transformation. He focuses on the convergence of analytics and AI, implementing semantic analytical mesh architectures and agentic engineering frameworks to deliver measurable business outcomes.

  Peeyush provides strategic leadership in building AI-ready enterprise data products, establishing data governance frameworks for responsible AI, and accelerating AI adoption through cloud-native architectures on AWS, Azure, and GCP. His expertise spans generative AI and LLM solutions, including work with OpenAI, Anthropic, and Hugging Face-alongside big data analytics, NLP, machine learning, and IoT implementations.

  He specializes in defining enterprise data strategies that incorporate data lakes, data fabrics, and data marts while establishing robust data governance to enhance organizational data maturity. Peeyush has led large-scale modernization initiatives, including cloud migrations, containerization, monolith-to-microservices transformations, cognitive automation, various flavors of RAG implementations, and agentic AI deployments for clients across the USA, Europe, the Middle East, and Australia.

  His approach combines strategic planning with hands-on technical leadership, defining transformation roadmaps that bridge business objectives with cutting-edge technology solutions through reference architectures, engineering standards, and best practices.

  A dedicated contributor to the technical community, Peeyush has served as a technical reviewer for several prominent books on Java, enterprise architecture, data, and cloud technologies. He actively participates in technical groups to share his expertise and support the next generation of technologists.

- **Kris Erickson** is a data scientist with The Home Depot, America's largest home improvement retailer. He is currently focused on the GCP stack, with special emphasis on BigQuery, Dataform, and applying Gemini Flash to the data via SQL. Kris is an active reader of science fiction. He also writes under the pen name *Eric Kay* and has recently published a fiction novel called *Above Dark Waters* about the intersection of AI therapy, brain privacy, and GenAI.

Acknowledgement

I would like to express my sincere gratitude to my family for their constant encouragement, patience, and unwavering support throughout the journey of writing this book. Their belief in my work has been my greatest source of motivation and strength.

I am deeply thankful to the publishing team for their guidance, professionalism, and dedication in bringing this book to completion. The process of conceptualizing, structuring, revising, and refining this manuscript has been a collaborative effort, enriched by the valuable insights of reviewers, technical experts, and editors whose suggestions significantly enhanced the quality and clarity of this book.

I would also like to acknowledge my colleagues, research collaborators, and academic peers who have contributed, directly and indirectly, through discussions, feedback, and shared experiences in the fields of data science, machine learning, and analytics. Their expertise and perspectives have greatly shaped the content and practical orientation of this crash course.

Finally, I extend my heartfelt appreciation to all students, professionals, and readers who continue to explore and apply data science in meaningful ways. Your curiosity, enthusiasm, and commitment to learning inspire authors like me to create structured, accessible, and impactful learning resources.

This book is dedicated to every learner striving to transform data into knowledge and insight into innovation.

Preface

Data is everywhere these days : in businesses, healthcare, education, research, and even in our daily lives. The book on data science and crash course was written to help readers build useful insights from data.

This book is designed for both beginners stepping into data science for the first time and professionals who wish to strengthen their foundations. It blends core concepts of statistics and mathematics with hands-on tools like Python, NumPy, Pandas, Matplotlib, and other essential libraries. From understanding structured and unstructured data to cleaning, analyzing, and visualizing datasets, the book walks through the complete data analysis process in a simple and approachable manner.

You will explore key ideas such as data preprocessing, visualization, supervised and unsupervised learning, predictive analysis, and even advanced topics like recommender systems, all supported with practical examples and exercises. Special emphasis is given to Python and its role in modern data analysis.

This book comprises of the following chapters:

Chapter 1: Introduction to Data Science — This chapter provides an overview of data science, tracing its history and evolution, and emphasizing its importance in various fields. It sets the stage for the rest of the book by explaining the scope and workflow of data science.

Chapter 2: Roles and Responsibilities of a Data Scientist — This chapter delves into the various roles within the data science field, highlighting the responsibilities and skills required for each position. It also discusses career pathways and offers a case study for practical understanding.

Chapter 3: The Necessity of Python in Data Science — This chapter explains why Python is the preferred language for data science, comparing it with other programming languages. It also covers the setup of the Python environment and introduces essential libraries.

Chapter 4: Introduction to Data Understanding — This chapter focuses on understanding different types of data and the importance of domain knowledge. It also covers various tools and techniques for data exploration.

Chapter 5: Data Preprocessing — This chapter covers the essential steps of data preprocessing, including cleaning, transformation, and feature engineering. It also introduces various tools and libraries used for preprocessing.

Chapter 6: Creating Synthetic Datasets in MS Excel — This chapter explains the importance of synthetic data and provides a step-by-step guide to creating synthetic datasets using MS Excel.

Chapter 7: Basics of Python Programming — This chapter introduces the fundamentals of Python programming, including syntax, variables, control structures, and functions.

Chapter 8: Working with Python Data Structures — This chapter covers Python's core data structures, including lists, tuples, dictionaries, and sets, and explains how to manipulate these structures.

Chapter 9: Data Analysis Process — This chapter outlines the steps involved in the data analysis process, from data collection to exploratory data analysis.

Chapter 10: Essential Python Libraries for Data Science — This chapter introduces essential Python libraries used in data science, including NumPy, Pandas, Matplotlib, and SciPy, with practical examples.

Chapter 11: Data Processing and Visualization — This chapter covers data processing techniques and introduces various tools for data visualization, including basic and advanced tools.

Chapter 12: Mathematical and Scientific Applications — This chapter focuses on the mathematical foundations and scientific applications of data science, including supervised and unsupervised learning techniques.

Chapter 13: Developing Recommender Systems — This chapter provides a comprehensive guide to building recommender systems, from basic concepts to advanced techniques and practical applications.

Chapter 14: Real-world Applications and Case Studies — This chapter explores various real-world applications of data science through detailed case studies, highlighting the practical use of data science techniques in different industries.

Chapter 15: Practical Examples and Exercises — This chapter provides hands-on projects and exercises to reinforce the concepts learned throughout the book, helping readers build a solid portfolio of data science projects.

Code Bundle and Coloured Images

Please follow the link to download the
Code Bundle and the ***Coloured Images*** of the book:

https://rebrand.ly/hc1i1nv

The code bundle for the book is also hosted on GitHub at
https://github.com/bpbpublications/Data-Science-Crash-Course.
In case there's an update to the code, it will be updated on the existing GitHub repository.

We have code bundles from our rich catalogue of books and videos available at **https://github.com/bpbpublications.** Check them out!

Errata

We take immense pride in our work at BPB Publications and follow best practices to ensure the accuracy of our content to provide an indulging reading experience to our subscribers. Our readers are our mirrors, and we use their inputs to reflect and improve upon human errors, if any, that may have occurred during the publishing processes involved. To let us maintain the quality and help us reach out to any readers who might be having difficulties due to any unforeseen errors, please write to us at: **errata@bpbonline.com**

Your support, suggestions and feedback are highly appreciated by the BPB Publications' Family.

Piracy

If you come across any illegal copies of our works in any form on the internet, we would be grateful if you would provide us with the location address or website name. Please contact us at **business@bpbonline.com** with a link to the material.

If you are interested in becoming an author

If there is a topic that you have expertise in, and you are interested in either writing or contributing to a book, please visit **www.bpbonline.com**. We have worked with thousands of developers and tech professionals, just like you, to help them share their insights with the global tech community. You can make a general application, apply for a specific hot topic that we are recruiting an author for, or submit your own idea.

Reviews

Please leave a review. Once you have read and used this book, why not leave a review on the site that you purchased it from? Potential readers can then see and use your unbiased opinion to make purchase decisions. We at BPB can understand what you think about our products, and our authors can see your feedback on their book. Thank you!

For more information about BPB, please visit **www.bpbonline.com**.

Join our Discord space

Join our Discord workspace for latest updates, offers, tech happenings around the world, new releases, and sessions with the authors:

https://discord.bpbonline.com

Table of Contents

CHAPTER 1
Introduction to Data Science

Introduction

Data science is a pioneering field that involves combining fields such as statistics, computer science, and domain-specific knowledge to extract meaningful insights from data. In today's era, a huge amount of data exists in different scenarios; hence, it is conducive to perform analytics on such data to derive useful information and make informed decisions.

This chapter discusses the history, evolution, and foundation of data science, giving a clear definition and key concepts used in it. It explores various fields that embody data science and how various problems may be solved and analyzed using it. We will also be looking at key figures who have contributed to the development of data science. Further we will discuss diverse application areas of data science and its impact on various sectors.

Data science involves various processes, such as data collection, data processing, data analysis and modeling, and the interpretation of results. This chapter will address some of the key challenges faced in data science today. Issues such as data quality, ethical considerations, and the scalability and performance of data systems are crucial to the successful implementation of data science initiatives.

By the end of this chapter, you will get the knowledge on basics of data science that serve as foundation for the more detailed and technical discussions that follow in subsequent chapters.

Structure

This chapter covers the following topics:

- Understanding data science
- History and evolution of data science
- Importance of data science in modern business
- Overview of data science workflow
- Key challenges in data science

Objectives

By the end of this chapter, you will be familiar with the basics of data science that serve as the foundation for more detailed and technical discussions that follow in subsequent chapters. This chapter aims to establish a solid understanding of the fundamental concepts of data science and to provide a comprehensive understanding of its importance in the modern world. Hence, after reading this chapter, you will be able to clearly understand data science and the various fields where it is applicable. This chapter details the history of data science, key figures in this field, and how this field has evolved and arrived at the current state where innovation meets various industries.

This chapter gives information about data science workflow, which includes number of steps followed while converting the raw text meaningful insights. At last, it addresses the challenges that are a part and parcel of data science, such as ensuring data quality, navigating ethical considerations, and managing the scalability and performance of data systems.

Understanding data science

Data science may be defined as the study of the extraction of meaningful information and knowledge from structured as well as unstructured data. It is an interdisciplinary field that utilizes techniques from various fields to analyze, process, and infer meaningful information from a raw text. Data scientists make use of different tools and techniques for the purpose of data analysis, such as statistical analysis, **machine learning** (**ML**), predictive modeling, etc.

Definition and key concepts

Data science is a multidisciplinary field that combines statistical methods, computational algorithms, and domain-specific knowledge to extract meaningful insights, patterns, and knowledge from both structured and unstructured data. It involves tasks such as, data collection and processing to analysis, modeling, and interpretation, ultimately transforming raw data into actionable intelligence.

Here are some key concepts:

- **Data collection**: It is a process of gathering data from various sources, which can include databases, sensors, social media, or web scraping. Effective data collection is crucial for ensuring the quality and relevance of the data used in the analysis.
- **Data cleaning**: After data collection, data is cleaned and preprocessed. This involves handling missing data, removing duplicates, correcting errors, and standardizing formats to ensure the data is accurate and ready for analysis.
- **Exploratory data analysis (EDA)**: It is the initial step in data analysis, where data scientists explore data's underlying structure, identify patterns, and generate

hypotheses. Techniques like summary statistics, visualizations, and correlation analysis are commonly used during this phase.

- **Statistical analysis**: It comprises applications for analyzing and interpreting data. This includes descriptive statistics (mean, median, mode), inferential statistics (hypothesis testing, regression analysis), and probabilistic models.
- **Data visualization**: It involves the use of visual tools like charts, graphs, and dashboards to represent data and findings in a way that is easy to understand and interpret. Effective visualization helps communicate insights and supports data-driven decision-making.
- **Predictive modeling**: This involves predicting future outcomes based on historical data. It is widely used in various applications, such as forecasting sales, predicting customer behavior, or identifying potential risks.

Interdisciplinary nature of data science

Data science is an interdisciplinary field that involves binding elements from various fields to tackle complex problems and generate useful insights from data.

The interdisciplinary nature of data science can be understood through its integration of knowledge and techniques from several key areas:

- **Statistics and mathematics**: Data science makes use of statistical methods and mathematical principles. Statistics provides the tools for understanding data distributions, estimating relationships, testing hypotheses, and making predictions. Mathematical concepts, such as linear algebra, calculus, and probability theory, are essential for developing and understanding models, algorithms, and data processing techniques.
- **Computer science and programming**: To excel in the field of data science, it is important to have good knowledge of algorithms, data structures, and software engineering. Programming skills are crucial for implementing data analysis, building ML models, and automating processes. Languages such as Python, R, and SQL are commonly used in data science for data manipulation, statistical analysis, and database management.
- **ML and artificial intelligence (AI)**: ML and AI are important components of data science that enable the development of algorithms that can learn from data and make predictions or decisions. These fields assist in design of algorithms that can process and learn from large datasets.
- **Data visualization**: With the help of data visualization, data scientists are able to present the complex data in the form of charts, graphs or interactive dashboards that makes it easy to understand. It helps in conveying the findings more clearly to stakeholders from non-technical backgrounds leading to better and informed decision-making process.

- **Ethics and social sciences**: The ethical implications of data science practices are conducive as data becomes more comprehensive in society. Ethical considerations include issues such as data privacy, consent, bias in algorithms, and the social impact of data-driven decisions. While working on data science, we should make sure that data science practices align with societal values and legal frameworks.
- **Operations research and business intelligence (BI)**: In the context of business, data science makes use of operations research and BI. Operations research is based on optimizing processes and decision-making within organizations. These fields help in improving operational efficiency, optimize resource allocation, and develop strategies that enhance business performance.

History and evolution of data science

The evolution of data science can be traced back to late 19th and early 20th centuries when statistics came into being. Pioneers like *Karl Pearson*, who developed the correlation coefficient, and *Ronald A. Fisher*, who laid the base for modern statistical methods with his work on experimental design and analysis of variance, were instrumental in introducing the mathematical tools required for data analysis. In the mid-20th century, *John Tukey*'s seminal work, EDA (1977), showcased the importance of exploring data to uncover underlying patterns and relationships. Tukey's approach laid the groundwork for modern data analysis techniques, which are now a core component of data science.

The emergence of computers in the mid-20th century marked a significant turning point in the evolution of data science. The development of electronic computers in the 1940s and 1950s enabled the processing of large datasets. Early computer scientists like *Alan Turing* and *John von Neumann* made critical contributions to the development of algorithms and computing theory, which are essential for data processing and analysis.

During the 1960s and 1970s, the field of computer science expanded rapidly with the development of **database management systems** (**DBMSs**) that allowed for efficient storage, retrieval, and manipulation of data. The creation of relational databases by *Edgar Codd* in the 1970s revolutionized the way data was organized and accessed, laying the foundation for modern data management practices.

Researchers like *Geoffrey Hinton, Yann LeCun, and Andrew Ng* made significant achievement by developing algorithms that could learn from data, leading to the creation of neural networks and other ML models. These models enabled computers to perform tasks such as image recognition, **natural language processing** (**NLP**), and predictive analytics, which are now integral to data science.

The 1990s saw the rise of data mining, a field focused on discovering patterns in large datasets. Techniques such as decision trees, clustering, and association rule learning became popular for extracting knowledge from data. Data mining laid the groundwork for the predictive modeling techniques that are now commonplace in data science.

Now, let us look at the birth of data science. The term began to gain importance in the early 2000s, when the proliferation of data lead to new opportunities and challenges.

In 2010s, the explosion of big data, was characterized by the three Vs: volume, velocity, and variety. The rapid growth of social media, mobile devices, and the **Internet of Things** (**IoT**) contributed to the generation of massive datasets. To manage and analyze this data, new technologies such as Hadoop and Spark were developed, that could perform the task of distributed computing and parallel processing.

Milestones in the development of data science

The development of data science is accompanied by several key milestones. These significant milestones include the following:

- **Birth of statistics:** The origins of data science was the result of development of statistical methods, which provided the mathematical foundation for data analysis. In the 17th century, *John Graunt* used statistical methods to analyze mortality rates. In the 19th century, *Carl Friedrich Gauss* introduced the method of least squares, which is important in regression analysis. The establishment of probability theory by *Pierre-Simon Laplace* led to advancement of mathematical tools that are available for analyzing data.

- **The advent of computing**: The invention of electronic computers in the 1940s revolutionized data processing. The development of the first computers, such as **Electronic Numerical Integrator and Computer** (**ENIAC**), enabled the automation of complex calculations, making it possible to handle large datasets. This period also saw the emergence of algorithms and computer science principles that would later become integral to data science.

- **Development of relational databases**: In 1970s relational databases was introduced by *Edgar Codd.* Codd's relational model for DBMS allowed for efficient storage, retrieval, and management of data. The **Structured Query Language** (**SQL**), developed shortly thereafter, became the standard for managing and querying relational databases, dramatically improving the ability to handle and analyze structured data.

- **The emergence of data mining**: Data mining emerged in the 1980s and 1990s as a field focused on discovering patterns and knowledge from large datasets. Techniques such as clustering, decision trees, and association rules were developed during this period, enabling more sophisticated analysis of data. This era also saw the rise of **business intelligence** (**BI**) tools, which began to automate the process of data analysis for decision-making. The **Cross-Industry Standard Process for Data Mining** (**CRISP-DM**) methodology was developed in the 1990s as a standard approach to data mining.

- **The birth of the term data science**: The term data science was popularized in the early 2000s, although it had been used informally before.

- **The rise of big data**: In the 2000s and 2010s, there was an explosion in the volume, variety, and velocity of data, often referred to as big data. It led to the development of new technologies such as Hadoop (2006) and Apache Spark (2014) for distributed data processing. Big data technologies enabled organizations to store, process, and analyze large datasets. The concept of data lakes also emerged to help in the storage of vast amounts of unstructured and structured data in a single repository.
- **Advancements in ML and AI**: AI and ML have become central to data science, with significant advancements in the 2010s. The development of deep learning, along with neural networks with many layers, allowed computers to achieve human-like performance in tasks such as image recognition, NLP, and autonomous driving. The creation of deep learning frameworks like TensorFlow (2015) and PyTorch (2016) has made it easier for data scientists to build and deploy ML models.
- **Democratization of data science tools**: Open-source programming languages like Python and R, along with libraries like Pandas, NumPy, and scikit-learn, became the standard tools for data scientists. The rise of cloud computing platforms like *AWS*, *Google Cloud*, and *Microsoft Azure* further facilitated access to powerful computing resources, enabling data scientists to work with large datasets and complex models.
- **Ethical and regulatory considerations**: As data science has become more popular in business and society, ethical and regulatory considerations have gained prominence. The introduction of regulations like the **General Data Protection Regulation** (**GDPR**) in 2018 highlighted the importance of privacy, data protection, and responsible data usage. Ethical concerns around bias in algorithms, data privacy, and the social impact of AI have prompted the development of guidelines and frameworks to ensure that data science is practiced responsibly.

Key figures and breakthroughs

The field of data science has been shaped by the contributions of numerous key figures and breakthroughs that have advanced the discipline. From early pioneers in statistics to modern innovators in ML and AI, these individuals and their work have been instrumental in the evolution of data science. Here are some of the most notable figures and their contributions:

- **John Tukey**: Tukey was an American statistician who is credited with coining the term data analysis. His book, *Exploratory Data Analysis* (1977), introduced techniques for understanding data before formal modeling or hypothesis testing. Tukey emphasized visual methods, such as box plots and stem-and-leaf plots, which are still widely used today. His approach laid the groundwork for modern data analysis techniques that focus on extracting patterns and insights directly from the data.
- **Ronald A. Fisher**: Fisher, an English statistician and geneticist, is considered as one of the founders of modern statistical science. His work in the early 20th century, particularly in the development of **analysis of variance** (**ANOVA**) and maximum

likelihood estimation, provided essential tools for analyzing and interpreting data. Fisher's principles of experimental design, including randomization and replication, remain fundamental to conducting scientifically rigorous studies and data analysis.

- **Edgar F. Codd**: Codd, an English computer scientist working at *IBM*, revolutionized data management with his development of the relational database model in the 1970s. His work laid the foundation for the structured organization and retrieval of data, which became the backbone of modern database systems. The introduction of SQL, based on Codd's model, transformed how data could be managed and accessed, enabling more sophisticated data analysis.
- **Geoffrey Hinton**: Hinton a British-Canadian cognitive psychologist and computer scientist, is widely recognized as one of the *godfathers* of deep learning. His research on artificial neural networks, particularly the backpropagation algorithm, has been fundamental to the development of deep learning.
- **Yann LeCun**: LeCun, a French computer scientist, made pioneering contributions to the development of **convolutional neural networks** (**CNNs**), which are specialized for processing grid-like data such as images. His work on CNNs has been instrumental in advancing the field of computer vision, enabling significant progress in tasks such as image recognition, object detection, and image segmentation. CNNs are now a cornerstone of deep learning applications in various domains.
- **Andrew Ng**: Andrew Ng, a Chinese-American computer scientist, is known for his work in AI, ML and online education. He co-founded Google Brain and led the development of **massive open online courses** (**MOOCs**).
- **DJ Patil and Jeff Hammerbacher**: DJ Patil and Jeff Hammerbacher, working at *LinkedIn* and *Facebook* respectively, recognized the need for a new domain that combined statistical analysis, programming skills, and domain expertise to extract actionable insights from large datasets.
- **Doug Cutting and Mike Cafarella:** Doug Cutting and Cafarella created Hadoop (in 2006) and big data technologies. Hadoop enabled the processing of vast amounts of data across distributed computer clusters, making it possible to analyze datasets that were too large for traditional systems.

Importance of data science in modern business

In today's rapidly evolving business landscape, data science has emerged as a critical tool for companies seeking to gain a competitive edge. Importance of data science in business include the following:

- **Enhanced decision-making**: Companies generate massive amounts of data daily, from customer interactions to operational metrics. Data science helps extract useful data, identify patterns, and make informed decisions. Predictive analytics help predict future trends, customer behaviors, and market shifts, enabling proactive decision-making.

- **Personalized customer experiences**: Data science plays an important role in understanding customer preferences and behaviors, allowing businesses to deliver personalized experiences.
- **Operational efficiency and cost reduction**: Data science helps optimize business operations and reduce costs. Through techniques like process mining, companies can analyze and improve their internal workflows, identify bottlenecks, and streamline operations. Predictive maintenance helps to identify equipment failures before they occur, reducing downtime and maintenance costs. Supply chain optimization helps companies manage inventory more effectively, reducing waste and ensuring that resources are allocated efficiently.
- **Risk management and fraud detection**: In industries like finance, insurance, and cybersecurity, data science is essential for managing risk and detecting fraud. Advanced ML algorithms can analyze transaction data in real-time to identify suspicious activities, such as fraudulent transactions or security breaches.
- **Innovation and product development**: By analyzing market trends, customer feedback, and competitor activities, businesses can identify gaps in the market and opportunities for innovation. Data-driven insights help in product development process, from initial concept to launch, ensuring that new offerings meet customer needs and stand out in the market.
- **Marketing and sales optimization**: Marketing and sales departments heavily rely on data science to optimize their strategies and maximize ROI. Data science is used in marketing and sales to segment audiences, personalize campaigns, and forecast sales.
- **Improved customer retention**: Customer retention is important for long-term business success. By analyzing customer behavior and engagement metrics, businesses can identify early warning signs of churn and take corrective action. Data science also enables companies to develop targeted retention strategies, such as personalized offers and loyalty programs, that help retain customers.
- **Competitive advantage**: Data science enables businesses to differentiate themselves by offering unique, data-driven insights or services that competitors cannot easily replicate. As industries become more competitive, the ability to leverage data science will increasingly determine which companies thrive and which fall behind. Modern BI platforms powered by data science help in providing real-time insights, predictive analytics, and interactive dashboards that help decision-makers at different levels of the organization.
- **Scalability and growth**: Data science tools and techniques, such as big data analytics and cloud computing, allow businesses to process and analyze large datasets efficiently, resulting in long-term growth, success, and sustainability.

Applications in different industries

Data science has varied applications in different sectors. These include:

- **Healthcare**: Data science can help in providing personalized medicine and treatment based on patients' genetic profiles, lifestyles, and medical histories. ML models analyze large datasets of patient information to identify patterns and predict the most effective treatments for specific conditions.

  Predictive analytics can be used to foresee patient outcomes, manage chronic diseases, and reduce hospital readmissions. Data science techniques, particularly deep learning, are applied in medical imaging to improve the accuracy of diagnoses. Algorithms can detect abnormalities in x-rays, MRIs, and CT scans with high precision, assisting radiologists in identifying diseases like cancer at earlier stages.

- **Finance and banking**: Financial institutions use data science and ML to detect fraudulent transactions in real-time. Data science is used in algorithmic trading, where automated trading systems use complex algorithms to execute trades at high speeds based on market data.

- **Retail and e-commerce**: Online retailers like *Amazon* and streaming services like *Netflix* use recommendation systems to suggest products and content to users based on their browsing and purchasing history. These personalized recommendations help in enhancing user experience and drive sales. Retailers use data science to optimize inventory management by predicting demand for products.

- **Manufacturing**: In manufacturing, data science is used for predictive maintenance, where ML models analyze data from equipment sensors to predict when a machine is likely to fail. This allows companies to perform maintenance before a breakdown occurs, reducing downtime and repair costs.

  Data science techniques are applied in quality control to monitor production processes and detect defects in real-time. By analyzing data from sensors and production lines, manufacturers can identify anomalies and address issues before they affect product quality. Manufacturers use data science to optimize their supply chains, from demand forecasting to inventory management.

- **Telecommunications**: These companies use data science to predict customer churn by analyzing customer behavior, service usage, and feedback. Data science helps telecom companies optimize their networks by analyzing data on network traffic, signal strength, and usage patterns. Telecom companies apply data science to detect and prevent fraud, such as unauthorized SIM card usage or subscription fraud. ML models can identify suspicious patterns in usage data and fraudulent activities.

- **Energy and utilities**: Data science is used in the management of smart grids, where data from sensors and meters is analyzed to optimize energy distribution. Predictive analytics can forecast energy demand, helping utilities balance supply and demand more effectively. Accurate forecasting allows for better integration of renewable energy into the grid, reducing reliance on fossil fuels.

- **Transportation and logistics**: In logistics, data science is used to optimize delivery routes by analyzing traffic data, weather conditions, and delivery schedules. This optimization reduces fuel consumption, lowers costs, and improves delivery times.
- **Media and entertainment**: Media companies use data science to understand audience preferences, viewing patterns, and content performance. Data science enables media companies to optimize their advertising strategies by analyzing audience demographics, behavior, and preferences. Targeted advertising campaigns can be created to reach the right audience at the right time, improving ROI.
- **Agriculture**: Data science is transforming agriculture through precision farming, where data from sensors, drones, and satellite imagery is used to optimize crop yields. Farmers can make data-driven decisions on irrigation, fertilization, and pest control, leading to more efficient and sustainable farming practices.
- **Supply chain:** Data science helps manage the supply chain by predicting demand, optimizing logistics, and reducing waste. Farmers use data science to predict weather patterns and forecast crop yields.
- **Education**: Educational institutions use data science to create personalized learning experiences for students. Data science is used to predict student dropout rates by analyzing factors such as attendance, grades, and engagement.

Impact on decision-making and strategy

Data science influences decision-making and strategy in modern organizations. By analyzing historical data, companies can identify trends, patterns, and correlations that might not be apparent through traditional methods. This data-driven approach reduces the reliance on gut feelings and allows decision-makers to base their strategies on concrete evidence. The impact of data science on decision-making and strategy includes the following:

- Companies can forecast future trends and outcomes based on historical data. Data science facilitates real-time decision-making by processing and analyzing data as it is generated. This capability is particularly important in fast paced industries such as finance, healthcare, and e-commerce, where timely decisions can significantly impact outcomes.
- Data science enables businesses to optimize their operations by identifying risks, inefficiencies, and areas for improvement. By analyzing data on processes, resource usage, and performance metrics, companies can streamline operations, reduce costs, and improve productivity. For example, in manufacturing, data science can be used

to analyze production line data to identify bottlenecks and optimize workflows. This leads to reduced downtime, lower production costs, and improved product quality. In logistics, data science can optimize delivery routes, reducing fuel consumption and ensuring timely deliveries.

- Sales teams can use data science to identify high potential leads, while customer service teams can analyze customer feedback to improve service quality.
- Data science provides real-time insights that enable companies to respond quickly to changing conditions. Whether it is adjusting to a sudden shift in market demand or responding to a competitor's new product launch, data-driven decision-making allows companies to stay ahead of the curve.

Overview of data science workflow

The data science workflow is a systematic process that involves several stages, responsible for transforming raw data into actionable insights and informed decisions. The key stages in the data science workflow are:

1. **Data collection**: It involves gathering raw data from various sources.
2. **Data cleaning and preprocessing**: Once data is collected, it often requires cleaning and preprocessing to ensure its quality and suitability for analysis.
3. **EDA**: It involves examining the dataset to understand its characteristics, patterns, and relationships.
4. **Feature engineering:** Feature engineering involves creating, selecting, or transforming features (variables) that will model building.
5. **Model building**: It is the process of selecting and training ML models to make predictions or classifications based on the data.
6. **Model validation and testing**: Model is applied on testing data and it is validated and tested; to ensure its proper functioning.
7. **Deployment**: Once a model is validated and tested, it is deployed into a production environment where it can make predictions or provide insights based on new data.
8. **Communication and reporting**: Proper documentation is done regarding the model training and testing and is well communicated.
9. **Feedback and iteration**: The final stage of the data science workflow involves gathering feedback and iterating or making improvements based on the feedback and new insights.

Data collection

Data collection is a foundational step in the data science workflow, which involves gathering raw data from various sources to address specific questions, solve problems, or generate insights. The quality, quantity, and relevance of the data collected significantly influence the success of subsequent stages in the data science process.

Data can be collected from a variety of sources, such as:

- **Internal data sources**: These include data generated within an organization, such as transaction records, customer databases, operational logs, and employee data. Internal data is often rich in detail and can provide valuable insights into business processes and performance.

- **External data sources**: External sources provide data that originates outside the organization, such as publicly available datasets, third-party data providers, and industry reports. This data can offer additional context, market trends, and competitive insights.

- **Web data**: Data collected from websites through web scraping or **application programming interfaces** (**APIs**) can include information such as user reviews, social media posts, and online behavior. This type of data can provide insights into customer sentiment and trends.

- **Sensors and IoT devices**: IoT devices and sensors generate real-time data from physical objects and environments.

- **Surveys and questionnaires**: They are used to gather subjective data, opinions, and feedback from users or customers. Data collected through controlled experiments may be used in scientific research and clinical studies.

Effective data collection requires addressing several challenges:

- Ensuring that the collected data is accurate, complete, and free from errors. Poor data quality can lead to unreliable analysis and incorrect conclusions.

- Protecting the privacy of individuals and complying with regulations such as GDPR and CCPA. Data collection methods must ensure that personal information is handled responsibly and securely.

- It is important to ensure that data collection methods are unbiased and representative of the target population.

- Combining data from multiple sources can be complex due to differences in formats, structures, and quality. Data integration techniques are required to harmonize and align data for analysis.

- Managing and processing large volumes of data can be challenging.

Data processing

Data processing is a crucial stage in the data science workflow that involves transforming raw data into a format suitable for analysis. The steps involved in Data processing include: data cleaning, data transformation, data integration, data enrichment, data reduction, data formatting and data validation:

1. **Data cleaning**: It involves identifying and correcting errors, inconsistencies, and inaccuracies in the dataset. This step ensures that the data is accurate, complete, and ready for analysis. Some key tasks in data cleaning include:

    a. **Handling missing values**: It involves addressing missing or incomplete data through imputation (replacing missing values with estimated values) or removal (discarding records with missing data).

    b. **Removing duplicates**: Identifying and eliminating duplicate records to ensure that each data point is unique and avoids redundancy.

    c. **Correcting errors**: Fixing data entry errors, inconsistencies, and inaccuracies. This may involve standardizing formats (e.g., dates, phone numbers), correcting typos, and resolving inconsistencies in categorical data.

    d. **Addressing outliers**: Identifying and handling outliers (values significantly different from the majority) that may affect the analysis.

2. **Data transformation**: Data transformation involves converting data into a format that is suitable for analysis. This step includes:

    a. **Normalization and scaling**: Adjusting the range of numerical values to ensure that features are on a comparable scale. Common techniques include min-max normalization and Z-score standardization.

    b. **Encoding categorical variables**: Converting categorical data (e.g., gender, product type) into numerical formats that can be used in statistical and ML models. Techniques include one-hot encoding and label encoding.

    c. **Aggregation**: Summarizing and combining data from multiple sources or records to provide a higher-level view. For example, aggregating daily sales data to monthly or yearly totals.

3. **Data integration**: Data integration involves combining data from different sources or datasets to create a unified dataset. This may involve merging tables, joining data on common keys, and aligning different data structures.

4. **Data enrichment**: This involves enhancing the dataset with additional information to provide more context and value. This may include:

   a. **Adding external data**: Integrating external data sources, such as demographic information or market trends, to provide additional insights.

   b. **Feature engineering**: Creating new features or variables from existing data that may improve model performance. For example, extracting date components (year, month) from a timestamp.

   c. Expanding the dataset by generating synthetic data or using techniques such as oversampling and undersampling to address class imbalances.

5. **Data reduction**: It involves reducing the size of the dataset while retaining its essential features. This step helps manage large datasets and improve computational efficiency. Key techniques include:

   a. **Dimensionality reduction**: Reducing the number of features in the dataset while preserving important information. Techniques include **principal component analysis** (**PCA**) and feature selection methods.

   b. **Sampling**: Selecting a representative subset of the data for analysis to reduce the dataset size and computational load. Sampling methods include random sampling, stratified sampling, and systematic sampling.

   c. **Aggregation**: Combining data to reduce granularity, such as aggregating transactional data to summary levels (e.g., monthly sales).

6. **Data formatting**: This involves organizing data into a structured format suitable for analysis. This includes:

   a. **Structuring data**: Arranging data into tables, columns, and rows in a structured format. This may involve creating relational databases, data frames, or other data structures.

   b. **Data types and conversion**: Ensuring that data types (e.g., integers, floats, strings) are correctly defined and converting data between types as needed.

   c. **File formats**: Saving and exporting data in appropriate file formats (e.g., CSV, JSON, Excel) for analysis and sharing.

7. **Data validation**: This stage ensures that the processed data meets the required quality standards and is suitable for analysis. Key tasks include:

   a. **Consistency checks**: Verifying that the data is consistent across different sources and formats. This includes checking for discrepancies and ensuring data integrity.

   b. **Accuracy verification**: Validating that the data accurately represents the real-world entities or phenomena it is supposed to represent.

   c. **Data profiling**: Analyzing the dataset to understand its structure, distribution, and quality. Data profiling helps identify anomalies, patterns, and areas that require further processing.

Data analysis and modeling

Data analysis is the process of systematically applying statistical and logical techniques to describe, illustrate, and evaluate data. The objective is to discover useful information, suggest conclusions, and support decision-making. Types of data analysis can be exploratory or confirmatory. They are described as follows:

- **EDA**: It is an initial phase of data analysis where the main aim is to explore the data without any preconceived notions. It involves summarizing the main characteristics of the data, often using visual methods like histograms, box plots, scatter plots, and correlation matrices. EDA helps in understanding the distribution, relationships, and potential anomalies in the data.

- **Descriptive statistics**: It involves summarizing and describing the main features of a dataset using metrics such as mean, median, mode, standard deviation, and variance. These statistics provide a quick overview of the data's central tendency, dispersion, and shape.

- **Inferential statistics**: It involves making inferences about a population based on a sample of data. Techniques such as hypothesis testing, confidence intervals, and regression analysis allow data scientists to draw conclusions and make predictions based on the data.

- **Visualization tools and techniques:** They include bar charts, line graphs, heatmaps, and scatter plots. They are used to represent data graphically. Visualizations make it easier to identify trends, outliers, and patterns that may not be immediately apparent in raw data.

Data modeling involves creating mathematical models that represent the relationships between variables in the data. These models are used to predict outcomes, classify data, and identify patterns. There are various types of models, including:

- **Predictive modeling**: Predictive models use historical data to make predictions about future events. Techniques include linear regression, logistic regression, decision trees, random forests, and neural networks. Predictive modeling is widely used in applications like sales forecasting, customer churn prediction, and risk assessment.

- **Classification**: Classification models are used to categorize data into predefined classes or labels. Common algorithms include decision trees, **support vector machines** (**SVM**), **k-nearest neighbors** (**KNN**), and deep learning models. Classification is commonly used in image recognition, spam detection, and medical diagnosis.

- **Clustering**: Clustering models group similar data points together based on their characteristics. Unlike classification, clustering is an unsupervised learning technique, meaning the model identifies groups without pre-labeled data. Techniques include k-means clustering, hierarchical clustering, and **Density-Based Spatial Clustering**

of Applications with Noise (**DBSCAN**). Clustering is used in market segmentation, customer profiling, and anomaly detection.

- **Time series models:** They analyze data points collected or recorded at specific time intervals. These models are used to forecast future values based on past trends. Techniques include **Autoregressive Integrated Moving Average** (**ARIMA**), exponential smoothing, and **long short-term memory** (**LSTM**) networks. Time series analysis is essential in financial forecasting, inventory management, and climate modeling.
- Dimensionality reduction techniques, such as PCA and **t-distributed Stochastic Neighbor Embedding** (**t-SNE**), are used to reduce the number of variables in the dataset while retaining important information. This simplifies the model and reduces computational complexity, making it easier to visualize and analyze high-dimensional data.

Model evaluation and validation

Once a model is built, it must be evaluated and validated to ensure its accuracy and reliability. This involves:

- **Training and testing**: The dataset is typically split into training and testing subsets. A model is trained on the training data and then tested on the testing data to evaluate its performance.
- **Performance metrics**: Various metrics are used to evaluate a model's performance, depending on the type of model. For regression models, metrics include **mean squared error** (**MSE**), **root mean squared error** (**RMSE**), and R-squared. For classification models, metrics include accuracy, precision, recall, F1 Score, and area under the ROC curve (AUC).
- **Overfitting and underfitting**: Overfitting occurs when the model performs well on the training data but poorly on new, unseen data, indicating that it has learned noise rather than the underlying pattern. Underfitting occurs when the model is too simple to capture the underlying pattern in the data.
- **Model tuning**: Hyperparameter tuning involves adjusting the model's parameters to improve its performance. Techniques like grid search, random search, and Bayesian optimization are used to find the optimal set of parameters.

Interpretation and communication of results

Interpretation and communication of results are critical steps in the data science workflow, where the insights derived from data analysis and modeling are translated into actionable information that can inform decision-making. The final step in data analysis and modeling is interpreting the results and communicating them effectively to stakeholders. This includes:

- **Interpretation**: Understanding the implications of the analysis and model results. For instance, identifying which variables are most influential in predicting outcomes or understanding the significance of certain patterns.
- **Communication**: Presenting the findings in a clear and understandable manner, often through reports, dashboards, and visualizations. Effective communication is crucial for ensuring that stakeholders can make informed decisions based on the data.
- **Making results actionable**: The main aim of data analysis and modeling is to translate insights into actions that can improve decision-making and drive outcomes. This involves:
    - **Recommendations**: Offering specific, data-driven recommendations based on the findings. For example, suggesting changes to marketing strategies, identifying target customer segments, or optimizing supply chain processes.
    - **Decision support**: Providing the information needed to support strategic decisions. This might include forecasting future trends, evaluating potential risks, or assessing the impact of different scenarios.

Key challenges in data science

Data science is an important field that can provide innovation, optimize operations, and provide deep insights across various domains. However, despite its many advantages, there are several challenges that are present in this field. These include:

- **Data quality and availability**: One of the most significant challenges in data science is ensuring that the data used for analysis is of high quality and readily available. Poor data quality can lead to inaccurate models, misleading insights, and faulty decision-making. Dataset must be complete. We must handle missing data through imputation, deletion etc. We should ensure that data is consistent that involves standardizing formats and resolving discrepancies. Data should be up to date. Outdated data can lead to poor decisions.
- **Ethical considerations**: Data science must abide by ethical considerations. This means that data must align with ethical standards to ensure fairness. Key ethical challenges include:
    - Protecting the privacy of individuals whose data is being analyzed is critical.
    - A model trained on biased data may make discriminatory decisions, leading to unfair outcomes.
    - The decisions made by data-driven models must be transparent and explainable.
- **Scalability and performance**: As data volumes grow exponentially, scaling data science solutions to handle large datasets efficiently becomes a significant challenge.

- **Integration of domain knowledge**: Data science requires the integration of domain knowledge. Without sufficient domain expertise, data scientists may misinterpret data or overlook critical aspects, leading to incorrect conclusions.
- **Collaboration and teamwork**: Data science projects require collaboration among diverse teams, including data scientists, engineers, domain experts, and business stakeholders. Effective collaboration is crucial, but it can be challenging due to differences in expertise, communication styles, and objectives.

Data quality and availability

Data quality and availability are basic elements in data science, directly influencing the accuracy, reliability, and usability of the insights derived from data analysis. Data quality refers to the condition of data in terms of its accuracy, completeness, reliability, relevance, and consistency. Data availability refers to the ease with which data can be accessed and used when needed.

Some key considerations for data availability include:

- **Accessibility**: Data should be easily accessible to those who need it without unnecessary hurdles.
- **Data integration**: It involves combining data from different sources into a unified format, allowing for comprehensive analysis.
- **Data sharing**: Data should be securely shared while maintaining privacy and confidentiality.

Ethical considerations

As data science evolves, the ethical implications of how data is collected, analyzed, and used have become increasingly important. Some key ethical considerations include the following:

- Protection of personal or sensitive information is of paramount importance. Individuals whose data is being collected and analyzed should be aware of how their data will be used. Only the data necessary for a specific analysis should be collected and used. Data minimization reduces the risk of privacy breaches and ensures that individuals' data is not exploited beyond its intended purpose.
- Data scientists must adhere to privacy regulations, such as the GDPR in *Europe* or the CCPA, which ensure ethical considerations when handling personal or organizational data.
- **Bias and fairness**: If the data on which training is performed comprises of biases, then it would lead to unfair or discriminatory outcomes.

- **Algorithmic bias**: Bias in algorithms can occur if the data used to train them reflects existing societal biases, such as those related to race, gender, or socioeconomic status. For instance, a hiring algorithm trained on historical data may inadvertently favor certain demographic groups over others. There should be transparency in decisions. Decisions derived should be explainable to stakeholders. Stakeholders should be able to understand how an algorithm arrived at a particular conclusion.

Scalability and performance

Scalability and performance are critical aspects of data science, particularly as the size and complexity of datasets continue to grow. As data science projects scale, the ability to efficiently process, analyze, and derive insights from large volumes of data becomes increasingly important.

Types of scalabilities include the following:

- **Vertical scalability**: This involves improving the capacity of individual machines by adding more resources, such as CPU, memory, or storage. Vertical scalability can enhance the performance of data processing on a single machine but may reach physical or cost limits.
- **Horizontal scalability**: Horizontal scalability involves distributing tasks across multiple machines or servers. By spreading the workload, horizontal scalability can handle significantly larger datasets and more complex computations, making it a preferred approach for big data processing.
- **Algorithmic scalability**: Scalable algorithms can manage large datasets without excessive increases in computational time or resource usage.

Performance in data science refers to the speed and efficiency with which data can be processed, analyzed, and used to generate insights.

The performance of ML models is often measured in terms of accuracy, precision, recall, and other metrics that reflect the model's ability to make correct predictions.

Efficient use of computational resources, such as CPU, GPU, memory, and storage, is crucial for maintaining performance as data scales. Performance and scalability should be continuously monitored to identify potential bottlenecks and areas for improvement. Automated tools can be used to monitor system performance, and regular performance tuning can ensure that systems remain efficient as they scale.

Conclusion

This chapter explored fundamental aspects of data science. We discussed key concepts, emphasizing the interdisciplinary nature of data science and specifying fields that are part of it. We also traced the history and evolution of data science, identifying significant milestones and breakthroughs that have shaped the field. Key figures who have contributed to the development of data science were also discussed, underscoring their influence on modern practices.

We examined the importance of data science in modern business, focusing on its applications across various industries and its profound impact on decision-making and strategic planning.

Finally, the chapter addressed key challenges that data scientists face, including issues related to data quality, availability, and ethical considerations. We also explored the scalability and performance of data science systems.

This chapter sets the stage for a detailed introduction to the basics of data science, helping readers with a solid understanding of the field's foundational elements and key challenges that are part of it.

In the next chapter, we will discuss about roles and responsibilities of a data scientist, various jobs available in the field of data science and the skills required to become a data scientist.

Exercises

1. Explain the definition and key concepts of data science, and discuss why it is considered an interdisciplinary field.
2. Describe the major milestones in data science development and key figures' contributions to the field.
3. Discuss the role of data science in driving business decisions and strategy across different industries. Provide examples to support your answer.
4. Outline the data science workflow, from data collection to the interpretation and communication of results, and explain the significance of each step.
5. What challenges do data scientists face when ensuring data quality and availability? Analyze the importance of data quality and availability in data science projects and discuss the common challenges encountered in this area.
6. Discuss the ethical challenges in data science, providing examples of ethical dilemmas that data scientists might encounter.
7. Explain the importance of scalability and performance in data science projects and discuss strategies to address these challenges.
8. Analyze how data science tools and techniques help organizations make informed decisions and develop strategies. Give real-world examples.
9. Explore the applications of data science in different industries and discuss the unique challenges and opportunities in each.
10. Explain why interpretation and communication of results are important in data science and how they influence the impact of data-driven insights.

CHAPTER 2
Roles and Responsibilities of a Data Scientist

Introduction

In today's data-driven world, the role of a data scientist has become important across industries, from healthcare and finance to marketing and technology. Data scientists are the architects of data-based decision-making, whose main job is to uncover insights from vast amounts of raw data and transform them into actionable strategies. Their work involves not only technical expertise but also critical thinking, creativity, and communication skills.

This chapter explores the core responsibilities and various job titles within the field of data science. We will look at the essential tasks a data scientist performs, including data collection and cleaning, statistical analysis, and communicating findings to stakeholders. In addition to specific roles, we will highlight the key skills required for data scientists, covering both the technical abilities such as programming, statistics, and **machine learning** (**ML**) and the soft skills that enable successful collaboration and problem-solving.

A discussion on career pathways will guide aspiring professionals through potential entry points and specialization areas within the field. Finally, the chapter concludes with a real-world case study: a day in the life of a data scientist. This will provide an inside look into their daily tasks, challenges, and the dynamic environment in which they operate, offering a practical perspective on what it truly means to be a data scientist.

Structure

This chapter covers the following topics:

- Core responsibilities of data scientists
- Data science job titles
- Skills required for data scientists
- Career pathways in data science
- Case study: A day in the life of a data scientist

Objectives

By the end of this chapter, readers will have a clear understanding of the roles and responsibilities of a data scientist. It discusses the foundational tasks that data scientists perform, including data collection, cleaning, analysis, and model building, ensuring data quality and accurate insights. This chapter discusses various roles within the data science field, such as data scientist, data analyst, data engineer, and ML engineer. Readers will also gain insights into technical and soft skills required for a data scientist and a case study of the day the day-to-day responsibilities of a data scientist by analyzing a real-world example, which illustrates the practical application of their skills and highlights common challenges data scientists face.

Core responsibilities of data scientists

A data scientist has various core responsibilities required for deriving insights from data and transforming them into actionable strategies. These responsibilities include gathering and preparing data, conducting statistical and ML analyzes, and effectively communicating findings to influence business decisions.

The following are essential responsibilities of a data scientist:

- **Data collection and cleaning**: Data collection and cleaning are the foundation of any data science project. Data scientists collect, process, and prepare raw data from various sources for analysis. This stage is important to ensure the data's accuracy, completeness, and relevance to the specific problem being tackled. Data cleaning involves addressing missing values, removing duplicates, handling outliers, and ensuring consistency across datasets.
- **Exploratory data analysis (EDA)**: This involves understanding the underlying structure of data underlying structure and extracting key insights to inform the next steps in the analysis. EDA helps uncover patterns, relationships, and potential issues within the data. Using graphs and charts we get a comprehensive view of data characteristics.
- **Statistical analysis and modeling**: It helps in transforming data into meaningful insights. It helps in building predictive models, identify trends, and support business decision-making.
- **Data-driven decision-making**: Data scientist performs decision-making using data-driven insights.
- **Model deployment and monitoring** Once models are built and validated, data scientists help in deploying them in production environments and provide same value of accuracy.
- **Collaboration**: Data scientists work within teams that include software engineers, product managers, business analysts, and other stakeholders to ensure that insights

and models are properly aligned with user needs and can be integrated into broader company operations.

- **Ethical and privacy considerations**: With data privacy regulations like GDPR and CCPA, data scientists must ensure their work complies with ethical standards and legal requirements. This involves handling data responsibly, especially when working with sensitive or personal information.

Data collection and cleaning

Data collection and cleaning are fundamental steps in the data science workflow. Data collection involves gathering information from various sources relevant to the problem being analyzed.

Sources of data collected include the following:

- **Primary data**: Data is collected through methods such as surveys, experiments, or direct observations.
- **Secondary data**: This includes data gathered from existing sources like databases, public records, research papers, and APIs. A web scraping is used to extract information from websites, using automated tools.

Types of data are as follows:

- **Structured data**: Data is organized in tables or spreadsheets. It includes numerical or categorical data easily searchable by databases.
- **Unstructured data**: This data includes text, images, videos, and audio files that lack a predefined format, requiring specialized methods for processing, such as **natural language processing** (**NLP**) for text or computer vision for images.
- **Semi-structured data**: Data with some organizational tags, like JSON or XML files, which offers a degree of structure but may need further cleaning to fit analysis formats.

Data cleaning, or preprocessing, is the process of preparing raw data for analysis by addressing errors, inconsistencies, and inaccuracies.

Data cleaning include the following stages:

- **Handling missing values**: Missing data can skew results if not addressed. Common methods include:
    - **Imputation**: Filling missing values with statistical metrics like the mean, median, or mode.
    - **Removal**: Dropping rows or columns with too many missing values, especially if they are unlikely to impact results.

- **Removing duplicates**: Duplicate entries can occur when data is merged from multiple sources or recorded multiple times.
- **Outlier detection**: Outliers are values significantly different from others in a dataset. They must be removed or transformed. Techniques such as Z-score, **interquartile range (IQR),** and visualization tools like box plots help identify them.
- **Data transformation**: Converting data into suitable formats using techniques such as standardizing units, normalizing data distributions, and encoding categorical variables.
- **Data type conversion**: Converting data to appropriate types (e.g., integers, floats, strings) ensures that analysis or modeling can be performed without errors.
- **Addressing inconsistencies**: Fixing inconsistencies, like differing date formats or spelling variations, ensures uniformity across datasets.

Statistical analysis and modeling

Statistical analysis and modeling are crucial components in data science, providing the framework for making sense of raw data, uncovering trends, identifying relationships, and creating predictive models. These methods transform data into actionable insights, enabling data scientists to support decision-making processes across various industries.

Core elements of statistical analysis include the following:

- **Descriptive statistics**: This foundational step involves summarizing and describing the main features of a dataset through metrics such as the mean, median, mode, variance, and standard deviation. These measures provide insight into the distribution, central tendency, and spread of data, helping data scientists understand its basic characteristics before proceeding to more complex analyses.
- **Inferential statistics**: Inferential statistics make it possible to draw conclusions about a larger population based on a sample dataset. Techniques such as hypothesis testing, confidence intervals, and significance tests help data scientists assess the reliability of findings and make data-driven predictions about broader trends.
- **Probability theory and distributions**: Probability distributions like the normal, binomial, and Poisson distributions help data scientists model real-world phenomena and understand data behavior under varying conditions.
- **Correlation and causation**: Understanding relationships between variables is central to statistical analysis. Correlation measures the degree of association between variables but does not imply causation. Determining causative links often requires experimental design or advanced statistical methods, such as randomized controlled trials or structural equation modeling, which are essential for drawing more accurate conclusions about relationships.

Key stages in statistical modeling include the following:

- **Data preparation**: Cleaning and preprocessing data is essential for effective statistical modeling. This involves handling missing values, removing outliers, and transforming variables, which ensures that the model receives high quality input for better results.
- **Model selection**: Choosing the right model depends on the specific goals and data characteristics. Some common statistical models include:
    - o **Linear regression**: Predicts continuous outcomes based on linear relationships.
    - o **Logistic regression**: It is used for binary classification problems, predicting categories such as yes/no or success/failure.
    - o **Time series models**: Such as **Autoregressive Integrated Moving Average (ARIMA)**, which forecast future values based on historical trends.
    - o **Clustering models**: Like k-means, which segment data into groups based on similarity.
- **Training and testing**: Data scientists split their data into training and testing sets to evaluate model performance. Cross-validation techniques, such as k-fold cross-validation, are used to ensure that the model generalizes well to new data by training it on different subsets and testing it across various splits.
- **Model evaluation**: Assessing a model's accuracy is important for ensuring its reliability. Different metrics are used depending on the model type:
    - o R-squared and **mean squared error** (**MSE**) for regression models.
    - o Accuracy, precision, recall and F1 Score for classification tasks.
    - o ROC curve and **area under curve** (**AUC**) for evaluating binary classification performance.
- **Hyperparameter tuning**: To improve model performance, data scientists adjust model parameters through methods like grid search or random search, optimizing factors like learning rate, depth of trees, or number of clusters.

Applications of statistical analysis and modeling include the following:

- **Business forecasting**: Time series analysis helps organizations forecast demand, sales, and supply chain requirements by examining past trends and predicting future values.
- **Customer segmentation**: Clustering algorithms identify customer groups with similar behaviors or preferences, aiding in targeted marketing and personalized recommendations.
- **Risk analysis:** Statistical models are used to assess financial risks, including credit scoring, fraud detection, and investment risk management.

- **Predictive healthcare**: Statistical models predict patient outcomes, diagnose diseases, and assess treatment efficacy, improving healthcare decision-making and patient care.
- **NLP**: Statistical methods in NLP help with sentiment analysis, topic modeling, and text classification, turning unstructured text data into valuable insights.

Communicating findings

Communicating findings is a crucial skill for data scientists, as it translates complex analyses into meaningful insights for decision-makers. Communicating findings involves storytelling, visualization, and clarity to bridge the technical and business worlds, ensuring that insights from data directly contribute to informed decisions.

Key elements of communicating findings are:

- **Understanding the audience**: The presentation according to the audience's level of technical knowledge, is essential. For non-technical stakeholders, such as executives, the emphasis should be on high-level insights, implications, and recommendations. For technical teams or peers, more detailed discussions on methodology, assumptions, and model performance must be performed.
- **Simplifying complex information**: Data science findings can involve intricate algorithms, statistical methods, and technical jargon. Using plain language, analogies, and structured explanations helps to make complex data accessible without losing the essence of the findings.
- **Using data visualization**: Visualization is a powerful tool that allows audiences to grasp patterns, trends, and outliers at a glance. Well-chosen charts, graphs, and dashboards are invaluable in simplifying complex data. Tools such as *Tableau*, *Power BI*, and Python libraries like Matplotlib and Seaborn help create clear, impactful visuals tailored to the data story.
- **Highlighting key insights and actions**: Identifying significant trends, anomalies, or risk factors, along with suggested actions is essential. Providing actionable insights helps stakeholders understand the impact and relevance of findings, enhancing their decision-making.
- **Emphasizing business value and impact**: Findings gain more relevance when they are in accordance with business objectives and outcomes. Explaining the financial, strategic, or operational impacts of data insights helps stakeholders see how data can drive business value. This includes outlining potential cost savings, efficiency improvements, or revenue generation opportunities.

Best practices for communicating findings include the following:

- Plan and structure the presentation
- Choose effective visuals

- Incorporate a story
- Practice and prepare for questions
- Engage the audience

Data science job titles

The field of data science encompasses a range of specialized roles, each focusing on different aspects of data collection, analysis, and ML. Prominent job titles within data science are:

- Data scientist
- Data analyst
- Data engineer
- ML engineer
- Data architect
- **Business intelligence** (**BI**) analyst
- **Quantitative analyst (Quant)**
- Data consultant
- **Chief data officer** (CDO)

Data scientist

A data scientist is a professional who transforms raw data into meaningful insights to help guide decision-making and problem-solving across industries. Data scientists employ a blend of skills in programming, statistical analysis, and domain expertise to interpret and communicate data in ways that are actionable and aligned with organizational objectives.

Key responsibilities of a data scientist are as follows:

- **Data collection and cleaning**: Collect data from internal and external sources. Process and clean data by handling missing values, removing outliers, and converting data into usable formats, ensuring a high quality dataset for analysis.
- **EDA**: Conduct exploratory analysis to understand data distribution and detect patterns, trends, or anomalies. Use statistical methods and visualization tools to uncover relationships, aiding in the formation of hypotheses and data-driven decisions.
- **Model building and testing**: Develop and validate ML models that align with business objectives.
- **Interpreting and communicating results**: Translate technical findings into actionable insights that can be understood by non-technical stakeholders. Create visualizations

and summaries that effectively convey the impact and significance of data-driven findings.

- **Deploying models and monitoring performance**: Collaborate with data engineering teams to implement models in production environments. Continuously monitor and update models to ensure they remain accurate and relevant over time.
- **Research and development**: Stay current with advancements in data science, ML, and AI. Experiment with new tools, algorithms, and methodologies to enhance data processes.
- **Data governance and ethics considerations**: A data scientist must ensure data privacy, security, and compliance with legal regulations while handling sensitive information. They are also responsible for promoting ethical AI use, minimizing bias, and ensuring transparency in data-driven decisions.

The following skills are required for a data scientist:

- **Programming**: Expertise in programming languages like Python and R, both of which are heavily used in data manipulation, ML, and statistical analysis.
- **Statistical analysis**: Understanding of statistics is essential, as it helps in hypothesis testing, regression analysis, and understanding patterns within data.
- **ML**: Familiarity with supervised and unsupervised learning techniques, including regression, classification, clustering, and deep learning.
- **Data wrangling and processing**: Proficiency in cleaning, transforming, and preparing data for analysis, which is crucial for model accuracy.
- **Data visualization**: Expertise in visualization tools like Matplotlib, Seaborn, Tableau, and Power BI allows data scientists to create informative and compelling visuals.
- **Big data technologies**: Knowledge of tools like Hadoop, Spark, and Kafka enables data scientists to handle massive datasets efficiently.
- **Cloud platforms:** Familiarity with cloud platforms like *AWS, Google Cloud Platform* and *Azure* supports data storage, scalability, and processing power.
- **Domain knowledge**: Understanding the specific business or industry context helps data scientists frame their analyses in ways that directly impact business decisions.

The typical career path for a data scientist ranges from entry-level roles to advanced executive positions:

- **Junior data scientist**: Entry-level role focused on data preparation, assisting with model development, and supporting more complex analyses.
- **Data scientist**: It involves end-to-end project ownership, including data gathering, model building, and insights communication.

- **Senior data scientist**: Leads data projects, collaborates with business teams, and provides mentorship to junior team members.
- **Lead data scientist/principal data scientist**: Oversees the organization's data science strategy, aligns data initiatives with business objectives, and mentors data teams.
- **CDO**: Executive level role responsible for the company's data-driven strategy and innovation, setting policies and overseeing data assets.

Data analyst

A data analyst is responsible for interpreting and analyzing data to provide insights that guide business decisions. Data analysts play a crucial role in understanding trends, making forecasts, and supporting strategic decision-making.

Core responsibilities of a data analyst include the following:

- **Data collection and preparation**: Data is collected from multiple sources, including databases, web scraping, APIs, and data warehouses. Data is cleaned and preprocessed, addressing issues like missing values, duplicates, and inconsistencies to ensure accuracy.
- **Data analysis and interpretation**: Descriptive and inferential statistical analyses are performed to uncover trends, patterns, and correlations in data. EDA is used to understand data distributions and identify key variables.
- **Data visualization**: Visualizations (e.g., bar charts, line graphs, heat maps) are created to effectively communicate data insights to stakeholders.
- **Reporting and communication**: Comprehensive reports, summaries, and presentations for key stakeholders, translating complex data insights into simple, actionable recommendations are prepared.
- **Identifying trends and anomalies**: Monitor **key performance indicators (KPIs)** and other metrics, identifying trends that can inform strategy. Detect anomalies or unusual patterns that may indicate business risks or opportunities.
- **Decision support and strategy development**: Work closely with decision-makers to inform strategy and policy by providing data-driven insights. Support cross-functional teams in understanding data implications, guiding projects, and strategic planning.

The following skills are required for a data analyst:

- **Data manipulation and analysis**: Data analysts should have proficiency in data manipulation using languages like SQL to extract and query data from databases. He should have familiarity with data processing libraries in Python (e.g., Pandas, NumPy) or R, which are essential for handling data and performing calculations.

- **Statistical knowledge**: Data analysts should have a strong understanding of statistics, including probability, hypothesis testing, regression analysis, and predictive modeling. He should be able to apply statistical techniques to interpret data and make informed predictions.
- **Data visualization and reporting**: A data analyst should be able to create visual representations using data visualization tools like Tableau, Power BI, or Google Data Studio of data.
- **Analytical and critical thinking**: A data analyst should have strong analytical thinking to understand complex data relationships and identify meaningful insights.
- **Problem-solving**: Data analysts should have the ability to approach data challenges systematically, breaking down complex problems into manageable steps.
- **Communication skills**: Data analysts should have proficiency in verbal and written communication to explain data insights to both technical and non-technical audiences.

Data engineer

A data engineer plays a crucial role in any data-driven organization by designing, building, and managing data pipelines and infrastructure that collect, store, and process large datasets. They are responsible for ensuring that data is accessible, clean, and well organized, which enables data scientists, analysts, and other stakeholders to draw meaningful insights and make data-driven decisions. Unlike data scientists who analyze and model data, data engineers focus on the architecture and processes that allow data to be efficiently used across the organization.

The core responsibilities of a data engineer include the following:

- **Data pipeline design and development**: Build and optimize data pipelines that allow for the efficient flow of data from different sources to storage and analysis systems.
- **Data collection and integration**: Work with APIs, databases, and streaming data sources to collect data from different platforms (e.g., databases, web services, IoT devices).
- **Data storage and management**: Develop and maintain data warehouses, data lakes, or other storage solutions suitable for big data environments.
- **Data cleaning and transformation**: Clean, transform, and structure raw data to make it suitable for analysis, a process known as **extract, transform, load** (ETL).
- **Collaboration with data scientists and analysts**: Collaborate closely with data scientists to understand their data requirements and ensure data pipelines and storage solutions support their needs.
- **Monitoring and maintenance**: Continuously monitor data pipelines and storage systems to detect and resolve issues, ensuring data availability and performance.

The following skills are required for a data engineer:

- **Strong programming skills**: Proficiency in programming languages like Python and Java for data pipeline development, as well as SQL for database management and query optimization. Familiarity with scripting languages such as Bash for automation and task scheduling.
- **Database management and design**: Expertise in relational databases (e.g., MySQL, PostgreSQL) and NoSQL databases (e.g., MongoDB, Cassandra) to handle both structured and unstructured data.
- **Big data technologies**: Proficiency with big data frameworks, including Apache Hadoop and Apache Spark, for processing and managing large datasets.

Data engineering workflow includes the following responsibilities:

- **Requirements gathering**: This step involves collecting data, performing data cleaning, and data preprocessing.
- **Data pipeline development**: Design, build, and test data pipelines, integrating data from diverse sources and transforming it into a format ready for analysis.
- **Data storage and optimization**: Storage systems should be structured and optimized for fast querying and analysis.
- **Data quality and monitoring**: Implement data quality checks and monitoring systems to detect and address any issues in the data pipeline.
- **Continuous optimization**: Regularly review and improve data architecture, pipelines, and storage to keep pace with new data sources, larger data volumes, and evolving analytical needs.

ML engineer

An ML engineer is responsible for developing, deploying, and maintaining ML models in production environments. They bridge the gap between data science and software engineering, enabling the practical application of ML techniques to solve real-world problems. ML engineers are responsible not only for designing models but also for ensuring these models operate at scale, are efficient, and deliver accurate predictions over time.

The core responsibilities of an ML engineer include the following:

- **Model design and development**: Develop ML models based on business needs, such as classification, regression, clustering, or deep learning models.
- **Data preprocessing and feature engineering**: Collaborate with data scientists and data engineers to preprocess and transform raw data into a format suitable for ML.

- **Deployment of ML models**: Deploy ML models into production environments, ensuring that they work efficiently and reliably.
- **Monitoring and maintenance**: Monitor models in production to ensure they perform well over time, identifying and addressing issues such as concept drift, where the data distribution changes, affecting model accuracy.
- **Collaboration with cross-functional teams**: Work closely with data scientists, software engineers, data engineers, and business stakeholders to align models with business goals.

Here are some skills required to become a ML engineer are as follows:

- **Strong programming skills**: Expertise in programming languages like Python, Java, Scala, or C++.
- **Deep understanding of ML algorithms**: Comprehensive knowledge of ML and deep learning algorithms.
- **Data handling and database management**: Proficiency in SQL for data extraction and manipulation, and experience with NoSQL databases like MongoDB for handling unstructured data.
- **Experience with deployment and automation**: Expertise in deploying ML models on cloud platforms
- **Model optimization and tuning**: Experience with techniques for hyperparameter tuning (e.g., grid search, random search, bayesian optimization) and model evaluation.
- **Problem-solving skills**: Strong analytical skills to debug, evaluate, and improve models, and problem-solving abilities to address issues that arise in model deployment and maintenance.

Skills required for data scientists

The role of a data scientist requires a combination of technical expertise, analytical thinking, and communication abilities. These skills collectively enable data scientists to uncover patterns in data, build predictive models, and drive data-based decision-making. The following points outline the essential skills every data scientist should develop to succeed in this dynamic field:

- Technical skills
- Soft skills
- Analytical skills
- Domain knowledge

Technical skills

Technical skills form the core foundation, enabling data scientists to handle, analyze, and model data to provide meaningful insights. These skills include programming, data manipulation, statistical analysis, ML, and more. Mastering these skills is essential for transforming raw data into actionable knowledge and solving complex problems. Here are the primary technical skills every data scientist should possess:

- **Programming proficiency**: Data scientists should have proficiency in programming, especially in Python.
- **Statistical analysis and probability**: Statistics and probability provide the theoretical foundation for data science, enabling data scientists to make inferences, test hypotheses, and validate the robustness of models. Knowledge in this area ensures that data scientists can design reliable experiments, interpret data accurately, and avoid false conclusions.
- **Data visualization**: Visualization helps data scientists explore data, identify patterns, and communicate findings effectively.
- **ML and modeling**: ML is a cornerstone of data science, enabling data scientists to create predictive models and discover hidden patterns in data. Knowledge of supervised, unsupervised, and deep learning methods allows data scientists to apply various models based on the data type and problem at hand.
- **Big data technologies**: Data scientist should have knowledge of big data technologies like Hadoop and Spark for efficient data processing.
- **Database management**: Databases are foundational in most data environments, making SQL a critical skill for data scientists. SQL is used to access, filter, and manipulate data stored in relational databases, allowing for efficient data analysis and retrieval.
- **NLP**: It is a branch of data science focused on analyzing human language data. NLP skills are essential for applications like sentiment analysis, chatbots, and machine translation, which require an understanding of linguistic structure and advanced ML techniques.
- **Software engineering and version control**: As data scientists often work in teams, skills in software engineering and version control (e.g., Git) are essential for collaborative coding, code maintenance, and managing code versions. Software engineering principles also help in writing optimized, modular, and reproducible code.

Soft skills

While technical proficiency is essential for data scientists, soft skills are equally crucial for excelling in the field. Soft skills enable data scientists to convey insights clearly, work effectively in teams, and build solutions that align with broader organizational goals. The key soft skills that can significantly enhance a data scientist's effectiveness and career growth are as follows:

- **Communication skills**: Effective communication is at the heart of data science. Data scientists often need to explain complex technical concepts to non-technical audiences, such as stakeholders or decision-makers. The ability to translate data insights into actionable recommendations helps bridge the gap between data teams and business units.
- **Problem-solving and critical thinking**: Data science involves tackling complex problems. Strong problem-solving skills enable data scientists to approach these challenges logically and creatively, identifying patterns, trends, and anomalies within data that can guide decision-making.
- **Collaboration and teamwork**: Data science projects often require input from various departments, such as engineering, marketing, and finance. Collaboration skills ensure that data scientists can work smoothly with these teams, aligning their work with organizational objectives and pooling knowledge for better outcomes.
- **Project management**: Data science projects can be complex, involving multiple phases like data collection, cleaning, analysis, and reporting. Project management skills help data scientists stay organized, meet deadlines, and manage resources effectively.
- **Adaptability and continuous learning**: The data science field is fast-evolving, with new tools, techniques, and best practices emerging frequently. Adaptability and a commitment to continuous learning enable data scientists to keep their skills current and remain competitive in the field.

Career pathways in data science

A career in data science offers diverse pathways and specializations, accommodating a variety of skill sets, interests, and ambitions. These pathways often start with foundational roles that lead to more specialized or advanced positions, allowing professionals to develop expertise in areas like ML, data engineering, analytics, or leadership. Various roles in the field of data science are as follows:

- Entry-level role
- Intermediate role
- Senior-level role

Entry-level to senior roles

The various roles exhibited by a data scientist include the following:

- **Entry-level roles in data science**: Data analyst, junior data scientist, BI analyst. They focus on data preparation, data cleaning, exploratory analysis, and reporting. Professionals in these positions use tools like Excel, SQL, Python, and visualization software to uncover insights and assist in decision-making processes.

- **Intermediate roles in data science**: Data scientist, data engineer, ML engineer. These professionals often take on more complex tasks that involve advanced analytics, model development, or data pipeline engineering. Data scientists in intermediate roles are responsible for creating predictive models and conducting deeper statistical analyses, while data engineers focus on building and managing data infrastructure to support large-scale data applications.

- **Senior level roles**: They include senior data scientist, lead data engineer, and principal data scientist. senior data scientists are responsible for overseeing projects, developing complex models, and ensuring the technical quality of deliverables. They guide junior and mid-level team members, offer strategic insights, and lead the technical execution of large-scale projects. Senior data scientists are trusted advisors within their organizations, valued for their ability to align data science goals with business strategies.

Specialization areas

Specialization in data science involves focusing on specific areas within the field to gain deep expertise and excel in solving industry-specific problems. As data science continues to expand across diverse sectors, specialization has become a critical path for data scientists aiming to enhance their skills, meet industry demands, and contribute impactful insights.

Data science is a broad, interdisciplinary field comprising programming, statistics, domain knowledge, and business-related information. Specializing in one area enables a data scientist to develop deeper knowledge and skills for a specific type of analysis or industry.

Here are some reasons why specialization can be advantageous:

- **Industry relevance**: Different industries have unique needs and data-related challenges. Specialization helps data scientists understand these requirements, making their work more relevant and impactful.

- **Advanced skills**: Focusing on a specific area allows data scientists to build advanced skills in particular techniques or tools, increasing their expertise and effectiveness.

- **Career growth**: Specialized skills are often in high demand, providing more opportunities for career advancement, increased earning potential, and roles with higher responsibility.

- **Focused problem-solving**: Specialization allows data scientists to address complex problems in depth and develop solutions that are highly targeted, making a tangible difference within an industry.

Case study: A day in the life of a data scientist

A day in the life of a data scientist may involve several activities, such as technical analysis, strategic planning, and collaborative communication. The role of data scientists generally follows a workflow that revolves around understanding and solving complex data-driven problems. The following are the tasks performed by a data scientist:

- **Planning and data exploration**: There is a team meeting where the data scientist meets with product managers, analysts, and engineers to discuss ongoing projects. The data scientist takes notes on areas requiring analysis, such as customer engagement metrics or conversion rates. After the meeting, the data scientist performs data extraction and data cleaning using Python.

- **Analysis and model development**: Once the data is cleaned, the data scientist performs analysis. Data scientist develops predictive models to forecast customer behavior based on the current data. For building a ML model, data scientists use libraries like scikit-learn or TensorFlow to setup and test algorithms, such as logistic regression or a neural network. Model accuracy, precision, and recall scores are then evaluated to determine which model performs best for the given data.

- **Collaboration and communication**: Data scientist collaborates with other departments to share insights. Data scientist also meet with the marketing team to discuss model predictions that indicate which products could perform well in future promotions.

- **Refinement and documentation data**: Scientists perform refinement such as adjusting hyperparameters or testing the model with additional data to improve its accuracy.

- **Documenting their work is essential**: They write detailed notes on the models used, assumptions made, data sources, and any insights gained from the analysis. This documentation ensures that others on the team can review, replicate, or refine the model if needed.

Real-world examples

Real-world problems solved by data scientist showcase how they apply their skills to solve concrete problems. Real-world scenarios where data scientists play a crucial role are as follows:

- **Predictive maintenance in manufacturing**: In the automotive industry, companies like *General Motors* use predictive analytics to anticipate machine failures and optimize maintenance schedules. Data scientists analyze sensor data from machinery to predict when parts may fail, reducing downtime and maintenance costs.

- **Fraud detection in finance**: Financial institutions employ data scientists to detect fraudulent transactions in real-time. By analyzing patterns of normal and suspicious transactions, data scientists create algorithms that detect anomalies.

- **Personalized recommendations in e-commerce**: Data scientists process vast amounts of customer interaction data and apply collaborative filtering, content-based filtering, and deep learning to recommend items based on each user's preferences, leading to higher user retention and increased sales.
- **Sentiment analysis in social media**: Data scientists use NLP to analyze posts and comments, detecting trends and customer sentiments in real-time. By categorizing sentiments as positive, negative, or neutral, data scientists provide actionable insights to marketing and product teams.
- **Predicting patient outcomes in healthcare**: Data scientists assess medical data, and apply predictive models to assess health risks. They then translate these predictions into insights that doctors use to improve patient outcomes and optimize hospital resources.
- **Supply chain optimization in retail**: Data scientists analyze data from suppliers, warehouses, and sales to predict demand and supply and improve inventory management. They use algorithms to optimize routes for faster delivery and minimize excess stock, saving costs and enhancing customer satisfaction.

Daily tasks and challenges

The daily tasks of a data scientist involve combining technical work with strategic decision-making and collaboration. Each day presents unique challenges as data scientists work to extract meaningful insights from data that drive business solutions.

Here is a detail of typical daily tasks and some common challenges data scientist's encounter:

- **Data collection and cleaning**: The first step in any data-driven project is gathering data, often from multiple sources. This involves extracting, transforming, and loading data from databases, APIs, or external sources. Data cleaning is essential to handle missing values, outliers, and inconsistencies, as clean data is the foundation of reliable analysis.
- **EDA**: Data scientists begin by exploring the dataset to understand its characteristics. EDA involves generating descriptive statistics, visualizing distributions, identifying patterns, and spotting any anomalies that may affect further analysis.
- **Feature engineering and selection**: Data scientists work on creating meaningful features to improve model performance. They may also select the most important features for modeling to reduce computational complexity and enhance interpretability.
- **Model development and training**: Data scientists apply ML algorithms or statistical models to their dataset. This includes selecting appropriate models, tuning parameters, and using techniques like cross-validation to ensure the model's performance and reliability.

- **Model evaluation and validation**: Evaluating models is critical to understanding their effectiveness. Data scientists use metrics such as accuracy, precision, recall, and F1 Score to assess performance and validate the models on unseen data to check for overfitting or underfitting.
- **Communication of findings**: Translating complex findings into clear, actionable insights for stakeholders is a key part of a data scientist's role. This might involve creating visualizations, presentations, or reports that make data-driven conclusions easy to understand and actionable for decision-makers.
- **Collaboration and cross-functional work**: Data scientists regularly work with product managers, software engineers, and other team members to align their findings with organizational goals. They also collaborate to ensure models are correctly deployed and integrated into products or services.
- **Continuous learning and development**: Given the rapid development in the field of data science, data scientists spend time each day updating their skills. This could involve studying new algorithms, testing out the latest libraries, or keeping up-to-date with industry trends.

Daily challenges one might include the following points:

- **Data quality issues**: Data may contain missing, duplicate, or inconsistent information, which can compromise model accuracy. Addressing these issues requires careful attention and often creative solutions, which can be time consuming.
- **Managing large datasets**: Handling large volumes of data is a technical challenge, as it requires robust infrastructure and optimized code. Data scientists often need to work with distributed systems or cloud platforms, which can add complexity.
- **Balancing model complexity and interpretability**: Finding the right balance between model performance and interpretability is challenging. While complex models (like deep neural networks) might yield high accuracy, they can be difficult to interpret, which complicates explaining the model's decisions to stakeholders.
- **Deployment and integration issues**: Transitioning from model development to deployment is often challenging, as models need to function seamlessly within production environments. This requires close collaboration with engineering teams and a good understanding of software integration.
- **Keeping up with rapid technological changes**: Data science is a fast-evolving field, with new tools, techniques, and algorithms constantly emerging. Data scientists must continuously learn and adapt, which requires time and dedication amid their daily responsibilities.
- **Bias and ethical concerns**: Ensuring that models are unbiased and ethically sound is increasingly important. Data scientists must be vigilant about potential biases in data

or models, which can lead to unfair or incorrect predictions, especially in sensitive applications like healthcare or hiring.

Conclusion

This chapter showcased the multiple roles and responsibilities of data scientists, describing how these professionals transform raw data into actionable insights that drive business decisions. The core responsibilities of a data scientist include data collection and cleaning, statistical analysis and modeling, and communicating findings. Further we discussed about various job titles within the data science field, including data scientists, data analysts, data engineers, and ML engineers, and highlighted the distinctions between these roles. Understanding these distinctions helps clarify the collaborative dynamics within data-driven teams and the unique skill sets each position brings to the table.

Additionally, this chapter explored the technical and soft skills required to excel in data science. Technical skills like programming, statistical knowledge, and ML expertise are essential for handling data complexities, while soft skills such as communication and problem-solving enable data scientists to work effectively across disciplines and present findings to diverse stakeholders. The chapter also covered career pathways in data science, outlining the progression from entry-level roles to specialized senior positions. This provides aspiring data scientists with insights into possible career trajectories and specialization areas. Finally, a case study titled *A day in the life of a data scientist* offered a practical perspective, illustrating the daily tasks and challenges data scientists face in real-world environments.

In the next chapter, we will discuss why Python is preferred over other programming languages in the field of data science. We will also discuss how to install Python. We will discuss various python libraries and community resources in the field of python.

Exercises

1. What is the significance of data cleaning in the data science process, and how does it impact the quality of the insights derived from data analysis?
2. Explain how data scientists use statistical models to solve real-world business problems. Provide examples of how these models can lead to better decision-making.
3. How does the role of a data scientist evolve as they gain experience and transition from entry-level to senior positions? Discuss the new responsibilities they take on.
4. Describe the relationship between data scientists and other data professionals, such as data engineers and ML engineers. How do they collaborate in a data-driven project?
5. What challenges might data scientists face when communicating their findings to non-technical stakeholders, and how can they overcome these challenges?

6. Discuss the technical skills that a data scientist needs in terms of programming languages, tools, and algorithms. How do these skills help in solving complex data problems?
7. In what ways do soft skills like problem-solving, critical thinking, and teamwork contribute to the success of a data scientist in a cross-functional team?
8. How do data science job titles, such as data analyst and data engineer, differ in terms of their focus and contributions to the data science workflow?
9. Reflect on the different career pathways available in data science. What factors should aspire data scientists consider when choosing a specialization area?

CHAPTER 3
The Necessity of Python in Data Science

Introduction

Today, it is very important to perform adequate data-driven decision-making. It is imperative to efficiently analyze, interpret, and derive valuable insights from enormous amounts of datasets. In the field of data science, Python is of paramount importance. The characteristics such as ease of understanding, versatility, portability, and extensive libraries make it viable for use in the field of data science and are preferred mainly by data scientists. Python has robust capabilities that are suited for advanced professionals, and it can include statistical analysis, **machine learning** (**ML**), and visualization, making it suitable for addressing complex problems quickly.

Furthermore, Python's open-source nature and an active global community ensure continuous development, support, and innovation. This chapter is based on the necessity of Python in data science, exploring why it has emerged as the only choice for professionals and enthusiasts. Due to its adaptable nature and comprehensive libraries such as NumPy, Pandas, Matplotlib, and scikit-learn, Python has revolutionized how data is processed and understood. All these features and capabilities have made Python a tool and a crucial enabler of success in data science.

Structure

This chapter covers the following topics:

- Choosing Python for data science
- Comparison with other programming languages
- Setting up Python environment
- Overview of Python libraries for data science
- Community and resources for learning Python

Objectives

By the end of this chapter, readers will be able to understand how Python serves as an indispensable tool in the field of data science. Its features of simplified syntax, versatility, extensive library, and open-source nature make it the most suitable and preferred language in the field of data science. Python is used to handle complex tasks in data science such as data collection, cleaning, analysis, and visualization. This chapter will discuss features of Python that make it the most preferred language compared to other languages. It will also discuss popular Python libraries like NumPy, pandas, Matplotlib, Seaborn, scikit-learn, and TensorFlow, emphasizing their roles in data science workflows. Python has become the industry standard for data science and is used by leading organizations and academic institutions worldwide. This chapter will discuss the installation of Python. It will also discuss online tutorials, courses, forums, and discussion groups dealing with Python in data science. By the end of this chapter, readers will be able to gain insight into why python is considered as the most preferred language for data science. They will be able to delve into various libraries of python in the field of data science. Lastly, they will know about the community and resources in the field of data science.

Choosing Python for data science

Python is one of the most popular programming languages in the field of data science. Its features, such as simplicity, versatility, and a rich ecosystem of libraries and tools, make it an ideal choice for data science professionals.

Here are some of the features of Python:

- **Ease of use and learning**: Python's simplicity and ease of understanding make it a preferred language by beginners and experienced programmers, which allows them to focus on solving problems rather than worrying about language complexity. This makes it accessible for people from diverse backgrounds, including mathematics, statistics, and business.
- **Comprehensive libraries**: Python comprises many libraries specifically designed for data analysis, manipulation, and visualization. These include:
    - NumPy for numerical computations and working with arrays.
    - Pandas for data manipulation and analysis, especially for tabular data.
    - Matplotlib and Seaborn for creating a wide range of visualizations.
    - Scikit-learn for ML and predictive modeling.
    - TensorFlow and PyTorch for deep learning and AI.
    - Statsmodels for statistical analysis.

These libraries significantly reduce the code and effort needed for complex data science tasks:

- **Community and support**: Python has one of the largest programming communities in the world. It is supported by extensive documentation, a wealth of tutorials and resources, active forums such as *Stack Overflow*, where data scientists can seek help, and continuous updates and innovations driven by the open-source community.
- **Versatility**: Python can be used across the entire data science workflow, including:
  - Data collection (via web scraping or APIs using libraries like Beautiful Soup and Requests).
  - Data cleaning and preprocessing.
  - **Exploratory data analysis** (**EDA**) and visualization.
  - Building and deploying ML models, and integrating with big data tools like Apache Spark.

  Python's versatility allows data scientists to switch between tasks without needing multiple languages or platforms.
- **Integration with other technologies**: Python can integrate with other languages and tools, such as big data frameworks like *Hadoop* and *Spark*, databases like *SQL*, *MongoDB*, and *Cassandra*, and cloud services for scalable storage and computing.
- **Cross-platform compatibility**: Python is platform-independent. Scripts written on one operating system (e.g., Windows) can run on another (e.g., Linux or macOS) with minimal adjustments, making it suitable for collaborative and diverse teams.
- **Scalability and flexibility**: Python can handle everything from small datasets to massive-scale computations and be able to derive beneficial results.

Advantages of Python

Python is a popular choice for data science due to its numerous advantages. Here are some key advantages of using Python in data science:

- **Simplicity**: Python's simplified syntax helps beginners and experienced professionals to focus on solving problems rather than being engrossed with complex syntax.
- **Extensive libraries and frameworks**: Python offers a wide range of libraries suitable for data science tasks:
  - **Data manipulation**: Pandas, NumPy
  - **Data visualization**: Matplotlib, Seaborn, Plotly
  - **ML**: Scikit-learn, TensorFlow, PyTorch, Keras

- **Statistical analysis**: SciPy, Statsmodels
- **Big data**: PySpark, Dask

These libraries simplify data cleaning, analysis, modeling, and visualization.

- **Strong community support**: Python has an extensive, active, and growing community of developers and data scientists who contribute to libraries, tools, and forums.
- **Cross-platform compatibility**: Python works seamlessly across platforms like Windows, macOS, and Linux, making it versatile for data science projects in varied environments.
- **Integration capabilities**: Python integrates well with other programming languages (e.g., R, C++) and databases (e.g., SQL, MongoDB). It also supports tools like Apache Hadoop and Apache Spark, enabling big data processing.
- **Open-source nature**: Python is free and open-source, reducing the cost barrier for individuals and organizations looking to adopt it.
- **Data visualization and reporting**: With libraries like Matplotlib, Seaborn, and Dash, Python enables effective data visualization and the creation of interactive dashboards for insights and reporting.
- **Scalability**: Python can handle large datasets and is scalable for big data applications when paired with distributed frameworks like Dask or PySpark.
- **Versatility in applications**: In addition to data science, Python is used in web development, automation, scripting, and more.
- **Rich ecosystem for ML and AI**: Python is best suited for ML and AI development, with frameworks like TensorFlow, PyTorch, and Keras enabling state of the art model building.
- **Support for Jupyter Notebooks**: Tools like Jupyter Notebook offer an interactive development environment for visualizing data and sharing findings in a notebook format.

Popularity and community support

Python is a popular language due to its flexibility, extensive libraries, ease of learning, and active community. It has become the dominant language in data science and has firm community support due to the following reasons:

- **Simplified syntax**: Python's syntax is simple and easy to understand making it accessible for beginners and professionals alike.
- **Extensive libraries and frameworks**: Python offers robust libraries for data manipulation (e.g., Pandas, NumPy), data visualization (e.g., Matplotlib, Seaborn,

Plotly), and ML (e.g., scikit-learn, TensorFlow, PyTorch), domain-specific libraries, such as Statsmodels for statistical modeling and Biopython for bioinformatics.

- **Versatility**: Python is a general-purpose programming language, making it ideal for tasks such as data analysis, web development, automation, or deployment of ML models.
- **Integration and interoperability**: Python integrates well with other languages and platforms. It can be easily combined with R or run on cloud services like *AWS*, *Google Cloud*, and *Azure*.
- **Growing adoption in the industry**: Python has become the language of choice for many companies, academic institutions, and researchers due to its ecosystem and scalability. It consistently ranks high in surveys like *Stack Overflow Developer Survey* and *Kaggle State of Data Science and Machine Learning*.

Active community support of Python includes the following:

- Platforms like Stack Overflow, GitHub, Reddit (r/learnpython), and Kaggle have active Python communities. Users can find solutions, contribute code, or discuss different problems.
- **Extensive documentation and tutorials**: Most Python libraries have extensive documentation, making it easier to understand and use. Tutorials and MOOCs (e.g., on *Coursera*, *edX*, and *YouTube*) help users learn Python for data science quickly.
- **Open-source nature**: Python is open-source, encouraging contributions from developers worldwide. Libraries are frequently updated, which ensures compatibility with modern tools and techniques.

Comparison with other programming languages

Python is one of the most popular programming languages in data science. This section will compare Python and other programming languages, revealing various strengths and limitations.

Python is a general purpose, with simplified syntax and extensive libraries (e.g., Pandas, NumPy). R is specifically for statisticians and is basically for statistical analysis and visualization. SQL is a domain-specific language explicitly used for querying and managing relational databases. Libraries for Python include scikit-learn, TensorFlow, PyTorch for ML, Matplotlib, and Seaborn for visualization. Libraries for R include: ggplot2, dplyr, caret, and tidyverse. Python has a large community and has broader applications beyond data science. R is used primarily in academic and Statistical fields. Python is used for large-scale applications and integrates well with other languages. R is used in in-memory computations and is suitable for small datasets. Python is used in ML, deep learning, data wrangling, and data integration. R is used in statistical modeling, EDA, and academic research. Python is slower than Julia for numerical computations due to dynamic typing. Julia is faster for numerical tasks and is close to C or Fortran in performance. Julia is used for scientific computing. Julia has smaller but rapidly growing in academic and scientific fields. Python is slower for performing matrix operations but can integrate C for speed. Matlab is used explicitly for performing matrix calculation. Python can efficiently perform all data science operations, such as data cleaning, manipulation, and visualization. This makes Python the most preferred language for data science.

R, SAS, MATLAB, Julia

R is used for statistical computing and data visualization. Libraries used for data analysis include dplyr, ggplot2, and caret. It has robust community support and resources such as RStudio and CRAN. R is suited for generating detailed, quality visualizations for EDA, statistical modeling, and testing. However, R is not able to perform efficiently with large datasets.

SAS is industry-based analytics software used in the corporate and financial sectors. It can handle large datasets and efficiently clean data.

MATLAB is used for numerical and matrix-based computations. MATLAB has a rich library for data analysis, signal processing, and ML. It is preferred in academic and engineering applications, engineering-based data analysis, signal processing and simulations, numerical modeling, and optimization. Its limitation is that it has a high cost of licensing.

Also, it provides less support for advanced ML. Julia is a high-performance language designed for numerical and scientific computing. Julia combines the ease of Python and the speed of compiled languages like C. It has a rich ecosystem for data science, with packages like DataFrames.jl and MLJ.jl. However, it supports smaller communities and fewer libraries than Python and R.

Advantages and disadvantages

Advantages of using Python in data science include the following:

- **Versatility and ease of use**: Python is beginner-friendly with a simple and readable syntax, which makes it accessible to data scientists from diverse backgrounds.
- **Extensive libraries**: Libraries like NumPy, Pandas, Matplotlib, Seaborn, and SciPy provide robust tools for data manipulation, visualization, and analysis. Advanced libraries such as TensorFlow, PyTorch, and scikit-learn are used for ML and deep learning needs.
- **Community support**: Python has an active and large community, ensuring quick support and abundant resources like tutorials, forums, and documentation.

- **Interoperability**: Python can be integrated with other languages (like R, C++, and Java) and tools, including databases, Hadoop, and Spark. It can be embedded in cloud platform workflows or data visualization tools like Tableau.
- **Diverse application**: Python can be used for data preprocessing, ML, deep learning, NLP, and even deployment of models in production.
- **Open-source and free**: Python is open-source, making it a cost-effective choice for personal and professional use.

Disadvantages of using Python in data science include the following:

- **Performance limitations**: Python is an interpreted language, making it slower than compiled languages like C++ or Java for computationally heavy tasks.
- **Memory consumption**: Python can be memory-intensive, which might not be ideal for massive datasets without optimization.
- **Dependency management**: Conflicts between library versions or dependencies can arise, especially when working on complex projects.
- **Less suitable for mobile and front-end development**: While Python is excellent for backend and data science applications, it is less effective for front-end or mobile application development compared to languages like JavaScript or Swift.
- **Limited for real-time applications**: Python's slower execution time can make it less suitable for real-time or latency-critical applications.

Setting up Python environment

Setting up a Python environment is a critical step in Python development. Here, are the steps involved in Installing Python.

Installing Python

Follow these steps to install Python:

1. **Install Python**: Check if Python is already installed: Open a terminal or command prompt and run: **`bash python --version`** or **`bash python3 --version`**.
2. **Download Python**: If Python is not installed, download it from the official website (**https://www.python.org/**).

   On Windows: Check the box to add Python to the PATH during installation.

   On macOS/Linux: Install Python using the package manager or the downloaded installer.

3. **Install a code editor or integrated development environment (IDE)**: Popular IDE include:
    - **VS Code**: Lightweight and extensible, with great support for Python.
    - **PyCharm**: An IDE with advanced debugging and project management.
    - **Jupyter Notebook**: Ideal for data analysis and interactive coding.

Virtual environments help isolate project dependencies. Steps to create a virtual environment:

1. **bash python -m venv myenv**: Replace `myenv` with your desired environment name.
2. **Activate the virtual environment**: On Windows: `bash myenv\Scripts\activate - On macOS/Linux:bash source myenv/bin/activate`.
3. **Deactivate the virtual environment**: `bash deactivate`
4. **Install Python Package**: Use `pip`, Python's package manager, to install dependencies: `bash pip install package_name`.
5. **To manage dependencies**: Create a `requirements.txt` file: `bash pip freeze > requirements.txt` Install dependencies from the file: `bash pip install -r requirements.txt`. We can also use Poetry. Poetry is a modern dependency management and packaging tool for Python. It simplifies and streamlines the process of managing project dependencies, packaging Python applications, and publishing them to repositories like PyPI.

Basic commands of Poetry:

- **poetry init**: Create a new `pyproject.toml` file.
- **poetry add numpy**: Add a dependency.
- **poetry install**: Install all dependencies.
- **poetry update**: Update dependencies to the latest versions.
- **poetry publish**: Publish your package.

Poetry uses a `pyproject.toml` file to declare and manage dependencies, making version control easy and clear.

We can also use **uv**, python package manager. **uv** is a fast and modern Python package manager developed by *Astral*. It is used in place of tools like pip, pip-tools, and even poetry, with a focus on speed, efficiency, and modern workflows.

Common commands used for python package manager:

- **uv pip install pandas**: Install a package using **uv** as a drop-in replacement for pip.
- **uv venv**: Create a new virtual environment.

- **uv pip freeze**: List installed packages.
- **uv sync**: Install dependencies defined in **`pyproject.toml`** and **`uv.lock`**.
- **Install Jupyter Notebook (optional)**: **`bash pip install notebook`**
- **Test your environment**: Create a simple Python script (**`hello.py`**): **`python print("Hello, Python!")`** Run the script: **`bash python hello.py`**
- **Install Git**: **`bash sudo apt install git`** # Linux **`brew install git`** # macOS we can initialize a Git repository and connect it to platforms like GitHub.
- **Install Anaconda**: A widespread distribution for data science with pre-installed libraries.

Choosing an integrated development environment

Choosing the right IDE depends on the specific needs, preferences, and the kind of development we are doing.

For Python, PyCharm, VS Code and Jupyter Notebook is preferred.

Popular IDEs are listed, as follows:

- **VS Code**: Its features include versatility, web development, lightweight, extensive, and a huge marketplace for plugins.
  - **Advantages of VS Code are listed here**:
    - It is free
    - Cross-platform
    - Excellent debugging
    - Git integration
  - **Disadvantage of VS Code are listed as follows:**
    - Might require manual configuration for advanced setups.
- **PyCharm**: It is used for Python development. It provides advanced tools for Python and Django:
  - **Advantages of PyCharm**:
    - Powerful debugging and testing capabilities
  - **Disadvantages**:
    - Professional version is paid

Overview of Python libraries for data science

Python offers a rich set of libraries that help in different aspects of data science, from data manipulation to visualization and ML. Here are some of the most popular Python libraries for data science, categorized by their primary use:

- **Data manipulation and analysis**: The Python libraries used primarily for data manipulation and analysis are as follows:
- **NumPy (https://numpy.org/)**: Core library for numerical computing. It supports multi-dimensional arrays and matrices, along with mathematical functions to operate on them.
- **Pandas (https://pandas.pydata.org/)**: Built on NumPy, it is widely used for data manipulation and analysis. It provides data structures like DataFrames and Series, making it easier to work with structured data.
- **Dask (https://dask.org/)**: Enables parallel computing and handles larger-than-memory datasets. It scales NumPy and Pandas for distributed environments.
- **Data visualization**: The Python libraries used primarily for data visualization are as follows:
    - **Matplotlib (https://matplotlib.org/)**: Fundamental plotting library. Other visualization libraries are often built on top of Matplotlib.
    - **Seaborn (https://seaborn.pydata.org/)**: Built on Matplotlib, it simplifies the creation of statistical graphics and is great for exploring data visually.
    - **Plotly (https://plotly.com/)**: Interactive plotting library that supports dashboards and 3D plots.
    - **Bokeh (https://bokeh.org/)**: Focused on creating interactive, web-ready visualizations.
    - **Altair (https://altair-viz.github.io/)**: Declarative statistical visualization library based on Vega and Vega Lite.
- **ML**: The Python libraries used primarily for ML are as follows:
    - **Scikit-learn (https://scikit-learn.org/)**: Comprehensive library for ML. Supports regression, classification, clustering, and preprocessing.
    - **XGBoost (https://xgboost.ai/) and LightGBM (https://lightgbm.readthedocs.io/)**: These are popular libraries for gradient-boosting algorithms.
    - **TensorFlow (https://www.tensorflow.org/)**: End-to-end open-source platform for ML.

  - **PyTorch (https://pytorch.org/)**: A flexible deep-learning library widely used for research and production.
  - **Keras (https://keras.io/)**: High-level neural network API that works as an interface for TensorFlow.
- **Data preprocessing**: The python libraries used primarily for data preprocessing are as follows:
  - **OpenCV (https://opencv.org/)**: Computer vision library for image processing.
  - **NLTK (https://www.nltk.org/) and spaCy (https://spacy.io/)**: Libraries for natural language processing tasks.
  - **Beautiful Soup (https://www.crummy.com/software/BeautifulSoup/) and Scrapy (https://scrapy.org/)**: Libraries for web scraping.
- **Statistical analysis**: The Python libraries used primarily for statistical analysis are as follows:
  - **SciPy (https://scipy.org/)**: Extends NumPy and includes optimization, integration, interpolation, and statistics modules.
  - **Statsmodels (https://www.statsmodels.org/)**: Focused on statistical modeling and hypothesis testing.
- **Big data and distributed computing**: The python libraries used primarily for big data and distributed computing are as follows:
  - **PySpark (https://spark.apache.org/docs/latest/api/python/)**: Python API for Apache Spark, used for big data processing.
  - **Dask (https://dask.org/)**: Distributed computation library that works seamlessly with NumPy and Pandas.
- **Deep learning**: The python libraries used primarily for deep learning are as follows:
  - **TensorFlow (https://www.tensorflow.org/) and PyTorch (https://pytorch.org/)**: The most commonly used frameworks for deep learning tasks.
  - **FastAI (https://www.fast.ai/)**: Built on PyTorch, simplifies training deep neural networks.
  - **Transformers (by Hugging Face) (https://huggingface.co/transformers/)**: Specialized for NLP and transformer models.

NumPy, Pandas, Matplotlib, SciPy, Seaborn

These are essential Python libraries for data science and numerical computing. Here is a brief overview of each:

- **NumPy**: It is used for numerical computing and working with arrays. It provides efficient multi-dimensional array objects and mathematical functions for linear algebra, statistics, etc. It provides high performance for operations on large datasets.
- **Pandas**: It is used for data manipulation and analysis. It provides data structures like Series (1D) and DataFrame (2D) for handling labeled and tabular data. It is used for data cleaning, merging, reshaping, and summarization.
- **Matplotlib**: It creates static, interactive, and animated visualizations in Python. It is used for line plots, bar charts, and scatter plots.
- **SciPy**: Builds on NumPy to provide advanced mathematical functions. It includes optimization, integration, interpolation, eigenvalue problems, and statistics modules. It is ideal for scientific computations.
- **Seaborn**: It is built on Matplotlib, designed for statistical data visualization. It provides a high-level interface for drawing attractive and informative statistical graphics.

Use cases for each library

Python libraries are powerful tools for simplifying coding tasks, and each library has specific use cases. Here is a breakdown of popular Python libraries and their primary use cases:

- **General purpose libraries**: The Python libraries for general-purpose tasks include the following:
  - **NumPy**:
    - **Use case:** Numerical computations, array manipulation, linear algebra, Fourier transforms.
    - **Example:** Scientific computing, building mathematical models.
  - **Pandas**:
    - **Use case:** Data manipulation and analysis, handling structured data.
    - **Example:** Working with tabular data in CSV or Excel files.
  - **Matplotlib**:
    - **Use case:** Data visualization.
    - **Example:** Creating line graphs, bar charts, and scatter plots.
  - **Seaborn**:
    - **Use case:** Statistical data visualization (built on Matplotlib).
    - **Example:** Heatmaps, violin plots, and pair plots for exploratory data analysis.

- **ML and AI**: The python libraries in the field of ML and AI include the following:
  - **Scikit-learn**: ML models and algorithms.
    - **Example**: Classification, regression, clustering, and dimensionality reduction.
  - **TensorFlow**: Deep learning and neural network models.
    - **Example**: Building complex models for image recognition and NLP.
  - **PyTorch**: Deep learning with dynamic computation graphs.
    - **Example**: Research and production-level AI models.
- **Data engineering**: The Python libraries in the field of data engineering include the following:
  - **SQLAlchemy**: Database interaction and **Object Relational Mapping** (**ORM**).
    - **Example**: Writing Python code to interact with SQL databases.
  - **PySpark**:
    - **Use case:** Big data processing and distributed computing.
    - **Example**: Data analysis on large datasets using Apache Spark.
  - **Dask**: Parallel computing for large-scale data.
    - **Example**: Handling computations that exceed memory limits.
- **Web development**: The Python libraries for web development include the following:
  - **Flask**: Building lightweight web applications and APIs.
    - **Example**: Developing a simple REST API.
  - **Django**: Full-stack web application development.
    - **Example**: Building a complete e-commerce platform.
- **Data science and statistics**: The Python libraries in data science and statistics include the following:
  - **SciPy**: Advanced mathematical functions for optimization, integration, and statistics.
    - **Example**: Solving differential equations.
  - **Statsmodels**: Statistical modeling and hypothesis testing.
    - **Example**: Performing regression analysis.
- **NLP**: The python libraries in the field of NLP are:

- **NLTK**: Text processing and linguistic analysis.
  - **Example**: Tokenization, stemming, and part-of-speech tagging.
- **spaCy**: Advanced NLP tasks with a focus on performance.
  - **Example**: Named entity recognition and dependency parsing.
- **Transformers (Hugging Face)**: Pretrained language models like BERT and GPT.
  - **Example**: Text generation, translation, and summarization.

- **Image processing**: The python libraries in the field of Image processing include the following:
  - **OpenCV**: Computer vision and image processing.
    - **Example**: Face detection, object tracking.
  - **Pillow (PIL)**: Basic image manipulation.
    - **Example**: Resizing and converting image formats.
- **Automation**: The Python libraries in the field of automation include the following:
  - **Selenium**: Browser automation and web scraping.
    - **Example**: Testing web applications or scraping data from websites.
  - **Beautiful Soup** Web scraping HTML and XML.
    - **Example**: Extracting data from web pages.

Community and resources for learning Python

Python is a popular programming language these days. Learning Python is an exciting journey, and the Python community is vast, welcoming, and resourceful.

Here are some communities and resources to help us learn Python effectively:

- **Python.org (https://www.python.org/community/)**: Official Python community site, where you can find mailing lists, forums, and user groups.
- **Python.org Tutorial (https://docs.python.org/3/tutorial/)**: The official Python documentation includes a beginner's guide.
- **freeCodeCamp Python Course (https://www.freecodecamp.org/learn/)**: Free, hands-on Python programming tutorials.
- **Real Python (https://realpython.com/)**: A mix of articles, tutorials, and video courses for all skill levels.

- **Codecademy Python Path (https://www.codecademy.com/learn/learn-python-3)**: Interactive and beginner-friendly (requires a subscription).
- **Online environments for coding and sharing Python projects. Kaggle (https://www.kaggle.com/)**: A platform for learning Python through data science and ML projects.
- **W3Schools Python Tutorial (https://www.w3schools.com/python/)**: An interactive and beginner-friendly way to practice Python concepts.
- **GitHub**: Explore repositories and contribute to open-source Python projects.

Online tutorials and courses

Learning data science using Python is a great choice due to the abundance of resources and its vast community. Here is a list of online tutorials and courses, including both free and paid options:

- **Kaggle courses**: Kaggle learn (**https://www.kaggle.com/learn**).
- **Google's data science and ML crash course**: Crash course on ML (**https://developers.google.com/machine-learning/crash-course**).
- **Coursera free courses**: Python for Everybody by the University of Michigan (**https://www.coursera.org/specializations/python**).
- **Real Python tutorials**: Real Python (**https://realpython.com/**) Beginner to advanced Python tutorials, many of which are free.

Forums and discussion groups

Forums and discussion groups are used where individuals with shared interests exchange ideas, ask questions, and share information. Whether you are a beginner or an expert, these platforms provide knowledge and opportunities for meaningful interaction. Here are some tips to help you navigate and contribute effectively:

- **Specialized forums**: Focused on a particular niche, such as technology, hobbies, or professional skills (e.g., Stack Overflow, Reddit communities).
- **General discussion boards**: Broader topics and casual discussions (e.g., Quora, Yahoo! Answers).
- **Social media groups**: Communities on platforms like *Facebook*, *LinkedIn*, and *Discord*. Here are some benefits of knowledge sharing, gaining insights or solving problems through crowd-sourced expertise, networking opportunities, skill development, enhanced communication, critical thinking, and problem-solving skills.

Conclusion

This chapter showcased the need for Python in data science. It discussed the key features of Python and how to draw the comparative differences between Python and other existing Programming languages. It took into account various strengths and weaknesses of using Python. This chapter also discussed Python libraries and their usages, such as NumPy, Pandas, Matplotlib, SciPy, and Seaborn. It also discussed different integrated development environments, community, and online resources contributing to Python and data science. In the next chapter, we will discuss data types, data collection techniques, data exploration, and case studies on data understanding in healthcare.

In the next chapter, we will study the types of data structured data vs unstructured data, data collection techniques, the importance of domain knowledge, tools for data exploration, and case studies of data understanding in healthcare.

Exercises

1. Explain the need for Python in data science. Why is Python preferred over other languages for data science?
2. Explain the advantages and disadvantages of using Python.
3. Explain the installation of Python in detail.
4. Write about online resources and the community of Python.
5. Give a contrast between Python and other programming languages.
6. Explain how Python can perform various data science operations efficiently.
7. Explain in detail about the IDE?
8. Explain in detail various Python libraries used in the field of data science.

Join our Discord space

Join our Discord workspace for latest updates, offers, tech happenings around the world, new releases, and sessions with the authors:

https://discord.bpbonline.com

CHAPTER 4
Introduction to Data Understanding

Introduction

In data science, we are committed to analyzing data and bringing about valuable insights from it. In this chapter, we are concerned about understanding the data type, whether structured data stored in databases or unstructured data like images and text. Understanding how to categorize different data types lays the foundation for effective data-driven decision-making. In data science, we deal with issues such as inconsistent formats, missing values, and complex structures, and we must drive thoughtful solutions. Data collection can take many forms, from traditional surveys and experiments to modern web scraping and **application programming interface** (**API**) integrations.

The primary goal of this chapter is to introduce the different types of data, know their characteristics, and explain techniques used for collecting, exploring, and understanding data. This chapter will also provide practical examples from the healthcare industry, emphasizing the importance of domain knowledge and collaboration with experts.

Every method has advantages, limitations, and best practices, making it essential for data scientists to select the appropriate approach based on the problem. Domain knowledge is crucial in interpreting the data correctly, asking the right questions in data collection, and deriving actionable insights. Collaboration with domain experts ensures data scientists leverage their technical skills while staying aligned with real-world challenges. Statistical methods and visualization tools enable data scientists to perform initial analyses, revealing hidden insights and guiding subsequent steps in the data science pipeline. This chapter also includes a case study related to the healthcare sector, demonstrating specific examples from the healthcare industry and mentioning the techniques used for data understanding.

Structure

This chapter covers the following topics:

- Structured vs. unstructured data
- Data collection techniques
- Importance of domain knowledge

- Tools for data exploration
- Case study on data understanding in healthcare

Objectives

By the end of this chapter, readers should be able to understand the difference between structured and unstructured data, identify their key characteristics, recognize the types of data, understand the advantages and challenges associated with both types of data, explore various data collection techniques like web scraping and APIs, know the importance of Domain Knowledge. Readers at the end of the chapter will gain a comprehensive understanding of how to handle different types of data, leverage appropriate tools, and incorporate domain knowledge to produce meaningful insights.

Structured vs. unstructured data

Data is the foundation for analysis and decision-making across various fields, and it can be categorized into two main types:

- **Structured data:** Structured data refers to data that is organized in a predefined format or schema. It is highly organized, often stored in tables or databases, and can be quickly processed and analyzed by computer systems. Structured data is typically quantitative and easy to search and manipulate because it follows a specific format with defined fields, such as numbers, dates, or strings.

  Features of structured data include the following:

  - Data is organized in rows and columns (e.g., in spreadsheets or relational databases). Since it follows a defined schema, structured data can be queried and analyzed easily using standard tools and languages like **Structured Query Language** (**SQL**).
  - Data types in structured data include numbers, dates, strings, and Boolean values that are stored in fields like integers, floats, and text.

- **Unstructured data:** Unstructured data refers to information that does not have a predefined format or structure. Unlike structured data, unstructured data is often textual, visual, or audio-based and may contain various types of content. It is typically harder to organize, search, or analyze directly. Still, it holds vast potential for insights when processed with advanced techniques such as **natural language processing** (**NLP**), **machine learning** (**ML**), or deep learning.

  Features of unstructured data are listed here:

  - Unstructured data does not adhere to a predefined model or schema, making storing and processing in traditional relational databases difficult.

- o This data often contains valuable insights, such as opinions, sentiment, and context, that cannot be easily represented in structured formats.
- o Unstructured data can include text, images, audio, video, and social media content.
- o Unstructured data can consume large amounts of storage space, especially when dealing with multimedia files or vast quantities of text.
- o Extracting valuable information from unstructured data is computationally intensive and often requires specialized software tools or platforms to clean, organize, and analyze the data.

Now, let us look at semi-structured data. In addition to structured and unstructured data, there is a category of semi-structured data somewhere in between.

Characteristics of semi-structured data are listed here:

- **Partially organized**: Semi-structured data contains tags or markers that separate different data elements but is not as organized as structured data.
- It may contain a flexible, evolving schema, such as data organized by key-value pairs or hierarchical structures. Examples of semi-structured data: XML Files, JSON Files etc.

Characteristics and examples

Structured data is organized into predefined models or schemas, typically represented in tables with rows and columns. Each row represents an entity, and each column represents a data attribute. Structured data can be queried using standard database languages like SQL making it efficient to retrieve specific information. It is commonly stored in relational databases, where tables can be linked via relationships (primary and foreign keys).

Examples of structured data:

- **Relational database**: Excel sheets or CSV files, log files (data generated by systems and applications, such as timestamps, status codes, and error messages stored consistently.)
- Tables in data management systems like *Microsoft Access* or *Google Sheets* that represent structured datasets for specific analysis or reporting.

Unstructured data does not follow a predefined format or schema, making it more difficult to categorize and analyze directly. Its content can be highly varied, ranging from text to multimedia (images, audio, video), and can contain both structured and unstructured elements. Unstructured data often provides deeper insights into qualitative information, such as opinions, emotions, behaviors, and context.

Semi-structured data lies somewhere in between. It has some organizational elements but does not conform to the strict structure of relational databases. It contains both unstructured content and some tags or markers that provide structure.

Semi-structured data does not have a fixed schema, but it contains markers (e.g., tags or key-value pairs) that allow for some degree of organization. It is often encoded in formats such as **JavaScript Object Notation** (**JSON**) or **Extensible Markup Language** (**XML**), which are readable and human-friendly but not strictly relational. Compared to unstructured data, semi-structured data is more straightforward to share across systems or platforms.

Challenges in handling each type

When working with various types of data, i.e. structured data, unstructured data, or semi-structured data, each comes with unique challenges. Let us look at some possible challenges:

- Performing data integration from different structured sources with varying schemas is challenging.
- There may be issues with missing, duplicate, or inconsistent values.
- Choosing the correct database (SQL vs. NoSQL) for better performance is a challenge.
- Unstructured data may involve processing complexities. It requires advanced techniques like NLP or computer vision.
- Unstructured data needs specialized systems for large files like images or videos.
- Annotating data for training AI models can be time-consuming.
- Extracting meaningful patterns can be challenging due to noise.
- In the case of semi-structured data, data formats can change over time.
- Requires specialized methods to handle semi-structured data patterns.
- Large spatial datasets demand high resources.
- Large graphs-based data require efficient storage and traversal algorithms.
- Blurriness or poor lighting conditions can impact analysis in the case of visual (image or video-based) data.
- Large audio files require significant space and resources.

Data collection techniques

Data collection is the first step in any data science project. The quality and accuracy of the data collected directly influence the effectiveness of any analysis, modeling, or decision-making process. Various techniques for gathering data exist, each suitable for different research questions, domains, and available resources.

Broadly, data collection techniques can be classified into two main categories:

- **Primary data collection**: Primary data collection involves directly gathering data from original sources.

- **Secondary data collection**: Secondary data collection uses data already collected and published by other researchers, organizations, or sources.

Here are the standard methods used for primary data collection:

- **Surveys**: Surveys are one of the most widely used techniques for gathering data. They typically collect information about people's attitudes, opinions, behaviors, and demographic characteristics. Surveys can be conducted through various mediums, including paper forms, online platforms, face-to-face interviews, and phone calls.

  Advantages of surveys:

  - Surveys allow for the collection of data from a large number of respondents, increasing the representativeness of the data.
  - Standardization responses are usually collected in a standardized manner, making it easier to analyze and compare data.
  - Surveys, especially online surveys, are cost-effective methods of data collection.

- **Experiments**: Experiments involve manipulating one or more variables to observe and measure the effects on other variables. This technique is handy when researchers aim to establish causal relationships between variables. Experiments are standard in fields like healthcare, psychology, and education.

  Types of experiments include the following:

  - Laboratory experiments
  - Field experiments

  Advantages of experiments include the following:

  - Experiments are the most reliable method for determining cause-and-effect relationships.
  - Researchers can manipulate variables to control for confounding factors.

- **Observations**: Observation is a qualitative data collection technique where researchers observe subjects in their natural environment without interference. Observations can be overt (where the participants are aware they are being observed) or covert (where the participants are unaware). This technique is often used in social sciences, psychology, and ethnographic studies.

  Advantages of observations include the following:

  - **Naturalistic data**: Observation allows researchers to collect data in natural settings without the influence of artificial conditions or bias.
  - **Contextual understanding**: Observations provide a rich context for understanding behaviors, interactions, and phenomena that might be missed in surveys or experiments.

- **Web scraping**: Web scraping is an automated method of extracting data from websites. It involves sending requests to web pages, downloading the content, and parsing it to retrieve relevant data. This technique is often used when the data is publicly available on the web but is not provided in structured formats like spreadsheets or databases.

  The advantages of web scraping include the following:

  - Web scraping can extract vast amounts of data from multiple websites quickly.
  - It enables collecting up-to-date information, such as news, prices, or social media data.

- **APIs**: APIs allow programs to interact with other software systems to retrieve data. Many platforms, like social media sites (e.g., *Twitter*, *Facebook*), weather services, and financial data providers, offer APIs that allow for easy access to structured data. Unlike web scraping, APIs are designed to provide reliable, machine-readable data in formats like JSON or XML.

  Advantages of APIs include the following:

  - **Structured data**: APIs typically provide data in a structured format, which makes it easy to process and analyze
  - APIs can retrieve data quickly and reliably without extensive web scraping or manual intervention.

- **Focus groups**: Focus groups are small, structured discussions involving participants discussing a specific topic or issue. They provide in-depth qualitative data on people's thoughts, attitudes, and perceptions. They are commonly used in market research, product development, and the social sciences.

  Advantages of focus groups include the following:

  - **Rich qualitative data**: Focus groups allow participants to express their opinions and feelings in a way impossible through surveys.
  - **Interactive discussions**: The group dynamic can spark new insights and ideas that individuals might not have considered independently.

- **Case study**: A case study is an in-depth investigation of a single individual, group, or organization. It typically explores complex issues in their real-life context. Case studies are commonly used in healthcare, business, and social science research.

  Advantages of case studies:

  - Case studies provide deep insights into the specific studied phenomena, including nuances and context.
  - They allow researchers to understand issues from multiple perspectives, combining qualitative and quantitative data.

- **Interviews**: Interviews involve direct questioning of individuals to gather information. They can be structured, semi-structured, or unstructured. Structured interviews have fixed questions, while semi-structured and unstructured interviews allow for more flexibility and depth in responses. Interviews are widely used in both qualitative and quantitative research.

  Advantages of interviews:

  - **Depth and detail**: Interviews provide the opportunity for deeper insights into complex issues and personal experiences.
  - **Flexibility**: Semi-structured and unstructured interviews allow for more flexibility and can explore new directions based on the participant's responses.

The choice of data collection technique depends on the research objectives, available resources, and the type of data needed. Each method comes with its own set of strengths and challenges, and often, a combination of techniques is used to gather comprehensive and high quality data.

Surveys and experiments

Surveys and experiments are two foundational data collection methods used extensively in data science and research across various domains.

A survey is a systematic method for collecting data from a predefined group of respondents. Surveys are typically used to gather opinions, attitudes, behaviors, and demographic information from a sample of individuals to make inferences about a larger population.

Types of surveys are listed here:

- **Questionnaires**: Surveys that involve written questions, which can be either open-ended or closed-ended (e.g., yes/no, multiple choice, Likert scale).
- **Interviews**: These are one-on-one interactions in which a researcher asks questions to the respondent, either in person or remotely (e.g., phone, video).
- **Online surveys**: Surveys can be distributed over the internet through tools like *Google Forms*, *SurveyMonkey*, or *Qualtrics*, making it easy to reach a large audience.
- **Telephone surveys**: Surveys conducted over the phone, often used for more personalized, in-depth responses.

Advantages of surveys are listed here:

- Surveys can reach a broad audience quickly, making it possible to gather data from large groups.
- Survey responses are typically standardized, making analyzing and comparing data across respondents easier.

- Online surveys, in particular, are low-cost data collection methods.
- Surveys can be tailored to collect qualitative and quantitative data depending on the questions' nature.
- Surveys can be anonymous, encouraging honest responses, especially for sensitive topics.

Here are some applications of surveys:

- **Market research**: Understanding consumer preferences, buying behavior, and satisfaction levels.
- **Public opinion polls**: Collecting data on the population's political views, social issues, or general attitudes.
- **Employee feedback**: Measuring job satisfaction, organizational climate, and areas for improvement within companies.
- **Healthcare research**: Surveying patients on health behaviors, treatment effectiveness, and healthcare accessibility.

An experiment is a controlled data collection method in which researchers manipulate variables to observe and measure their effects. Experiments are used to establish causal relationships between variables by systematically testing hypotheses.

Types of experiments:

- Laboratory experiments
- Field experiments
- A/B testing (split testing)
- **Randomized controlled trials** (**RCTs**)
- Descriptive experiments
- Controlled experiments
- Hypothesis testing
- **Exploratory data analysis** (**EDA**)
- Simulation-based experiments
- ML experiments
- Cross-validation experiments
- Factorial experiments
- Longitudinal experiments
- Quasi-experimental design

- Single-blind study
- Double-blind study

Here are some advantages of experiments:

- Unlike observational studies, experiments can establish cause-and-effect relationships between variables.
- By manipulating variables and controlling confounding factors, experiments allow for more precise conclusions.
- Well-designed experiments can be replicated to confirm results, increasing the reliability of findings.
- Experiments can be adapted to various fields, such as healthcare, marketing, psychology, and education.
- Experiments often produce high quality, reliable data because they are designed to isolate specific variables of interest.

Here are some applications of experiments:

- Testing the efficacy of new drugs, treatments, or medical devices through clinical trials.
- Running A/B tests to determine which version of a product, advertisement, or website drives more conversions or engagement.
- Investigating human behavior and cognitive processes by manipulating variables like stress, sleep, or social interactions.
- Experimenting with teaching methods, curriculum designs, or learning tools to determine what produces the best educational outcomes.

Surveys are beneficial for gathering large-scale data on respondents' attitudes, opinions, and behaviors. They offer flexibility and efficiency but are limited in establishing causality. On the other hand, experiments allow researchers to test hypotheses and establish causal relationships by manipulating variables in a controlled environment, but they can be more complex and resource-intensive. Depending on the research goals and available resources, surveys and experiments can play crucial roles in providing valuable insights that help decision-making and innovation.

Web scraping and APIs

Web scraping and APIs are two essential methods for collecting data from the web. These techniques enable data scientists and analysts to access a vast amount of publicly available data, which can be used to build models, conduct analysis, and extract insights.

Web scraping refers to the automated process of extracting data from websites. It involves fetching web pages and extracting specific content, such as text, images, tables, or links. Web scraping is especially useful when publicly available data is not easily accessible through structured formats like CSV, XML, or JSON.

Let us look at how web scraping works:

- The process starts by sending an HTTP request to the target web page.
- Once the page is fetched, the HTML content is parsed to extract the necessary data.
- Specific data is identified using HTML tags, CSS selectors, or XPath queries to extract text, numbers, or other elements.

The extracted data is then cleaned, formatted, and stored in a structured format, like a database, CSV file, or spreadsheet.

Applications of web scraping:

- **Market research**: Gather product prices, customer reviews, and competitor analysis.
- **Sentiment analysis**: Extracting data from social media or news websites to perform sentiment analysis on public opinion.
- **Real-time data extraction**: Collecting real-time information from sources like stock market prices, weather updates, or sports scores.
- **Content aggregation**: Collecting and aggregating content from multiple news websites or blogs for content curation.

An API is a set of rules and protocols that allows one software application to communicate with another. APIs provide structured, reliable access to data and services, allowing data scientists to retrieve data from remote sources consistently and in an organized manner. Unlike web scraping, APIs provide data in machine-readable formats like JSON or XML, which makes them easier to process and integrate into data workflows.

This is how APIs work:

- A client (data scientist or application) sends an HTTP request to the API endpoint, specifying the data it needs.
- < UNK> To ensure secure access, many APIs require authentication, such as an API key, OAuth token, or username/password.
- The server processes the request and returns the requested data in a structured format, often JSON or XML.
- The response is parsed and processed, and the data is integrated into the analysis or model-building process.

The working of API is shown in *Figure 4.1*:

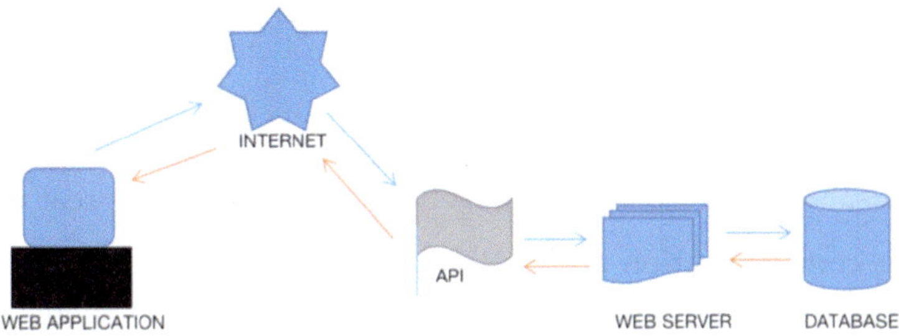

***Figure 4.1**: Working of API*

Here are the advantages of using APIs:

- APIs typically provide data in a structured format, such as JSON or XML, making it easier to parse and use.
- APIs are faster and more reliable than web scraping, as they are designed for data retrieval and typically provide up-to-date information.
- APIs offer a standardized way of accessing data, ensuring the data format and structure remain consistent.
- Using an API generally adheres to the provider's terms of service, reducing legal and ethical concerns associated with scraping.

Importance of domain knowledge

Domain knowledge is a critical component of data science that significantly enhances the effectiveness of data-driven decision-making. Domain knowledge ensures that the data is interpreted and applied correctly in the real-world context. Understanding the industry or field specific nuances allows for more accurate analysis, better model-building, and, ultimately, more actionable insights.

The following are the advantages of having domain knowledge:

- **Defining the problem correctly**: Without a clear understanding of the problem's context, data scientists may solve the wrong problem or analyze irrelevant data. Domain experts help define the key questions and challenges that the analysis should address.
- **Identifying relevant features and data**: Domain knowledge guides data scientists in selecting important variables for addressing the problem. It can also assist in filtering out irrelevant or noisy data, improving the model's performance.

- **Interpreting data correctly**: Data can have different meanings depending on context. Without domain knowledge, data scientists may misinterpret the data or fail to recognize meaningful patterns for solving the problem.
- **Building better models**: Domain knowledge enhances the development of ML models by helping data scientists choose the right algorithms and techniques. It also aids in designing features and transformations that capture the data's real-world complexity.
- **Enhancing communication and collaboration**: Data science is often a collaborative process involving teams of data scientists, engineers, business analysts, and domain experts. Domain knowledge allows data scientists to communicate more effectively with domain experts, facilitating smoother collaboration and better results.
- **Ensuring ethical and relevant use of data**: Data science projects, especially those dealing with sensitive data, require careful ethical considerations. Domain experts provide a framework for understanding the societal, legal, and moral implications of using data in specific contexts, ensuring that data-driven decisions are responsible and compliant with regulations.
- **Improving model validation and evaluation**: Model validation is essential to any data science project. Without domain knowledge, the process of validating models can be misaligned with the real-world application of the model's output. Domain experts help define appropriate validation metrics and interpret the results in the industry context.
- **Increasing the efficiency of data collection**: Data scientists rely on clean, relevant, and comprehensive data for analysis. Domain experts assist in determining the most effective methods for data collection by identifying what data is critical, how it should be gathered, and what external factors may influence data quality.

Examples of domain knowledge across different industries include the following:

- **Healthcare**: Domain knowledge in healthcare involves understanding medical terminology, clinical practices, and regulatory guidelines. Medical experts guide data scientists in analyzing patient health data, identifying relevant features (e.g., comorbidities), and interpreting results within a clinical context.
- **Finance**: Financial experts understand market dynamics, investment strategies, and risk assessment principles.
- **Retail**: Retail experts know consumer behavior, inventory management, and sales forecasting. They assist data scientists in analyzing customer purchase data and designing targeted marketing strategies or supply chain optimizations.
- **Manufacturing**: Domain experts in manufacturing are familiar with production lines, machinery, and quality control. They help data scientists in predictive maintenance, supply chain optimization, and process improvements by defining relevant features and interpreting sensor data.

Understanding context and relevance

In data science, understanding the context and relevance of data is fundamental to deriving meaningful insights and making informed decisions. Context refers to the circumstances or background that define and give meaning to data, while relevance pertains to the importance of specific data in addressing a particular problem or objective.

The importance of understanding context includes the following:

- **Defining the problem statement**: Context helps identify the underlying issue or question the analysis seeks to address.
  - **Example**: In healthcare, understanding a patient's medical history (context) is crucial for predicting disease outcomes.
- **Identifying relevant data**: Context guides the selection of datasets and meaningful features to the problem.
  - **Example**: For weather forecasting, atmospheric pressure and humidity are more relevant than demographic data.
- **Avoiding misinterpretation**: Data can lead to incorrect conclusions or inappropriate actions without context.
  - **Example**: A spike in product sales may be misinterpreted as organic growth without understanding seasonal demand trends.
- **Ensuring ethical use**: Context helps assess the moral implications of data usage, preventing unintended harm or biases.

The importance of relevance in data science includes the following:

- **Focus on problem specific data**: Relevance filters out unnecessary information, streamlining analysis and improving efficiency.
  - **Example**: Vehicle count data are relevant in a study on urban traffic, while meteorological data may not always be.
- **Enhancing model performance**: Relevant features reduce noise and improve the accuracy of statistical models and machine learning algorithms. Square footage and location are highly relevant for predicting house prices, whereas the seller's age is not.
- **Improved decision-making**: Relevant data provides actionable insights, enabling data-driven strategies.
  - **Example**: Retailers analyzing relevant purchase patterns can optimize inventory management.

Here are steps to understand context and relevance include the following:

1. **Engage with domain experts**: Collaborating with professionals who have deep knowledge of the domain ensures that data is interpreted accurately.
    - **Example:** Partnering with medical staff when analyzing patient records ensures relevant clinical factors are considered.
2. **Define clear objectives**: Establish specific goals and questions that the data analysis aims to address.
    - **Example**: A marketing team focuses on understanding customer churn rather than general sales trends.
3. **Perform EDA**: Use statistical summaries and visualizations to explore data characteristics and identify meaningful patterns.
    - **Example**: EDA can reveal outliers in financial data that might indicate fraud.
4. **Review metadata and source information**: Metadata details data origin, collection methods, and intended use, offering essential context.
    - **Example**: Understanding survey design helps assess the reliability and bias in survey data.
5. **Consider external factors**: Consider broader contextual elements, such as economic trends, cultural norms, or industry practices.
    - **Example**: Economic downturns might affect sales data in ways unrelated to product quality.

Understanding context and relevance is fundamental to effective data science. It ensures that analysis is grounded in the problem's real-world environment, leading to meaningful insights and actionable outcomes. By combining technical expertise with domain knowledge and continuously reevaluating context, data scientists can maximize the impact and accuracy of their work.

Collaboration with domain experts

Collaboration with domain experts is a vital component of successful data science projects. While data scientists bring technical expertise in analytics, machine learning, and programming, domain experts provide the contextual knowledge necessary to interpret the data and ensure its relevance to specific business or scientific objectives. This synergy bridges the gap between raw data and actionable insights, resulting in more accurate, meaningful, and impactful outcomes.

Here are some reasons why collaboration with domain experts is useful:

- **Contextual understanding**: Domain experts possess deep knowledge about the industry, field, or problem being addressed. They help identify the most critical variables, patterns, and anomalies, ensuring data relevance.

  - **Example**: In healthcare, a medical professional can guide a data scientist on the significance of biomarkers in patient datasets.
- **Defining the problem statement**: Clear and precise problem definitions are crucial in data science. Domain experts help articulate goals and constraints from a practical perspective.
  - **Example**: A financial expert can specify fraud detection needs regarding transaction types and risk factors.
- **Data validation and quality assessment**: Domain experts assess data quality, accuracy, and completeness. They identify missing or irrelevant data that could lead to flawed conclusions.
  - **Example**: In agriculture, an agronomist ensures that satellite data on crop health aligns with on-ground conditions.
- **Feature engineering**: Domain knowledge is critical for identifying and creating meaningful features for machine learning models.
  - **Example**: An engineer might recommend features like peak load times or weather conditions affecting power usage in energy.
- **Interpreting results**: Statistical models and machine learning algorithms generate patterns that need to be interpreted in context. Domain experts validate whether results align with practical expectations and industry standards.
  - **Example**: In retail, a marketing specialist interprets customer segmentation results to design effective campaigns.
- **Ethical considerations**: Domain experts help identify ethical concerns, ensuring data usage complies with industry regulations and societal norms.
  - **Example**: In legal analytics, a lawyer ensures that algorithms used for case prediction respect privacy laws and avoid biases.

Collaboration with domain experts is critical for the success of data science projects. It ensures that the analysis aligns with real-world needs, enhances the accuracy and applicability of models, and addresses ethical considerations. By fostering interdisciplinary teamwork, organizations can maximize the value of their data science initiatives and achieve more meaningful, actionable results paid.

Tools for data exploration

Data exploration is a critical phase in the data science process. It allows analysts and data scientists to understand the structure, characteristics, and nuances of the data before advanced analysis.

Tools used for data exploration are listed here:

- **Python**: Python is one of the most popular programming languages for data exploration due to its versatility and extensive ecosystem of libraries.

  Key libraries include:

  - **Pandas**: Provides data structures for efficient manipulation of structured data, such as DataFrames.
  - **NumPy**: Offers fast numerical computations for array and matrix operations.
  - **Matplotlib and Seaborn**: Enable data visualization to understand patterns and relationships.

- **R**: R is a powerful statistical analysis and data visualization programming language.

  Key libraries include the following:

  - **dplyr**: Simplifies data manipulation tasks like filtering, grouping, and summarizing.
  - **tidyr**: Helps with reshaping and tidying data for easier analysis.
  - **ggplot2**: Creates high quality, publication-ready visualizations.

- **Tableau**: Tableau is a user-friendly visualization tool that simplifies the exploration of large datasets. It includes a drag-and-drop interface for creating interactive charts and dashboards, real-time connectivity with databases, and cloud storage.

- **Microsoft Power BI**: Power BI is a robust business intelligence tool for data exploration and visualization.

- **Apache Spark (with PySpark)**: Apache Spark is a distributed computing framework, and PySpark enables its use with Python for handling large-scale data exploration. A data engineer uses PySpark to explore log files from a web application, identifying usage patterns and performance bottlenecks.

- **Jupyter Notebooks**: Jupyter Notebooks is an open-source tool for interactive computing and data exploration. It supports multiple languages, including Python and R. It integrates with visualization libraries for inline plots. It can also document workflows alongside code and outputs.

- **Konstanz Information Miner (KNIME)**: KNIME is an open-source data analytics platform with a visual workflow interface. It supports drag-and-drop workflow creation without coding and Integrates with R, Python, and machine learning libraries.

- **RapidMiner**: RapidMiner is a data preparation, exploration, and predictive modeling platform. It is a no-code environment with drag-and-drop functionality and advanced statistical tools for descriptive analysis.

- **Google Data Studio**: Google Data Studio is a cloud-based tool for visualizing and exploring data. It generates Interactive reports and dashboards for real-time exploration.
- **Statistical Analysis System (SAS)**: SAS provides robust tools for data exploration, statistical analysis, and reporting. It handles large and complex datasets efficiently and supports advanced statistical methods and visualization.

Data exploration is the foundation of practical data science workflows. The right tool enables professionals to uncover patterns, spot anomalies, and gain insights early. Organizations can streamline analysis and make informed, data-driven decisions by selecting appropriate tools based on the data and task requirements.

Statistical tools

Statistical tools are indispensable in data science. They provide methods and techniques for analyzing, interpreting, and drawing conclusions from data. These tools enable data scientists to uncover patterns, test hypotheses, and make predictions based on quantitative insights.

The importance of statistical tools includes the following:

- **Data analysis**: Simplify complex datasets for better understanding.
- **Hypothesis testing**: Evaluate assumptions and test their validity.
- **Predictive modeling**: Build models to forecast future trends.
- **Decision-making**: Provide data-backed insights for informed decisions
- **Quality assurance**: Improve processes through statistical control.

Popular statistical tools include the following:

- **R**: It is a programming language tailored for statistical analysis and visualization. It has extensive libraries like ggplot2, dplyr, and caret for data manipulation and modeling. It is used for hypothesis testing, regression analysis, and time series forecasting.
- **Python**: It is a versatile programming language with libraries such as NumPy, SciPy, Statsmodels, and Pandas for statistical computations. It performs various statistical functions and integrates with machine learning frameworks like scikit-learn.
- **SAS**: It is a powerful tool for advanced analytics and statistical modeling. It handles large datasets efficiently and includes regression, clustering, and multivariate analysis features. It is commonly used in healthcare, finance, and clinical research.
- **Statistical Package for the Social Sciences (SPSS)**: This user-friendly statistical analysis software is primarily used in the social sciences. It has advanced options for survey analysis, factor analysis, and hypothesis testing. It is suitable for academic research and market surveys. A sociologist uses SPSS to analyze data from a national study on education.

- **Excel**: An essential yet widely used tool for data handling and statistical calculations. It is ideal for small datasets and quick exploratory analysis. A small business uses Excel to calculate monthly sales trends and forecasts.
- **Stata**: A statistical software package used in economics, sociology, and biostatistics. It is often used for econometric modelling and healthcare data analysis.
- **MATLAB**: It is a high-level data analysis and modelling computing environment. It has extensive support for matrix-based calculations and integrates with toolboxes for statistical and ML analysis. It is used in engineering, image processing, and predictive modelling.
- **Minitab**: It is software specializing in quality improvement and Six Sigma projects. It provides tools for control charts, process capability, and **design of experiments** (**DOE**).
- **JMP**: Developed by SAS, JMP combines statistical analysis with interactive data visualization. It provides tools for multivariate analysis, reliability studies, and exploratory data analysis.
- **Gretl**: It is a free and open-source tool for econometric analysis. It is used for econometric modeling in academia and policy research.

Statistical tools are the backbone of data science, enabling the extraction of meaningful insights from raw data. Each tool has its strengths and is suited for specific tasks, industries, or levels of expertise. By selecting the appropriate tool, data scientists can perform accurate analyses, make data-driven decisions, and contribute to solving real-world problems.

Visualization tools

Visualization tools play a crucial role in data science by transforming raw data into visual representations that are easier to interpret and analyze. These tools enable data scientists, analysts, and stakeholders to identify patterns, trends, and anomalies, facilitating better decision-making.

Here are the key visualization tools commonly used in data science:

- **Tableau**: Tableau is a leading data visualization tool known for its user-friendly interface and robust capabilities for creating interactive dashboards. It provides drag-and-drop functionality for creating charts, graphs, and maps. It integrates with various data sources, including spreadsheets, databases, and cloud platforms.
- **Power BI**: Microsoft developed it. Power BI is a powerful business analytics tool that integrates seamlessly with *Microsoft Office* applications. It supports advanced analytics with integration into Azure and other Microsoft services. It allows users to publish reports and share insights across teams.

- **Matplotlib (Python library)**: Matplotlib is a widely used Python library for creating static, animated, and interactive visualizations. It supports advanced styling and control over plot elements. It integrates well with other Python libraries like Pandas and NumPy.
- **Seaborn (Python library)**: It is built on Matplotlib. Seaborn simplifies the creation of visually appealing statistical graphics and provides predefined themes for professional-looking visuals.
- **Plotly**: It is an open-source library for creating interactive web-based visualizations. It supports Python, R, and JavaScript and provides interactive charts such as 3D plots, geographic maps, and time series graphs.
- **ggplot2 (R library)**: ggplot2 is a popular R library for creating declarative visualizations based on the grammer of graphics.

Case study on data understanding in healthcare

A regional hospital aims to improve patient outcomes for diabetes management by analyzing data from its **electronic health records** (**EHRs**). The hospital wants to understand the factors influencing patient readmissions within 30 days after discharge, as high readmission rates affect patient health and hospital performance metrics. The following steps are involved in data analysis in the field of healthcare:

1. **Data collection**: The hospital collects data from its EHR system, including patient demographics, Such as age, gender, and ethnicity.
2. **Data profiling and exploration**: The dataset is profiled to understand its structure and quality. For example, the Average age of diabetes patients is 55, and the median HbA1c level is 8.2%. 22% of patients were readmitted within 30 days, and 5% of records had missing HbA1c values.
3. **Outliers**: A few patients may have extremely long stays (>30 days), likely due to complications.
4. **Data cleaning and preprocessing**: This involves handling missing values. Missing HbA1c values may be imputed using the mean for patients in the same age group. Records with missing discharge notes may be flagged for manual review. Outliers may be retained as they indicate critical cases. Numerical variables, such as HbA1c levels and income, are normalized for better comparability.
5. **Visualization and pattern identification**: Heatmap may be used for correlation analysis. A strong correlation was found between high HbA1c levels and readmissions. A moderate correlation was observed between comorbidities (e.g., hypertension) and readmissions. A bar chart of readmission by age group may be drawn.

6. **Insights and recommendations**: Based on the analysis, the following insights may be found: Patients with HbA1c > 9% should be enrolled in intensive diabetes management programs. Discharge plans should include follow-up appointments within 7 days for patients with multiple comorbidities.

Specific examples from healthcare industry

Here are some specific examples of how data understanding techniques are applied in the healthcare industry:

- **Identifying patient trends with data profiling**:
  - A hospital wants to analyze admission trends for patients with chronic illnesses. Using descriptive statistics to summarize patient demographics (e.g., age, gender, comorbidities).
  - Analyzing admission frequency for chronic conditions like diabetes or hypertension.
  - Data profiling reveals seasonal spikes in admissions, such as higher asthma cases during pollen heavy months.
- **Visualizing disease incidence using heatmaps**:
  - A public health agency tracks disease outbreaks by region. It creates a heatmap to visualize the prevalence of diseases like influenza across different geographical areas, using time series visualizations to track outbreaks over time.
  - Heatmaps highlight regions with unusually high infection rates, enabling targeted interventions.
- **Handling missing data in patient records**:
  - A clinic analyzing patient data discovers incomplete records, such as missing BMI or blood pressure values.
  - Imputing missing BMI values using the average BMI for patients of similar age and gender.
  - Removing incomplete records if the proportion of missing data is significant. Cleaned data ensures accurate insights into patient health trends and treatment outcomes.
- **Exploring relationships between medication and recovery rates**: A pharmaceutical company studies the effectiveness of a new medication for managing blood pressure. Using scatter plots, it explores the relationship between dosage and reduction in systolic blood pressure, calculating correlation coefficients to quantify the strength of this relationship. Results show a strong correlation, validating the efficacy of the new drug.

- **Quality assessment of diagnostic data**:
    - o A radiology department evaluates the quality of image data for machine learning applications in cancer detection. It assesses completeness by verifying that all patients have corresponding metadata (e.g., age, diagnosis) and ensures consistency in imaging formats (e.g., DICOM files).
    - o Improved data quality supports reliable AI model development for cancer detection.
- **Domain collaboration for feature understanding**: A data scientist analyzes patient outcomes collaborates with doctors to interpret lab test results. It consults with physicians to understand the significance of biomarkers like HbA1c for diabetes patients.
- **Detecting anomalies in patient monitoring data**: Wearable devices track patient vitals, such as heart rate and oxygen levels.
- **Visualizing drug usage trends**: A healthcare provider monitors the prescription patterns over time. Line charts may show the monthly trend in opioid prescriptions across hospitals.
- **Sampling data for predictive models**: A hospital may develop a predictive model to identify patients at risk of readmission. Using stratified sampling to ensure representation of patients with varying conditions.
- **Case study**: EHR Analysis for patient care optimization is a healthcare organization wants to optimize resource allocation based on patient data from EHRs. Visualization tools may be used to map patient flow across departments.

Techniques used for data understanding

Data understanding is a critical step in the data science process that involves exploring and analyzing data to comprehend its structure, content, and quality.

The following points are techniques used for data understanding:

- **Data profiling**: Involves examining the data to understand its structure, distribution, and patterns. This includes computing measures like mean, median, variance, and standard deviation to summarize data attributes, analyzing the occurrence of different values in categorical variables, identifying data types (e.g., numerical, categorical, date/time), and checking consistency in formats.
- **Data visualization**: Visualization techniques provide a graphical representation of data, making it easier to detect trends, patterns, and anomalies. Common visualization methods include: histograms and box plots.

- **Data cleaning and validation**: Understanding data often uncovers quality issues that require cleaning. This step involves: Handling missing values, removing duplicates and eliminating outliers.
- **EDA**: It is a systematic approach to understanding data using statistical and visualization techniques.

It involves the following:

- **Univariate analysis**: Examining one variable at a time to understand its distribution and central tendencies.
- **Bivariate analysis**: Exploring relationships between two variables using correlation coefficients or cross-tabulations.
- **Multivariate analysis**: Understanding interactions among multiple variables using advanced methods like PCA.
- **Data quality assessment**: Evaluating data quality ensures reliability and accuracy. Key aspects include completeness, consistency, and accuracy.
- **Domain-specific techniques**: Domain expertise is essential for contextualizing data. Techniques include Feature Understanding and collaborating with domain experts to understand what each variable represents data labeling, relevance assessment.
- **Data sampling**: When working with large datasets, sampling techniques are used to create a smaller, representative subset for initial analysis. Random sampling means selecting data points randomly to avoid bias. Stratified sampling means dividing data into strata (groups) and sampling proportionally.
- **Data annotation and documentation**: Metadata Analysis means reviewing information about data (e.g., source, date of collection). Annotation is adding labels or comments to describe features, outliers, or decisions made during understanding.
- **Correlation and dependency analysis**: Understanding relationships among variables helps in feature selection and hypothesis formulation.
- **Data distribution analysis**: Analyzing data distribution helps to understand the shape, center, and spread of the data. It is crucial for selecting the right statistical models and transformations. For e.g., Skewness measures the asymmetry of the distribution of values. This is shown in *Table 4.1*:

Skewness value	Distribution shape
≈ 0	Symmetrical (normal)
> 0	Positively skewed (right-tailed)
< 0	Negatively skewed (left-tailed)

Table 4.1: *Skewness vs distribution shape*

Kurtosis measures the tailedness or peakedness of the distribution compared to a normal distribution. This is shown in *Table 4.2*:

Kurtosis value (excess)	Shape	Characteristics
≈ 0	Mesokurtic	Normal tails and peak
> 0	Leptokurtic	More extreme outliers
< 0	Platykurtic	Fewer outliers, flat peak

Table 4.2: *Interpretation of Kurtosis*

- **Data visualization dashboards**: Interactive dashboards provide a comprehensive data view through visual summaries and real-time analytics. Example: Tools like Tableau or Power BI.

Conclusion

This chapter provides a foundational understanding of the data types and how to obtain meaningful insights from the given data set. It describes structured data, which is highly organized and stored in tabular formats, and unstructured data, such as text, images, and videos, that lack a predefined format. Both types' challenges and unique characteristics are explored, emphasizing the importance of selecting the right tools and techniques for handling them. The chapter also delves into data collection techniques, covering traditional methods like surveys and experiments and modern approaches such as web scraping and APIs. It highlights the strengths and limitations of each method while addressing the ethical considerations and challenges in ensuring data quality.

This chapter explores the importance of domain knowledge and explains how understanding the context and relevance of data enhances interpretation and decision-making. Collaboration with domain experts is discussed as a vital component in bridging the gap between technical analysis and practical application. The chapter also discusses tools for data exploration, such as statistical analysis tools and visualization platforms, which play a critical role in uncovering patterns, trends, and insights. This chapter also discusses a case study in healthcare demonstrating the application of these principles in a real-world context. It explores how structured and unstructured data are utilized, the methods employed for collection, and the techniques used for exploration and understanding. The next chapter discusses about data cleaning, data transformation techniques, feature engineering, data preprocessing tools and libraries.

Exercises

1. Explain the difference between structured and unstructured data. Provide relevant examples for both.
2. Discuss the challenges faced when handling unstructured data compared to structured data.

3. Why is it important to correctly identify whether data is structured or unstructured before analysis?
4. How does the storage and processing of structured data differ from unstructured data?
5. Describe a real-world scenario where both structured and unstructured data are used together.
6. Describe the role of web scraping and APIs in modern data collection. Include ethical considerations.
7. Why is it important to validate the quality of data collected through APIs or web scraping?
8. How can poorly collected data impact the outcomes of a data science project? Provide an example.
9. Explain how advancements in technology have transformed data collection techniques over the years.
10. Explain the role of domain knowledge in identifying outliers or anomalies in data.
11. How do visualization tools help in the process of data exploration? Provide examples of popular tools.
12. What are the key steps involved in performing exploratory data analysis (EDA) on a new dataset?
13. Discuss two challenges faced when dealing with unstructured data and suggest possible solutions.
14. Provide examples of structured and unstructured data in a business context and explain how they are utilized differently.
15. Explain the role of APIs in data collection. How do they simplify access to real-time data?
16. Describe the ethical considerations involved in web scraping. How can data scientists ensure responsible use?
17. Discuss the role of domain experts in data interpretation and decision-making. Provide an industry-specific example.
18. Why is domain knowledge crucial for identifying relevant features in a dataset? Illustrate with a practical example.
19. What role do data visualization tools like Tableau or Power BI play in simplifying data understanding for stakeholders?

Chapter 5
Data Preprocessing

Introduction

Today, data-driven decisions are highly dependent on the insights that we draw from data, which in turn is dependent on the quality of data. Raw data, which is collected from various sources, is often incomplete, inconsistent, or noisy, making it unsuitable for direct analysis or modeling. Hence, data preprocessing is essential and serves as the foundational step in data science or ML. Data preprocessing involves cleaning, transforming, and preparing data to ensure it is accurate, complete, and ready for analysis.

By addressing challenges like missing values, inconsistent formats, and irrelevant features, this step ensures that the data is both meaningful and usable for deriving actionable insights. This chapter explores the essential techniques and tools for effective data preprocessing. From handling missing data to transforming variables and engineering features, we explore the strategies that enhance the reliability and predictive power of models. We also discuss popular tools and libraries like Pandas and scikit-learn that help in preprocessing tasks. We also discuss a case study focusing on retail data, highlighting real-world challenges and solutions.

In this chapter, we will understand the importance of data preprocessing and recognize the critical role it plays in ensuring the quality and usability of data for analysis and ML models. Additionally, we will also look at data cleaning techniques, identify different types of missing data, and apply appropriate methods to handle missing values effectively.

Structure

This chapter covers the following topics:

- Data cleaning
- Data transformation techniques
- Feature engineering
- Data preprocessing tools and libraries
- Case study: Preprocessing in retail data

Objectives

By the end of this chapter, readers will learn about data transformation techniques and understand and implement strategies such as normalization, standardization, and encoding categorical variables to prepare data for analysis. They would be able to apply feature engineering methods, develop skills in creating new features, and select the most relevant ones to enhance model performance.

Data cleaning

Data cleaning is the process of identifying and rectifying errors, inconsistencies, and inaccuracies in a dataset to ensure it is suitable for analysis or machine learning tasks.

Raw data often contains missing values, outliers, or incorrect entries due to errors in data collection, storage, or integration. Without data cleaning, our analysis' accuracy can be compromised.

Data cleaning not only involves dealing with missing values but also handling other challenges, such as:

- Identification and removal of duplicate records.
- Identification and dealing with the outliers.
- Standardizing formats such as dates, currencies, and text fields.
- Correction or elimination of incorrect entries i.e. typographical errors, impossible entries (e.g. negative ages).

Follow these steps to perform data cleaning:

1. **Understanding the context**: Knowledge of domain information can be used to interpret and address data issues appropriately.
2. **Perform documentation**: All the records of cleaning steps must be maintained to ensure reproducibility and transparency.
3. **Use automation**: Utilize libraries like Pandas for efficient data cleaning workflows.
4. **Validate results**: Ensure that the cleaned data aligns with the original intent and preserves its integrity.

Types of missing data

Dataset may involve missing data values. The following are the types of missing data:

- Presence of missing data in datasets can significantly impact the quality of analysis and modelling if not handled appropriately. Missing data is broadly categorized into three types:

- **Missing completely at random (MCAR)**: Data is considered MCAR if the missingness has no relationship with any other observed or unobserved variable in the dataset.
- **Missing at random (MAR)**: Data is classified as MAR when the missingness is systematically related to some observed data but not to the missing data itself. The missing values can be predicted using other variables in the dataset.
- **Missing not at random (MNAR)**: Data is MNAR when the missingness is related to the value of the missing data itself.

Let us look at the importance of identifying the type of missing. Understanding the type of missing data is essential for selecting appropriate handling techniques. Not identifying and dealing with the missing data can introduce bias, reduce statistical power, and lead to inaccurate conclusions. Analysts and data scientists should assess the patterns of missingness using statistical tests and visualizations to determine the most effective strategies for managing missing data.

Techniques for handling missing data

Handling missing data is a very important aspect of data preprocessing. The approach to dealing with missing values largely depends on the type and extent of the missing data, as well as the impact of missing data on the analysis.

Here are common techniques for dealing with the missing data:

- **Deletion techniques**: When the missing data is not extensive, deletion is a simple method to remove incomplete records or variables. However, it should be used carefully to avoid biased analysis or excessive data loss.

  Here are some deletion techniques:

  - **Listwise deletion**: It involves removing entire rows that have any missing values in any column. It is simple to implement; no need for complex imputation. It can lead to a significant reduction in sample size if many rows have missing values, reducing statistical power and potentially introducing bias if the missing data is not random.
  - **Pairwise deletion**: Instead of deleting an entire row, pairwise deletion uses available data for each pair of variables involved in the analysis. It removes only the missing values for specific analyses and retains more data compared to listwise deletion. However, it can lead to inconsistencies across analyses, as the number of available data points may vary between different variables.
  - **Column deletion**: It involves removing entire columns that contain a high percentage of missing values or are not critical for the analysis. It simplifies the dataset when columns are not helpful or highly incomplete. However, the loss of potentially valuable information if critical variables are removed.

- **Imputation techniques**: Imputation is the process of filling in missing data with substituted values. Imputation methods vary based on the nature of the data and the relationships between observed and missing values.

  Here are some imputation techniques:

  - **Mean imputation**: It replaces missing numerical values with the mean of the observed data in that column.
  - **Median imputation**: It replaces missing numerical values with the median, often used for skewed data.
  - **Mode imputation**: It replaces missing categorical values with the most frequent category (mode).
  - **Forward/Backward fill**: In time-series data, missing values can be filled using the previous (forward fill) or subsequent (backward fill) available value.
  - **K-nearest neighbors (KNN) imputation**: KNN imputation estimates missing values based on the values of the nearest neighbors, considering other available data points. It is more accurate than mean/median imputation, especially for complex data patterns. It is computationally expensive, particularly with large datasets.
  - **Multivariate imputation by chained equations (MICE)**: It is a sophisticated method where missing values are imputed multiple times using regression models based on other variables. This process iteratively refines imputations.
  - **Regression imputation**: Involves predicting missing values using a regression model based on other variables in the dataset.
  - **Expectation-Maximization (EM) algorithm**: The EM algorithm uses an iterative process to estimate missing data values by maximizing the likelihood of observed data while accounting for missingness.

Data transformation techniques

Data transformation techniques involve modifying the data into a format that is suited for analysis or machine learning models. It ensures that the data is consistent, scaled appropriately, and ready for modelling.

The following are common data transformation techniques used in data preprocessing:

- **Normalization and standardization**: Both normalization and standardization are techniques used to scale numerical data, ensuring that features with different units or scales do not disproportionately affect the model's performance. Normalization involves rescaling the data to fall within a specific range, typically [0, 1]. This is done by subtracting the minimum value of the feature and dividing by the range (maximum-minimum).

- **Log transformation**: Log transformation is a technique used to address data that is highly skewed or has extreme values. By applying a logarithmic function, the data is compressed, reducing the impact of large values. The log transformation cannot handle zero or negative values. Therefore, the data must be adjusted accordingly (e.g., by adding a constant to the data before applying the log transformation).
- **Box Cox transformation**: The Box Cox transformation is a more general method that can be used to stabilize variance and make the data more normally distributed. This technique is particularly useful for data that exhibits heteroscedasticity (non-constant variance).
- **Categorical data transformation**: Categorical data needs to be transformed into numerical format before it can be used in most machine learning models. The transformation methods ensure that categorical features are treated in a way that preserves their relationships with the target variable.
- **One-hot encoding**: One-hot encoding creates a binary column for each possible category value in a categorical feature. A *1* is assigned to the column corresponding to the feature's value, and *0s* are assigned to the other columns.
- **Label encoding**: Label encoding converts each category in a categorical feature into a unique integer. For example, *Red* might become 1, *Green* becomes 2, and *Blue* becomes 3.
- **Ordinal encoding**: Ordinal encoding is a method used for ordinal categorical data (where categories have an inherent order). The categories are assigned numerical values according to their order. For example, *Low, Medium, High* can be encoded as 0, 1, 2.
- **Binning (discretization)**: Binning is the process of converting continuous variables into categorical variables by grouping the values into discrete intervals or bins. This can make it easier to analyze and interpret data, especially for algorithms that struggle with continuous data.

Data transformation is a vital part of the data preprocessing process. By performing scaling, normalizing, or encoding the data appropriately, analysts can ensure that their data is suitable for analysis and modeling.

Normalization and standardization

Normalization and standardization are two common techniques used to scale numerical data before sending it to machine learning algorithms. These techniques are essential because many ML models (e.g., KNN, neural networks, gradient descent-based algorithms) perform better when the data is on a similar scale.

Normalization, also known as **min-max scaling**, is the process of rescaling the feature values to a fixed range, typically [0, 1]. This ensures that all the feature values are on the same scale, making it easier for machine learning models to learn from the data.

Follow these steps to perform normalization:

1. Identify the minimum and maximum values for the feature.
2. Subtract the minimum value from each data point.
3. Divide the result by the range (max value - min value) to scale the data between 0 and 1.

Here are the advantages of normalization:

- It is simple and easy to implement.
- It works well when the data does not contain outliers, as it directly maps the data to a fixed range.
- It is essential for algorithms that rely on distance metrics (e.g., KNN, k-means clustering).

Here are the disadvantages of normalization:

- Sensitive to outliers. If the data contains extreme values, normalization can skew the results since the scaling is based on the minimum and maximum values.
- The transformed data is limited to a predefined range (e.g., [0, 1]), which can sometimes be undesirable for algorithms requiring data with a broader range or different scales.

Standardization is also called as Z-score normalization. It involves rescaling the data such that it has a mean of 0 and a standard deviation of 1. Unlike normalization, standardization does not bound the data to a specific range but instead centres the data around 0 and scales it based on its variance.

Follow these steps to perform standardization:

1. Calculate the mean and standard deviation of the feature.
2. Subtract the mean from each data point.
3. Divide the result by the standard deviation to scale the data to have a mean of 0 and a standard deviation of 1.

Here are the advantages of standardization:

- It is more robust to outliers compared to normalization because the scaling is based on the standard deviation, which is less affected by extreme values than the minimum and maximum.
- It is ideal for algorithms that assume data is normally distributed (e.g., linear regression, logistic regression, SVM).

- It does not constrain data to a specific range, making it more suitable for models that require a broader scale.

Here are the disadvantages of standardization:

- It does not bound the data within a specific range, which may be undesirable for some algorithms.
- It can cause issues when the data is not normally distributed, as the mean and standard deviation may not accurately reflect the central tendency and spread of the data.

Normalization and standardization are both important preprocessing steps in the data pipeline. Normalization scales data to a specific range, making it ideal for algorithms that depend on distance calculations. Standardization transforms data into a form with zero mean and unit variance, which is helpful for many machine learning algorithms that assume normally distributed data.

Encoding categorical variables

Categorical variables represent categories or labels, are an essential part of many datasets. However, machine learning algorithms generally require numerical input, so categorical variables must be transformed into a numerical format before they can be used in most models. There are several techniques for encoding categorical variables, depending on the nature of the categorical variable (nominal or ordinal) and the type of model being used.

Here are some common techniques for encoding categorical variables:

- **One-hot encoding**: It is a popular technique for converting nominal categorical variables (those without any inherent order) into a format that machine learning algorithms can process. It creates binary columns for each category, where each column represents a unique category and contains a 1 if the observation corresponds to that category, and 0 otherwise. Dummy variables are binary (0 or 1) variables created to represent categorical variables (variables with discrete categories) in a numeric format so that they can be used in statistical models and machine learning algorithms. Dummy variables are created using one-hot encoding.

  Example: Suppose we have a categorical variable **`Color`** with three categories: **`Red`**, **`Green`**, and **`Blue`**. One-hot encoding would create three new columns: **`Color_Red`**, **`Color_Green`**, and **`Color_Blue`**.

  Each data point would be represented as follows:

```
Color    Color_Red  Color_Green  Color_Blue
Red          1           0            0
Green        0           1            0
Blue         0           0            1
```

Here, the new binary columns are the dummy variables. Here are some advantages of one-hot encoding:

- o It works well with nominal data (where categories have no order).
- o It allows machine learning algorithms to treat each category independently without introducing false ordinal relationships.
- o It prevents models from assuming any arbitrary ranking between categories.

Here are some disadvantages of one-hot encoding:

- o It can lead to high-dimensional datasets if there are many unique categories, resulting in increased computational complexity (e.g., when dealing with categorical variables with many unique values, such as **`City`**).
- o It may lead to sparse matrices, where most of the values are 0, increasing memory usage.

- **Label encoding**: It involves assigning a unique integer to each category in a categorical variable. This method is particularly suitable for ordinal data (where categories have a meaningful order, like **`Low`**, **`Medium`**, and **`High`**).

  Example: Consider an ordinal feature **`Education Level`** *with categories:* **`High School`**, **`Bachelor's`**, **`Master's`**, **`Ph.D`**.

  Label encoding would assign the following integer values:

```
Education Level   Encoded Value
High School            0
Bachelor's             1
Master's               2
Ph.D.                  3
```

  Each observation is now represented by the corresponding integer value.

  Here are some advantages of label encoding:

  - o It is simple to implement and efficient in terms of memory usage.
  - o It is suitable for ordinal data, where the encoding reflects the inherent ordering of the categories.

  Here is a disadvantage of label encoding:

  - o For nominal data; this approach may lead to unintended consequences. The model could misinterpret the integer values as having a natural order or ranking (e.g., **`"Red" = 0`**, **`"Green" = 1`**, **`"Blue" = 2`**), which can introduce bias into the model.

- **Ordinal encoding**: It is similar to label encoding, but it is specifically used for ordinal categorical variables, where the order of categories matters (e.g., `Low`, `Medium`, `High`). For an ordinal variable `Income Level` with the categories `Low`, `Medium`, and `High`, ordinal encoding might assign the following integers:

Income Level	Encoded Value
Low	0
Medium	1
High	2

  Here are some advantages of ordinal encoding:

  - It preserves the natural order in ordinal data.
  - It is simple and memory-efficient.

  Here is a disadvantage of ordinal encoding:

  - Like label encoding, using ordinal encoding on nominal data may introduce artificial order, leading to biased models.

- **Binary encoding**: It is a combination of label encoding and one-hot encoding, and it is useful for categorical variables with a high number of categories. The categories are first label-encoded, then each encoded value is converted into its binary representation.

  Example: Consider a categorical feature `Product Type` with categories: `A`, `B`, `C`, `D`, `E`. After label encoding, the values would be:

Product Type	Label Encoded Value	Binary Encoding
A	0	000
B	1	001
C	2	010
D	3	011
E	4	100

  Here are some advantages of binary encoding:

  - It is more efficient than one-hot encoding for high-cardinality categorical variables (those with many unique values).
  - It reduces the dimensionality compared to one-hot encoding.

  Here is a disadvantage of binary encoding:

  - The binary encoding may still not work well if there is a very large number of categories, as the number of binary digits (columns) increases.

- **Frequency or count encoding**: Frequency encoding replaces each category with the number of times it appears in the dataset. This technique is useful when the frequency of each category carries some meaningful information. For example, consider a feature `City` with categories: `New York`, `Los Angeles`, and `Chicago`.

  The frequency encoding would replace each category with the number of occurrences of each city in the dataset:

  ```
  City          Frequency Encoding
  New York              10
  Los Angeles           5
  Chicago               3
  ```

  Here are some advantages of frequency or count encoding:

  - Simple to implement.
  - It is useful when the frequency of the categories carries meaningful information.

  Here is a disadvantage of frequency or count encoding:

  - The frequency encoding may introduce bias if the category frequency is not meaningful for the model.

- **Target encoding (mean encoding)**: Target encoding involves replacing each category with the mean of the target variable for that category. This method is often used in regression problems where the goal is to predict a continuous value. For example, Consider a categorical feature `Category` and a target variable `Sales`.

  Each category in the `Category` feature is replaced with the mean sales for that category:

  ```
  Category      Target Encoding
  A                     150
  B                     250
  C                     350
  ```

  In this case, the `Target Encoding` for `Category A` would be the mean of `Sales` for `Category A`

  Here are some advantages of target encoding:

  - It is useful when there is a correlation between the categorical variable and the target variable.
  - It helps reduce dimensionality compared to one-hot encoding.

  Here is a disadvantage of target encoding:

  - It can lead to overfitting if not handled properly, especially in cases of small sample sizes. This is often mitigated by applying regularization techniques.

Feature engineering

Feature engineering is the process of using domain knowledge and data analysis techniques to create, transform, and select features that improve the performance of a machine learning model. Features are the input variables that a machine learning model uses to make predictions, and well-designed features can significantly enhance a model's predictive power. Feature engineering typically involves creating new features from existing data, selecting the most relevant features, and transforming data into a more suitable format for analysis. It is often considered one of the most critical steps in the machine learning pipeline, as the quality of the features directly impacts model performance.

Follow these steps for feature engineering:

1. **Understanding the data**:
   a. Analyze the data to understand its structure, relationships, and distributions.
   b. Use domain knowledge to identify potential features that could influence the target variable.
2. **Creating new features**:
   a. Generate new variables from existing data that may capture additional information or insights. Examples: Combining multiple features (e.g., creating a **`BMI`** feature from **`Weight`** and **`Height`**).
   b. Extracting useful components from date or time fields (e.g., extracting the day of the week or the hour from a timestamp).
3. **Transforming features**:
   a. Apply mathematical transformations or scaling techniques to make the data more suitable for modeling.
   b. Techniques include normalization, standardization, and encoding categorical variables.
4. **Selecting features**:
   a. Identify and retain the most relevant features while removing redundant or irrelevant ones.
   b. Techniques include correlation analysis, feature importance from models, and dimensionality reduction methods like PCA.
5. **Validating features**: Test the impact of newly engineered features on model performance through cross-validation or holdout testing.

The importance of feature engineering includes the following:

- Improves model accuracy.
- Reduces overfitting.
- Enhances interpretability.
- Handles complex relationships.

Here are some techniques in feature engineering:

- **Feature creation**: Combine or transform existing features to create new ones.
- **Feature transformation**: Transform existing features into formats more suitable for modeling.

  Techniques for feature transformation include:

  - **Log transform**: For skewed distributions.
  - **Box Cox transform**: For stabilizing variance and making data more normally distributed.
  - **Binning**: Converting continuous variables into categorical bins.
- **Feature scaling**: Normalize or standardize numerical features to ensure consistent scaling. Techniques for feature scaling include:
  - Min-max scaling.
  - Z-score normalization.
- **Handling missing data**: Impute missing values using techniques such as mean, median, or mode substitution, or advanced methods like KNN imputation.
- **Encoding categorical variables**: Convert categorical variables into numerical representations using one-hot encoding, label encoding, target encoding, or binary encoding.
- **Feature selection**: Identify and retain the most impactful features using techniques such as:
  - **Filter methods**: Correlation analysis, mutual information.
  - **Wrapper methods: Recursive feature elimination (RFE).**
  - **Embedded methods**: Feature importance from tree-based models like random forest or XGBoost.
- **Dimensionality reduction**: Reduce the number of features while retaining essential information using techniques like PCA, t-SNE (for visualization), and autoencoders.

Creating new features

Feature generation or Feature construction, involves deriving additional variables from existing data to improve the performance of ML models.

Let us look at the importance of feature construction:

- **Improve model accuracy**: New features often enhance the predictive power of the model.
- **Capture hidden relationships**: Deriving new features can uncover relationships between variables not evident in the raw data.
- **Simplify data representation**: Combining or transforming features can make the data more interpretable and easier for models to process.
- **Reduce noise**: Aggregated or transformed features may reduce noise and outliers, improving model robustness.

Common approaches to feature construction include the following:

- **Mathematical transformations**: Apply mathematical operations to existing features to create new ones.
- **Combining features**: Combine multiple features to generate interaction terms or summary statistics.
- **Temporal features**: Extract information from time-based data, such as dates or timestamps.

  Examples: Extract day, month, year, or time of day from a timestamp, calculate elapsed time (e.g., time since the last purchase), Identify seasonal or periodic patterns (e.g., day of the week or holiday periods).
- **Text features**: Extract information from text data using **natural language processing** (**NLP**) techniques.

  Examples: Word or character count in a text field, Sentiment scores from a product review and Frequency of specific keywords or n-grams.
- **Categorical features**: Encode categorical data in a way that adds meaningful information.

  Examples: Group categories by their statistical importance (e.g., combining rare categories into any other category) or assign numerical values based on domain knowledge or data patterns.
- **Domain-specific features**: Use domain knowledge to create features tailored to the specific context or industry.

- **Statistical features**: Use statistical summaries of data to create features.

  Examples: Mean, median, standard deviation, or variance of numerical features.

- **Binning**: Group continuous numerical data into discrete bins.

  Examples: Age groups: convert numerical age into categories like *child, teen, adult, and senior.* Categorize income into low, medium, and high ranges.

- **Lag features (time-series data)**: Create lagged variables that represent past values of a feature.

  Examples: Previous day's sales or stock price like rolling averages or rolling maximum values.

- **Feature interactions**: Combine features to capture interactions or dependencies between variables.

Feature selection methods

Feature selection is the process of identifying and selecting the most relevant features from a dataset that contribute to the predictive performance of a ML model. It involves removing redundant, irrelevant, or noisy features to improve the efficiency and effectiveness of the model. Feature selection reduces model complexity, prevents overfitting, and enhances interpretability. It is especially critical when working with high-dimensional datasets where irrelevant features overwhelm useful information.

The importance of feature selection includes the following:

- Improved model performance
- Reduced overfitting
- Increased interpretability
- Lower computational cost

Categories of feature selection methods

Feature selection techniques are broadly categorized into three types:

- **Filter methods**: Filter methods rely on statistical tests and metrics to evaluate the relevance of features independent of the machine learning model. They are simple and fast.

- **Wrapper methods**: Wrapper methods evaluate subsets of features by training and testing a ML model. These methods search for the optimal feature set by iteratively adding or removing features and assessing model performance.

Types under wrapper methods include the following:

- o **Forward selection**: Starts with no features and adds features one by one based on their contribution to model performance.
- o **Backward elimination**: Starts with all features and removes the least significant features iteratively.
- o Recursive feature elimination (RFE): Uses a model (e.g., linear regression or decision trees) to rank features and recursively eliminates the least important ones.

- **Embedded methods**: Embedded methods incorporate feature selection into the model training process. These methods combine the benefits of filter and wrapper techniques by using algorithms that penalize irrelevant features during training.

Data preprocessing tools and libraries

Data preprocessing is a crucial step in the field of ML, and several tools and libraries have been developed to simplify and automate this process. These tools are used for data cleaning, transformation, feature engineering, and feature selection, making it easier for data scientists to prepare their datasets for analysis and modeling.

Python libraries for data preprocessing include the following:

- **NumPy**: It is used for numerical computation.

  The following are the key features of NumPy:

  - o Efficient handling of large arrays and matrices.
  - o Used for mathematical operations for data transformation (log, exponential, etc.).
  - o Provide tools for handling missing values (**`np.nan`**).

  Example:

  ```
  ```python import numpy as np
  # Normalization
  data = np.array([1, 2, 3, 4, 5])
  normalized_data = (data - np.min(data)) / (np.max(data) - np.min(data))
  ```

- **Feature-engine**: It is used for feature engineering and preprocessing.

  Key features of Feature-engine are:

  - o Encoding categorical variables.
  - o Handling missing data.
  - o Variable transformations (log, power, etc.).
  - o Outlier removal.
  ```

Example:

```
from feature_engine.encoding import OneHotEncoder
encoder = OneHotEncoder()
transformed_data = encoder.fit_transform(data)
```

- **PySpark (Spark MLlib)**: It is used for distributed data processing for large datasets.

  Key features of PySpark include the following:

  - Scalable handling of big data.
  - Data preprocessing, feature engineering, and transformation at scale.
  - Support for machine learning pipelines.

  Example:

```
from pyspark.ml.feature import StringIndexer
data = {
    'Name': ['Alice', 'Bob', 'Charlie', 'David', 'Ella', 'Frank',
'Grace', 'Hannah', 'Ian', 'Jack'],
    'Age': [25, 30, np.nan, 22, 29, 35, np.nan, 40, 26, np.nan],
    'City': ['New York', 'Los Angeles', 'Chicago', np.nan, 'Houston',
'Phoenix', 'Philadelphia', 'San Antonio', np.nan, 'San Diego'],
    'Salary': [50000, 60000, 55000, 48000, np.nan, 62000, 70000, np.nan,
58000, 65000]
}
df = pd.DataFrame(data)
indexer = StringIndexer(inputCol="category", outputCol="categoryIndex")
indexed = indexer.fit(df).transform(df)
```

Tools for data visualization and exploration include the following:

- **Matplotlib and Seaborn**: These are used to identify patterns and anomalies in data during preprocessing.

  For example:

```
import seaborn as sns
sns.heatmap(df.isnull(), cbar=False) # Visualizing missing data
```

- **Tableau and Power BI**: These are interactive tools for visualizing datasets to identify data quality issues. They are used in the early stages of preprocessing to guide cleaning efforts.

The following are some specialized libraries for data cleaning:

- **OpenRefine**: It is a standalone tool for cleaning and transforming messy data. Key Features include the following:

- o Deduplication and clustering of data.
- o Parsing unstructured data into structured formats.
- o Transformations using custom expressions.

- **Dask**: It is a parallel computing library that extends Pandas to large datasets. Key features of Dask are:
  - o Handles datasets larger than memory.
  - o Parallel processing for faster preprocessing.

Libraries for advanced preprocessing techniques include the following:

- **TensorFlow and PyTorch**: They provide frameworks for deep learning that include preprocessing utilities for image, text, and structured data.

  Example (TensorFlow):

```
import tensorflow as tf
# Normalization
normalized_data = tf.keras.utils.normalize(data, axis=1)
```

- **NLTK and spaCy**: It is used for preprocessing textual data. Key features include the following:
  - o It is used for tokenization, lemmatization, and stemming.
  - o It is used for removing stop words.
  - o It is used for part-of-speech tagging.

  Example (NLTK):

```
from nltk.tokenize import word_tokenize
tokens = word_tokenize("This is an example sentence.")
```

Tools for automation in data preprocessing include the following:

- **Feature tools**: It is used for automated feature engineering. Key features include the following:
  - o Generates features automatically based on relationships in the data.
  - o Handles time-based features and hierarchies.
- **Auto-sklearn and H2O.ai**: These are automated ML platforms that include built-in preprocessing pipelines. They handle tasks like missing data imputation, feature scaling, and encoding automatically.

Data preprocessing is an important task in a data science project. Depending on the size of the dataset, the type of preprocessing required, and the computational resources available, the right tool or library should be used. With the help of these tools, data scientists can ensure their datasets are clean, structured, and ready for advanced analysis and modeling.

Python libraries

Pandas and scikit-learn Python provide libraries that are used to perform data preprocessing efficiently. Let us look at them in detail:

- **Pandas**: It is used for data manipulation and analysis. Key features of Pandas:
    - It is used for reading and writing data in various formats (CSV, Excel, JSON, SQL, etc.).
        - Handling missing data using methods like **`fillna`**, **`dropna`**, and **`interpolation`**.
        - Data transformation using functions like **`apply`**, **`map`**, and **`aggregation`**.
        - Handling categorical data through encoding techniques like **`get_dummies`**: Merging, grouping, and reshaping datasets.
- **Scikit-learn**: It is used for ML and data preprocessing.

  Key features of scikit-learn are:
    - Normalization and standardization using **`StandardScaler`** and **`MinMaxScaler`**.
    - Encoding categorical variables with **`OneHotEncoder`** and **`LabelEncoder`**.
    - Handling missing values with **`SimpleImputer`** and **`KNNImputer`**.
    - Dimensionality reduction using PCA and feature selection techniques.

  Example:

```
from sklearn.preprocessing import StandardScaler
scaler = StandardScaler()
scaled_data = scaler.fit_transform(data)
```

Practical examples and applications

Real-world datasets generally comprise inconsistencies, missing values, or irrelevant information, making the preprocessing task essential.

Preprocessing tasks in a data science project include the following:

- **Handling missing data**: For example, patient datasets often have missing values for features like blood pressure or cholesterol levels. For numerical data, we can use mean or median imputation. For categorical data (e.g., gender or symptoms), we can use mode or predictive methods.

- **Normalization and standardization**: Features like income and credit score have different scales, affecting the model's performance. We can normalize or standardize numerical data to bring all features to the same scale.

  Example:

```
from sklearn.preprocessing import StandardScaler
credit_data = [[50000, 700], [60000, 750], [45000, 680]]
scaler = StandardScaler()
standardized_data = scaler.fit_transform(credit_data)
```

- **Encoding categorical variables**: Customer data contains categorical variables like gender or region. We can use one-hot encoding to convert these variables into the numerical format.

  Example:

```
from sklearn.preprocessing import OneHotEncoder
customer_data = [['Male'], ['Female'], ['Female']]
encoder = OneHotEncoder(sparse_output=False)
encoded_data = encoder.fit_transform(customer_data)
```

- **Feature engineering**: Create new features to capture user behavior.

  Example:

```
import pandas as pd
data = {'CustomerID': [1, 2, 1], 'PurchaseAmount': [100, 200, 50]}
df = pd.DataFrame(data)
df['TotalSpent'] = df.groupby('CustomerID')['PurchaseAmount'].
transform('sum')
```

- **Preprocessing for image data**: Images may vary in size, brightness, and orientation, affecting recognition models. Preprocessing on images may be performed by resizing, normalizing pixel values, and applying augmentations like rotation or flipping:

```
import tensorflow as tf
image = tf.keras.preprocessing.image.load_img('face.jpg', target_
size=(128, 128))
image_array = tf.keras.preprocessing.image.img_to_array(image) / 255.0
```

- **Data cleaning**: Text data contains noise like special characters, URLs, and emojis. Clean the text using tokenization, removal of stop words, and stemming or lemmatization.

Case study: Preprocessing in retail data

Data collected from retail operations is often incomplete and inconsistent, making preprocessing a critical step for extracting meaningful insights. In this case study, we explore the preprocessing steps for retail data, focusing on a hypothetical scenario of a retail company analyzing customer purchase patterns to improve marketing strategies.

Real-world examples

A large retail chain with stores across multiple regions wants to optimize inventory management to minimize stockouts and reduce overstocking

The dataset may contain the following columns:

- `CustomerID`
- `PurchaseDate`
- `ProductID`
- `Category`
- `Price`
- `Quantity`
- `Location`

These are the steps we perform during data preprocessing:

1. **Data cleaning**: Data cleaning is one of the essential parts of data preprocessing. It involves the following:

    a. **Handling missing data**: For example, missing values in `Price` and `Location`. We can use the mean or the median to impute missing `Price` values.

    b. **Removing duplicates**: Duplicate rows lead to inflated metrics like sales.

    c. **Correcting date formats**: Inconsistent date formats in `PurchaseDate` can cause parsing errors.

2. **Data transformation**:

    a. **Normalization**: Normalize the `Price` column to scale values between 0 and 1.

    b. **Enabling categorical variables**: Non numeric columns like `Category` and `Location` cannot be directly used in models.

3. **Feature engineering**: Extract new insights by deriving meaningful features. Identifying high value customers.

4. **Results and insights**: After preprocessing, the clean and structured dataset enabled the company to generate analyses or forecasts and predict sales trends.

Challenges and solutions

There are many challenges encountered during preprocessing. Some of these challenges and their solutions are elaborated upon here:

- **Handling missing data**: Missing data is generally found in most datasets, and its improper handling can lead to biased results or poor model performance. Missing values might result from system failures, data corruption, or human errors during data collection.

  Solution:

  - Use statistical methods like mean, median, or mode imputation for numerical data.
  - Apply algorithms like (KNN) or regression-based imputation for more accurate estimates.
  - Consult experts to decide whether missing values represent meaningful absence or require imputation.

- **Data inconsistencies**: Datasets often contain inconsistencies in formats, units, or naming conventions. For instance, dates might have varying formats, or categories like **`electronics`** and **`Electronics`** might appear separately.

  Solution:

  - **Standardization**: Use libraries like Pandas to convert dates, strings, and numerical values into consistent formats.
  - **Validation rules**: Define rules to check and correct inconsistencies in real-time.
  - **Automated scripts**: Create reusable scripts for format normalization across datasets.

- **Dealing with outliers**: Outliers can distort statistical metrics and impact the performance of machine learning models. They may result from data entry errors or represent true but extreme observations.

  Solution: Use visualizations (e.g., box plots) and statistical measures like the IQR or Z-scores to identify outliers.

- **High-dimensionality**: Datasets with too many features (high-dimensionality) can make modeling computationally expensive and lead to overfitting.

  Solution: Dimensionality Reduction by using techniques like PCA.

Conclusion

Data preprocessing is a critical step in data science and ML. The raw data needs to be transformed into a clean, consistent, and usable format for analysis and modeling. This chapter has discussed essential components of data preprocessing, data cleaning, Various techniques for handling missing values, data transformation techniques, and data preprocessing tools and libraries such as Pandas and sci-kit.

Finally, this chapter also discussed the retail data preprocessing case study and the challenges and solutions involved in preparing data for analysis. By performing data preprocessing, data scientists and machine learning practitioners can ensure that their models are built with greater accuracy and derive more conducive insights.

In the next chapter, we will discuss about creation of synthetic dataset, its creation in MS Excel, its advantages and disadvantages.

Exercises

1. Explain the importance of data preprocessing in data science and ML. Why is it considered a foundational step?
2. What are the different types of missing data, and how do they impact the analysis process? Provide examples.
3. Describe the advantages and disadvantages of using mean, median, and mode imputation techniques for handling missing values.
4. Discuss the role of normalization and standardization in data transformation. How do they differ?
5. Explain the process and importance of encoding categorical variables. Compare techniques such as one-hot encoding and label encoding.
6. What is feature engineering, and how does it enhance the predictive power of machine learning models?
7. What are feature selection methods? Discuss at least two techniques commonly used in feature selection.
8. Explain the concept of multicollinearity and its implications in feature selection. How can it be addressed?
9. Discuss the use of Python libraries like Pandas and scikit-learn for data preprocessing. What are their key functionalities?
10. Provide an example of how missing data can be handled using the Pandas library. Include relevant code snippets.
11. Explain the role of the StandardScaler and MinMaxScaler classes in scikit-learn. When would you use each?
12. What are the challenges faced during data preprocessing in real-world scenarios? Provide examples from different industries.
13. Describe a situation where forward fill or backward fill imputation might be the most appropriate method for handling missing data.
14. Why is it important to address outliers during data preprocessing? Explain methods for detecting and handling outliers.
15. In the context of preprocessing retail data, what specific challenges might arise, and how can they be addressed?

CHAPTER 6
Creating Synthetic Datasets in MS Excel

Introduction

This chapter explores the concept of synthetic data, its significance, and the various methods for creating synthetic datasets. It discusses the advantages and limitations of artificial data. It also discusses real-world applications and case studies of synthetic data that have led to innovation across various industries.

The primary objectives of this chapter are to learn about the concepts of Synthetic Data, its significance, and how it differs from real-world data in terms of generation, usage, and application. This chapter explores various techniques for generating synthetic data, including random data generation, data augmentation, and advanced methods such as **generative adversarial networks** (**GANs**). It provides a practical, hands-on approach to generating synthetic data using Microsoft Excel, utilizing functions such as **`RAND()`**, **`RANDBETWEEN()`**, and logical formulas. Further, we will discuss the advantages of using synthetic data include overcoming data privacy issues, mitigating class imbalance, and enhancing model performance. Finally, it discusses applications, case studies, and the ethical challenges and considerations that arise when working with synthetic data, particularly in fields where data privacy and fairness are crucial.

Structure

This chapter covers the following topics:

- Introducing synthetic data
- Methods for creating synthetic data
- Tools for synthetic data generation
- Step-by-step guide in MS Excel
- Limitations of synthetic data
- Practical applications

Objectives

Synthetic data refers to artificially generated data that mimics the statistical properties and patterns of real-world datasets without directly exposing sensitive or confidential information. As data privacy, accessibility, and scalability become increasingly important, synthetic data has emerged as a powerful alternative to traditional data collection methods.

By the end of this chapter, readers will have a thorough understanding of synthetic data, its generation, and its practical application in data science projects.

Introducing synthetic data

Today, with advancements in the field of data science, it is imperative to have high quality data available, which ultimately determines the success of machine learning models and analytical projects. However, obtaining real-world data is challenging. There may be issues related to data privacy, security, and scarcity of relevant data in specific domains. These issues are hurdles in the way of innovation and the development of effective models. This problem can be resolved by using synthetic data.

Synthetic data refers to artificially generated datasets that have the statistical properties, structures, and relationships found in real-world data. Unlike traditional datasets, synthetic data can be created without requiring sensitive or proprietary information, offering a valuable alternative for model training, testing, and research. It provides data scientists with the flexibility to generate large volumes of data, overcome privacy concerns, and improve model performance when accurate data is scarce or inaccessible.

Importance of synthetic data

In the field of data science, synthetic data is of significant importance across various industries and applications. Synthetic data comes into play when real data is scarce, inaccessible, or cannot be used due to privacy issues. In practice, synthetic data is often used along with real data. Synthetic data is often used in early-stage development, model testing, and training, while real data is important for final validation and deployment. A balanced use of both helps to build more robust, scalable, and ethical ML systems.

Synthetic data however, allows data scientists to generate large, well-balanced, and fully labeled datasets quickly and inexpensively.

The synthetic data, generated through algorithms or models, mimics real-world data without requiring actual data collection, which can often be expensive, time-consuming, or challenging to obtain. As the need for vast and diverse datasets grows, synthetic data becomes indispensable.

The following are the reasons of having a synthetic dataset:

- **Overcoming data scarcity**: Real-world data are scarce, incomplete, or expensive to collect. For example, in fields such as healthcare or finance, gathering sufficient high quality data can be challenging due to privacy constraints or limitations on data access. Synthetic data is a solution that can fill the gap, allowing ML models to train effectively even when real data is lacking.
- **Privacy preservation and data securit**y: Due to increasing concerns over data privacy, synthetic data allows organizations to provide data without compromising sensitive information. This is important in industries that deal with personal, financial, or medical data, such as healthcare, banking, and insurance.
- Using synthetic datasets, organizations can comply with data protection laws such as the **General Data Protection Regulation** (**GDPR**) in *Europe* or the **Health Insurance Portability and Accountability Act** (**HIPAA**) in the *United States*, ensuring that real personal data is not exposed or misused during model training or testing.
- **Enabling edge case simulations**: Real-world datasets may lack in coverage of rare or extreme scenarios, which may be critical for the success of certain applications.

  For instance, in autonomous driving, data representing rare traffic situations or adverse weather conditions, such as snowstorms, may be missing. Synthetic data enables the generation of these rare scenarios. Synthetic data is handy in domains such as robotics, autonomous vehicles, and **natural language processing** (**NLP**), where simulating these cases can be challenging.
- **Reducing bias in datasets**: In ML, data bias can lead to biased models, which may produce unfair or inaccurate results. Real-world data may contain inherent biases. Synthetic data can be used to create balanced datasets that eliminate biases.
- **Testing and model validation**: Synthetic data is handy in testing and validating models. It is crucial in testing edge cases, stress-testing algorithms, or evaluating models under varying conditions.
- **Speed and cost efficiency**: Generating synthetic data is a faster and more cost-efficient process. It reduces the need for manual data collection, cleaning, and labelling, which are often expensive and error-prone tasks.
- **Enabling scalability in data generation**: As data needs grow, the ability to scale the generation of datasets becomes essential. Synthetic data can be scaled quickly and efficiently.

  For example, in simulation-based training for robotics or autonomous systems, synthetic environments can generate vast quantities of data, allowing for rapid testing and refinement of models without being constrained by the physical world.

Use cases and advantages

Synthetic data is becoming increasingly valuable across various industries and applications. By generating artificial datasets that closely resemble real-world data, synthetic data allows organizations to overcome challenges related to data scarcity, privacy, and bias.

The following are the use cases and advantages of synthetic data:

- **Training ML models**: One of the most common use cases for synthetic data is training machine learning models when actual data is unavailable, scarce, or expensive to collect.

  For example: In the case of autonomous driving, the synthetic dataset may comprise scenarios with various road conditions, weather patterns, and traffic situations. This enables autonomous vehicles to learn how to navigate rare or hazardous driving conditions that may not be represented in real-world datasets.

- **Data privacy and security**: In fields where data privacy is critical, such as healthcare, finance, or social media, synthetic data helps ensure that models can be trained without exposing sensitive personal information.

- **Simulating rare events and edge cases**: Synthetic data can be used to simulate rare events that would be impractical to collect through traditional means. For example, in the case of flood prediction or fire detection, generating synthetic data for rare events, such as specific weather patterns, can help train ML models

- **Bias mitigation in data**: Real-world data can often be biased or unrepresentative of the entire population, leading to skewed machine-learning models. Synthetic data offers a way to address and correct these biases.

- **Testing and model validation**: Testing machine learning algorithms, software systems, or simulation models often requires vast amounts of diverse input data. However, it may be impractical to collect sufficient real-world data for this purpose, especially for testing edge cases or conducting stress tests.

- **Software testing**: Developers can use synthetic data to simulate a wide range of user behaviors, inputs, or system failures, helping them test software systems without relying on real user data. For example, synthetic transaction logs can be generated to test e-commerce platforms.

Ethical considerations

While synthetic data offers a powerful solution to many challenges in data science, its use raises several ethical considerations. As synthetic data becomes increasingly integral to AI and machine learning applications, it is crucial to consider the potential implications for privacy, fairness, transparency, and accountability.

Here are some of the key ethical issues that arise when working with synthetic data:

- **Accuracy and representation of synthetic data**: One of the fundamental ethical concerns in using synthetic data is ensuring that it accurately represents the characteristics of the real-world data it is intended to mimic. If synthetic data is poorly generated or fails to accurately reflect the nuances of real data, it can lead to flawed models that perform poorly or even harm certain groups.
- **Risk of misrepresentation**: Synthetic data that does not adequately reflect the complexities and distribution of real-world data may mislead ML models. For example, if the synthetic data used to train a facial recognition system is not diverse enough or does not capture certain environmental factors, the resulting model may perform poorly in real-world applications, leading to misidentifications or bias.
- **Data quality**: Generating synthetic data that accurately mimics real-world distributions requires sophisticated techniques, and any inaccuracies in the synthetic data generation process can lead to systemic problems, especially if the data is used in high-stakes applications like healthcare, finance, or criminal justice.
- **The conceptual approach**: Developers must ensure that the synthetic data generation process is transparent and that the synthetic data is rigorously tested for accuracy and validity. It is essential to continually compare synthetic datasets with real-world data to identify potential discrepancies.
- **Bias in synthetic data**: If synthetic data is generated from biased models or based on unbalanced real-world datasets, the synthetic data can inherit and amplify these biases.

  For example: Suppose a synthetic dataset for hiring algorithms is generated based on historical employment data that reflects gender or racial disparities. In that case, it may perpetuate those biases, resulting in unfair hiring decisions. Developers must ensure that synthetic data generation processes address potential bias. This includes proactively creating balanced datasets that represent diverse demographic groups and continuously monitoring and testing the models for fairness. There must be a commitment to reducing systemic biases and promoting equality through the careful design of datasets.
- **Transparency and accountability**: The use of synthetic data raises concerns about transparency and accountability, particularly in sectors where decisions driven by machine learning models have high consequences for individuals and society.
- **Deepfakes and manipulation**: One of the most notorious examples of synthetic data misuse is the creation of deepfakes manipulated media (audio, video, or images) that appear realistic but are entirely synthetic. Deepfakes can be used to spread misinformation, manipulate public opinion, or cause harm to individuals by creating fabricated evidence or defamatory content.

- **Deceptive practices**: Synthetic data may also be used in ways that are intentionally deceptive, such as generating fake datasets to mislead investors, regulators, or researchers. In the context of corporate research, the use of synthetic data to falsely portray the efficacy of a product or to hide adverse effects is a serious ethical concern.

Methods for creating synthetic data

Creating synthetic data involves generating artificial datasets that resemble real-world data but are not directly derived from actual observations. There are several methods and techniques for generating synthetic data, each suited for different types of data (e.g., numerical, categorical, image, text) and various applications, such as training ML models, ensuring privacy, or simulating rare events.

Here are some of the most common methods for creating synthetic data:

- **Random data generation**: One of the most straightforward methods for generating synthetic data is random data generation. In this approach, data points are generated based on specified statistical distributions, ensuring that the synthetic data adheres to certain statistical properties commonly found in real-world datasets.
- Data points are generated randomly within a specified range, adhering to predefined probability distributions, such as the normal (Gaussian), uniform, exponential, or binomial. It can involve generating numerical data, like age, salary, or temperature, or categorical data, such as binary labels (yes/no) or classes (red/blue/green).
- **Numerical data**: Generating synthetic financial transaction data for testing fraud detection algorithms by creating random spending amounts based on normal or uniform distributions.
- **Categorical data**: Generating synthetic demographic data, where the gender and age are randomly assigned from predefined categories.
- **Data augmentation**: Data augmentation is a technique often used in the context of image data but can also be applied to text and audio. It involves applying various transformations to existing data to create new synthetic instances.

Data augmentation is performed in the following ways:

- **For images**: Apply transformations like rotation, flipping, scaling, cropping, color adjustment, or adding noise to create new synthetic images from original ones.
- **For text**: This may involve paraphrasing, swapping words, or replacing words with synonyms, enabling the generation of multiple versions of the same input text.
- **For audio**: Methods like pitch shifting, time stretching, or noise injection can be used to generate new audio samples.

Generative models

Generative models use advanced machine learning techniques to generate new data points that are statistically similar to real-world data. These models learn the underlying patterns and distributions of a given dataset and use this knowledge to generate new, synthetic instances.

Two widely used generative models are GANs and **variational autoencoders** (**VAEs**):

- **GANs**: A GAN consists of two neural networks, a generator and a discriminator. The generator creates synthetic data, while the discriminator attempts to differentiate between real and synthetic data. Over time, the generator learns to create increasingly realistic data.
- **VAEs**: They are a type of deep learning model that learns to encode data into a lower-dimensional latent space and then decodes it to generate new, synthetic instances that resemble the original data.

  GANs are frequently used to generate realistic images, such as creating synthetic faces (e.g., **https://thispersondoesnotexist.com/**) or simulating medical images like **Magnetic Resonance Imaging** (**MRI**) scans.

  VAEs can be used in NLP for generating realistic text sequences, like creating synthetic news articles or product descriptions.

Simulation and modeling

Simulating real-world systems or processes can be an effective method for generating synthetic data, particularly in fields such as robotics, autonomous vehicles, and scientific research.

Data is generated through simulations based on predefined models or systems. These models can simulate physical, environmental, or even social systems and generate synthetic data-based on the behavior patterns of these systems.

For example, traffic simulations can generate synthetic data on car movements, weather, or road conditions, while financial models may simulate stock prices based on economic variables.

Here are some various ways of creating synthetic data:

- **Synthetic data using rule-based systems**: Synthetic data can be generated using rule-based systems or expert knowledge. This method involves specifying rules that govern how data should behave and then using these rules to create data points.

  Experts define the relationships and constraints between variables (e.g., *Age must be between 18 and 100, Income must be greater than $30,000 for individuals aged 50+)*. The system then creates synthetic data points that adhere to these rules while mimicking the overall distribution and characteristics of the actual dataset.

  - For example, in marketing, synthetic customer data (e.g., age, income, occupation) are generated based on predefined business rules and constraints to simulate different customer segments.

- **Differential privacy**: For applications involving the generation of privacy-preserving data, differential privacy techniques can be used to generate synthetic data that maintains the statistical properties of the original data while preserving sensitive information.

  Differential privacy involves adding controlled noise to data, ensuring that individual records cannot be re-identified while still allowing for valuable insights from the data. Synthetic data can be generated by introducing noise into the dataset, ensuring that individual data points are not identifiable while maintaining aggregate trends.

  - For example, in healthcare, creating synthetic patient data with privacy guarantees that can be used for research without exposing any real patient information.

Random data generation

Random data generation is one of the simplest and most commonly used methods for creating synthetic data. It involves producing new data points randomly within a specified range or according to a particular statistical distribution. This method is often employed when there is a need for large volumes of data for testing, simulation, or initial model development when actual data is unavailable or unsuitable.

Random data generation relies on the use of mathematical distributions to simulate random variables. These distributions dictate how the data is generated based on specific parameters, such as the mean, variance, or shape of the distribution.

The process typically consists of the following steps:

1. **Specify the distribution**: Choose a statistical distribution (e.g., normal, uniform, exponential) that best describes the kind of data you are generating.

2. **Set the parameters**: Define the parameters of the distribution, such as the mean and standard deviation for a normal distribution or the range for a uniform distribution.

3. **Generate the data**: Using a random number generator, create data points that follow the chosen distribution. Each generated data point represents a synthetic instance that conforms to the statistical characteristics of the specified distribution.

4. **Format the data**: Optionally, the generated data can be formatted into specific structures, such as tables or datasets, to meet the needs of downstream applications (e.g., feeding the data into a model for training or simulation).

Common types of distribution

Here are some common types of distributions for random data generation:

- **Uniform distribution**: Data points are distributed evenly across a defined range.
    - **Example**: Generating ages between 18 and 100 with equal likelihood for any age in that range.
- **Normal (Gaussian) distribution**: Data points follow a bell-shaped curve, with most values clustered around a central mean.
    - **Example**: Generating heights of people where most individuals are around 5'8", with fewer people being much taller or shorter.
- **Exponential distribution**: Frequently used to model time between events in a process that occurs at a constant rate (e.g., time between customer arrivals or system failures).
    - **Example**: Generating the time between two arrivals of customers at a store.
- **Poisson distribution**: Typically used to model counts or the number of occurrences of an event in a fixed interval of time or space.
    - **Example**: Generating the number of calls received by a customer service center in an hour.
- **Binomial distribution**: Used for generating binary outcomes, like success/failure, with a fixed number of trials and a constant probability of success.
    - **Example**: Simulating the results of flipping a coin 10 times and counting the number of heads.

Advantages of random data generation

Here are some advantages of random data generation:

- **Simplicity**: Random data generation is easy to implement and does not require complex models or algorithms.
- **Cost-effective**: It allows for the generation of large volumes of data without the need for real-world data collection, which can be expensive or time-consuming.
- **Testing and simulation**: Useful for testing software, algorithms, and models when real data is either unavailable or too costly to obtain.
- **Customization**: You have control over the statistical properties of the data, such as the distribution shape, mean, variance, and range, which allows for tailored synthetic data for specific use cases.

Limitations of random data generation

Limitations of random data generation include the following:

- **Lack of realism**: Random data may fail to capture the complexity, correlations, and dependencies found in real-world data, leading to unrealistic or flawed models.
- **Bias and over-simplification**: If the chosen distribution does not adequately represent the real data, the generated synthetic data may introduce bias or oversimplify the problem.
- **Limited usefulness for complex scenarios**: In cases where the relationships between variables are highly complex (e.g., interactions between multiple features), random data generation may not produce data that accurately reflects these dependencies.
- **No contextual meaning**: Synthetic data generated randomly may lack meaningful context or semantics, particularly in fields such as healthcare, where data relationships have profound real-world implications.

Data augmentation techniques

Data augmentation is a technique used to artificially expand the size of a dataset by creating modified versions of existing data points. This is particularly useful in machine learning, especially when dealing with limited data or imbalanced datasets. By applying various transformations, data augmentation introduces variability into the data, which helps improve the robustness of ML models and prevent overfitting.

Data augmentation can be applied to various types of data, including image data, text data, and audio data, with each type having its own specific augmentation techniques.

Let us explore the various techniques for data augmentation across different domains.

Image data augmentation techniques

In computer vision, data augmentation is widely used to increase the diversity of training images without the need to collect additional real-world data. By applying transformations such as flipping, rotating, and zooming, new training samples are created that still retain the essential characteristics of the original data.

Standard techniques for image data augmentation include the following:

- **Rotation**: Randomly rotating images by a specified angle (e.g., between -30° to +30°) to account for different orientations.
- **Flipping**: Horizontally or vertically flipping the image to simulate different perspectives.

- **Scaling (zooming)**: Zooming in or out on the image to simulate varying distances between the camera and the object.
- **Translation**: Shifting the image in the x and y directions to simulate different viewpoints.
- **Shearing**: Slant the image along an axis.
- **Brightness and contrast adjustment**: Randomly adjusting the brightness, contrast, or saturation to simulate different lighting conditions.
- **Adding noise**: Introducing random noise (e.g., Gaussian noise) into the image to simulate variations caused by environmental factors or sensor limitations.
- **Color jittering**: Slightly altering the color properties of an image (e.g., adjusting hue or saturation) to compensate for variations in lighting or camera settings.

Text data augmentation techniques

Data augmentation for text is commonly used in NLP to improve the performance of models, especially when training data is limited. Various techniques can be applied to text data to create new, meaningful sentences or phrases that are semantically similar to the original content.

Here are some standard techniques for text data augmentation:

- **Synonym replacement**: Replace words in a sentence with their synonyms using a thesaurus or pre-trained models like Word2Vec or GloVe.
- **Random insertion**: Insert randomly selected words into the sentence at random positions. These words can be related to the topic or domain of the sentence.
- **Random deletion**: Randomly delete words from a sentence to simulate noisy or incomplete input.
- **Text paraphrasing**: Rewriting a sentence or paragraph in a different way while preserving its original meaning. This can be achieved by using rule-based systems, pre-trained models (like GPT-3), or paraphrasing tools.
- **Back translation**: Translating the text to a different language and then translating it back to the original language. This introduces slight changes in sentence structure while maintaining the meaning.
- **Sentence shuffling**: In longer texts, sentences or paragraphs may be shuffled randomly to introduce variety in the data while maintaining logical meaning.
- **TF-IDF replacement**: Text augmentation can be done by replacing low TF-IDF words (less important) with synonyms or contextually similar terms, keeping the sentence meaning intact.

- **Contextual embeddings**: We can use contextual embeddings to replace words with similar meaning in the same context, avoiding the semantic drift caused by traditional synonyms.

Audio data augmentation techniques

In the domain of speech recognition or sound classification, data augmentation techniques are also employed to modify audio data. These techniques help train models that can handle different conditions and variabilities that might be encountered in real-world environments.

Here are some common techniques for audio data augmentation:

- **Time stretching**: Stretching or compressing the audio in time without affecting the pitch, simulating variations in the speed of speech or sounds.
- **Pitch shifting**: Changing the pitch of the audio while keeping the tempo intact. This can simulate different speaking tones or audio pitch variations.
- **Noise injection**: Adding background noise (e.g., white noise or environmental sounds) to simulate real-world conditions like crowds or street noise.
- **Volume adjustment**: Adjusting the volume of the audio to simulate different recording conditions or audio levels.
- **Speed perturbation**: Altering the speed of the audio (by speeding it up or slowing it down) to simulate various speaking rates or performance conditions.
- **Reverberation**: Adding echoes or reverberation to the audio to simulate different room acoustics.

Tools for synthetic data generation

Tools for synthetic data generation may be categorized based on the following:

- Data type (tabular, image, text, time series, etc.).
- Domain (e.g., healthcare, finance).
- Technique (statistical modeling, rule-based, generative AI).

Some of the tools that produce tabular data include the following:

- **Synthetic Data Vault (SDV)**:
  - Supports relational, multi-table, and single-table data
  - GAN and Bayesian-based generation
  - Privacy-preserving models

- **Conditional Tabular GAN (CTGAN) from SDV**:
  - GAN-based model for tabular data
  - Handles imbalanced distributions well
- **Scikit-learn make_classification / make_regression**:
  - Generates synthetic classification and regression datasets for testing ML models
- **DataSynthesizer**:
  - Supports both independent attribute mode and correlated attribute mode
  - Good for privacy-focused applications
- **YData synthetic**:
  - Offers CTGAN and Gaussian Copula models
  - Works well for time series data
  - Python SDK, Jupyter support
- **MOSTLY AI**:
  - No code platform
  - Strong GDPR compliance
  - Generates highly realistic, privacy safe data

Some of the tools that produce image data include the following:

- **Albumentations**:
  - Fast image augmentation library
  - Useful for expanding real image datasets
- **Synthetica**:
  - 3D-rendered synthetic image generation
  - Used for autonomous driving, retail
- **Unity Perception toolkit**:
  - Synthetic scene generation for training vision models
  - Used with Unity engine
- **NVIDIA Omniverse Replicator**:
  - Photorealistic synthetic image generator
  - Used in robotics and manufacturing
- **StyleGAN/StyleGAN2**:
  - GAN-based generator for high quality synthetic faces and images

Some of the tools that produce text data include the following:

- **TextAttack**:
  - o Generates paraphrases and adversarial examples using contextual models.
- **NLPAug**:
  - o Augments text using BERT, WordNet, spelling errors, etc.
- **BackTranslation**:
  - o Translates text into another language and back for natural paraphrasing.
- **Parrot Paraphraser**:
  - o Uses T5 or Pegasus for high quality paraphrasing.
- **GPT (OpenAI, LLaMA, etc.)**:
  - o Can generate synthetic natural language text on demand.

Some of the tools that produce time series data include the following:

- **YData Synthetic**:
  - o Specializes in time series generation (GAN-based)
- **TimeGAN**:
  - o GAN-based model specifically designed for generating sequential time series
- **Gretel.ai**:
  - o Offers synthetic time series generation for industrial data

Some of the domain-specific synthetic data generation tools include the following:

- **Healthcare domain**: Synthea generates realistic, simulated patient health records
- **Finance domain**: MOSTLY AI, Gretel.ai, which is used for synthetic financial transactions, credit scores
- **Autonomous driving domain**: CARLA, LGSVL Simulator, which generates driving scenarios and synthetic video/image data

Most commonly used synthetic data generation tool is Excel. It is a manual or semi-automated synthetic data creation for structured/tabular data. Excel is easily understood, accessible, and intuitive for non-programmers. It is considered good tool for small-scale prototyping or teaching data science concepts. However, it is not scalable for large datasets and lacks support for unstructured data, e.g., images and text.

Step-by-step guide in MS Excel

In this section, we will discuss how to generate synthetic data in Microsoft Excel using built-in functions and formulas. This process will focus on creating simple synthetic datasets for various use cases, such as demographics, sales, or financial data.

Example 1, generating random numbers in Excel

Excel has built-in functions to generate random numbers which can be used to create synthetic data.

Two common functions are:

- **RAND()**: Generates a random decimal number between 0 and 1.
- **RANDBETWEEN(bottom, top)**: Generates a random integer between a specified minimum (**`bottom`**) and maximum (**`top`**) value.

Example 2, creating a synthetic employee dataset

Let us create a synthetic dataset for employee data with columns like **`Employee ID`**, **`Age`**, **`Salary`**, and **`Department`**. We will use **`RAND()`** and **`RANDBETWEEN()`** to generate these values:

1. **Create column headers**:
   a. Open a new Excel spreadsheet.
   b. In cells **`A1`** to **`D1`**, type the following headers:
   ```
   A1: Employee ID
   B1: Age
   C1: Salary
   D1: Department
   ```
2. **Generate Employee IDs**: In cell **`A2`**, enter the following formula to generate sequential Employee IDs:
   ```
   =ROW()-1
   ```
   a. This formula will give each row a unique ID starting from **`1`**.
   b. Drag the fill handle (the small square at the bottom right corner of the cell) down to fill the column with employee IDs.
3. **Generate random ages**:
   a. In cell **`B2`**, enter the following formula to generate a random age between **`18`** and **`60`**:
   ```
   =RANDBETWEEN(18,60)
   ```

b. Drag the fill handle down to generate ages for all employees.

4. **Generate random salaries**:

   a. In cell **C2**, enter the following formula to generate a random salary between $30,000 and $120,000:

   ```
   =RANDBETWEEN(30000,120000)
   ```

   b. Drag the fill handle down to generate salaries for all employees.

5. **Assign random departments**:

   a. In cell **D2**, enter the following formula to assign random departments (**Sales**, **Engineering**, or **Marketing**):

   ```
   =CHOOSE(RANDBETWEEN(1,3), "Sales", "Engineering", "Marketing")
   ```

   b. This formula uses **RANDBETWEEN(1,3)** to pick a number between **1** and **3**, and the **CHOOSE()** function assigns a department based on the number.

   c. Drag the fill handle down to assign departments for all employees.

6. **Final dataset**:

   Your final synthetic employee dataset should look something like the following table:

Employee ID	Age	Salary	Department
1	32	45000	Engineering
2	29	54000	Marketing
3	45	65000	Sales
4	38	70000	Sales
5	52	80000	Engineering

Table 6.1: Synthetic employee dataset

Generating date data

You can also create synthetic date data using Excel's **TODAY()** function or by generating random dates.

Refer to the following steps:

1. **Creating a date range**:

   a. In cell **E1**, type **Hire Date**.

   In cell **E2**, enter the following formula to generate a random date between January 1, 2010, and December 31, 2020: **=RANDBETWEEN(DATE(2010,1,1), DATE(2020,12,31))**

   b. Drag the fill handle down to generate a hire date for each employee.

2. **Format the date**:
   a. Select the column with dates (e.g., column **`E`**).
   b. Right click and choose **Format Cells.**
   c. In the **Number** tab, select **Date** and choose your preferred date format.
   d. Now, you will have a column with synthetic hire dates that vary within the specified range.
3. **Using functions to create more complex data**: Let us say you want to create a synthetic product sales dataset with columns like **`Product Name`**, **`Units Sold`**, **`Unit Price`**, and **`Total Sales`**:
   a. **Create column headers**: In cells **`A1`** to **`D1`**, type the following headers:
      i. **`A1: Product Name`**
      ii. **`B1: Units Sold`**
      iii. **`C1: Unit Price`**
      iv. **`D1: Total Sales`**
   b. **Generate product names**:
      i. In cell **`A2`**, use the **`CHOOSE()`** function to generate product names. For example:
         ```
         =CHOOSE(RANDBETWEEN(1,3), "Laptop", "Smartphone", "Tablet")
         ```
      ii. Drag the fill handle down to generate product names for all rows.
4. **Generate units sold**:
   a. In cell **`B2`**, use the **`RANDBETWEEN()`** function to generate random values for units sold between **`1`** and **`500`**:
      ```
      =RANDBETWEEN(1,500)
      ```
   b. Drag the fill handle down to generate units sold for all products.
5. **Generate unit prices**:
   a. In cell **`C2`**, use the **`RANDBETWEEN()`** function to generate unit prices:
      ```
      =RANDBETWEEN(100,1000)
      ```
   b. Drag the fill handle down to generate unit prices.
6. **Calculate total sales**:
   a. In cell **`D2`**, use the following formula to calculate total sales:
      ```
      =B2*C2
      ```
   b. This multiplies the units sold by the unit price to calculate total sales for each product.
   c. Drag the fill handle down to calculate total sales for all products.

7. **Final sales dataset**: Your final synthetic product sales dataset will look like this:

Products name	Units sold	Unit price	Total sales
Laptop	120	899	107880
Smartphone	250	599	149750
Tablet	80	450	36000
Smartphone	300	550	165000
Laptop	50	999	49950

Table 6.2: Synthetic product sales dataset

Randomizing data with advanced functions

You can also combine Excel's more advanced functions for complex data generation. For instance, if you want to generate random email addresses based on the employee names and departments:

1. **Generate random names**:
   a. In cell `F1`, type `Name`.
   b. In cell `F2`, use the formula to generate random names (e.g., combining first and last names):
   ```
   =CHOOSE(RANDBETWEEN(1,3), "John Doe", "Jane Smith", "Michael Johnson")
   ```
   c. Drag the fill handle down to generate names.
2. **Generate random email addresses**:
   a. In cell `G1`, type `Email`.
   b. In cell `G2`, use the following formula to create email addresses based on the names and `departments:=LOWER(LEFT(F2,FIND("",F2)-1)&"."&RIGHT(F2,LEN(F2)-FIND(" ",F2))&"@"&LOWER(D2)&".com")`
   c. This formula concatenates the first and last name, adds the department, and generates a corresponding email address.
   d. Drag the fill handle down to generate email addresses.
3. **Saving the data**:
   a. Once you have generated synthetic data in Excel, save your file for future use:
   b. Click on **File | Save As**.
   c. Choose the location, enter a filename, and save it as an Excel workbook (`.xlsx`).

d. Using Microsoft Excel's built-in functions like **RANDBETWEEN(), RAND(), CHOOSE(),** and simple formulas, one can easily generate synthetic datasets for various use cases.

Using function and formulas

In this section, we will focus on how to use functions and formulas in Microsoft Excel to generate synthetic data. These techniques are helpful when creating simulated datasets for analysis, testing, or training machine learning models. The functions we will cover include those for generating random numbers, dates, text, and combinations of these.

We will create synthetic data in several domains, including employee records, sales data, and dates, utilizing Excel's powerful built-in functions.

In the upcoming subsections, we will be looking at examples of generating random numbers using Excel functions.

Using RANDBETWEEN() for random numbers

Now, let us look at using **RANDBETWEEN()** for random numbers:

- **Function**: **=RANDBETWEEN(bottom, top)**
- **Description**: This function generates a random integer between the **bottom** (minimum) and **top** (maximum) values you provide.

Example: Generate employee ages using the following steps:

1. In cell **A1**, type **Age** to create the column header.
2. In cell **A2**, use the following formula to generate a random age between **18** and **60**:

   =RANDBETWEEN(18,60)

3. Drag the fill handle (small square at the bottom-right of the cell) down to generate random ages for more rows.

Using RAND() for random decimal numbers

Let us look at using **RAND()** for random decimal numbers:

- **Function**: **=RAND()**
- **Description**: This function generates a random decimal number between 0 and 1.

Example : Generate random salaries as decimal values using the following steps:

1. In cell **B1**, type **Salary** to create the column header.

2. In cell **B2**, use the following formula to generate a random decimal salary between $30,000 and $100,000:

```
=RANDBETWEEN(30000,100000) * RAND()
```

3. This formula multiplies the base salary range with a random decimal between 0 and 1, simulating variations in salary.

4. Drag the fill handle down to generate random salaries.

To generate random dates within a specific range, Excel provides the **RANDBETWEEN()** function along with the **DATE()** function.

Using RANDBETWEEN() with DATE() for random dates

Here we will look at Using **RANDBETWEEN()** with **DATE()** for random dates:

- **Function**: **=RANDBETWEEN(DATE(year,month,day), DATE(year,month,day))**
- You can use **RANDBETWEEN()** to randomly select dates between two specified dates by passing **DATE()** values as arguments.

Example: Generate random hire dates using the following steps:

1. In cell **C1**, type **Hire Date** to create the column header.
2. In cell **C2**, use the following formula to generate random hire dates between January 1, 2015, and December 31, 2020:

```
=RANDBETWEEN(DATE(2015,1,1), DATE(2020,12,31))
```

3. Drag the fill handle down to generate random hire dates for multiple employees.

Generating random text using CHOOSE() and RANDBETWEEN()

You can also generate random text values based on predefined lists, using the **CHOOSE()** function in combination with **RANDBETWEEN()**.

Using CHOOSE() for random text data:

- **Function**: **=CHOOSE(RANDBETWEEN(1, n), "Option1", "Option2", ..., "OptionN")**
- **Description**: **CHOOSE()** selects a value from a list of options, with the list indexed by a randomly generated number from **RANDBETWEEN()**.

Example: Assign random departments using the following steps:

1. In cell **D1**, type **Department** to create the column header.
2. In cell **D2**, use the following formula to randomly assign an employee to one of three departments: "**Sales**," "**Marketing**," or "**Engineering**":

```
=CHOOSE(RANDBETWEEN(1,3), "Sales", "Marketing", "Engineering")
```

3. Drag the fill handle down to assign departments to other employees.

Combining functions to create more complex synthetic data

You can combine Excel functions to create more complex synthetic datasets. For example, let us combine random employee names, departments, and salaries.

Example: Generating full employee records:

1. **Create column headers**:
   - In `A1`, type `Employee ID`.
   - In `B1`, type `Employee Name`.
   - In `C1`, type `Age`.
   - In `D1`, type `Department`.
   - In `E1`, type `Salary`.
2. **Generate employee IDs**:
   a. In cell `A2`, type `1`, and in cell `A3`, type `2`.
   b. Select both cells, then drag the fill handle down to generate a sequential list of employee IDs.
3. **Generate random employee names**:
   a. In cell `B2`, use the formula to randomly pick a name from a `list:=CHOOSE(RANDBETWEEN(1,5), "John Smith", "Jane Doe", "Alex Johnson", "Maria Garcia", "David Lee")`
   b. Drag the fill handle down to generate names for each employee.
4. **Generate random ages**:
   a. In cell `C2`, use `=RANDBETWEEN(18,60)` to generate random ages.
   b. Drag the fill handle down to generate ages for each employee.
5. **Assign random departments**:
   a. In cell `D2`, use the formula:

   ```
   =CHOOSE(RANDBETWEEN(1,3), "Sales", "Marketing", "Engineering")
   ```

   b. Drag the fill handle down to assign departments.

6. **Generate random salaries**:
   a. In cell `E2`, use the formula:
   ```
   =RANDBETWEEN(30000,120000)
   ```
   b. Drag the fill handle down to generate salaries.
7. **Using formulas for data calculation**: After creating synthetic data, you might want to perform calculations on it. For example, calculating `Total Sales` based on `Units Sold` and `Unit Price`.
8. **Calculate total sales, as follows**: Create column headers:
   - In `A1`, type `Product Name`.
   - In `B1`, type `Units Sold`.
   - In `C1`, type `Unit Price`.
   - In `D1`, type `Total Sales`.

Generate product names

Follow these steps to generate product names:

1. In cell `A2`, use `=CHOOSE(RANDBETWEEN(1,3), "Laptop", "Smartphone", "Tablet")` to randomly assign product names.
2. Drag the fill handle down to generate product names.
3. **Generate units sold**:
   a. In cell `B2`, use `=RANDBETWEEN(1,500)` to generate random units sold.
   b. Drag the fill handle down.
4. **Generate unit prices**:
   a. In cell `C2`, use `=RANDBETWEEN(100,1000)` to generate random unit prices.
   b. Drag the fill handle down.
5. **Calculate total sales**:
   a. In cell `D2`, use the formula to calculate total sales for each product:
   ```
   =B2*C2
   ```
   b. Drag the fill handle down to calculate the total sales for all products.

6. **Using TEXT() for formatting:**

   a. You can also use the **`TEXT()`** function to format numeric data into readable text formats. This is especially useful when generating synthetic data like dates or currency.

   b. **Example 7**: Format as currency:

      - In cell **`E2`**, you might want to format the salary as currency. Use the formula:

```
=TEXT(E2, "$#,##0")
```

This will display the salary in the format: $45,000.

Using Excel functions and formulas provides a powerful way to create synthetic data for a wide range of use cases, from simple employee records to more complex datasets like sales and financial data. By combining random number generation, text manipulation, and basic arithmetic calculations, you can generate realistic synthetic data without needing external tools.

Practical examples

In this section, we will explore several practical examples of generating synthetic data using Excel functions. These examples will help you apply the techniques covered in previous sections to create datasets for employee records, sales data, financial data, and more. These datasets can be used for data analysis, training machine learning models, or demonstrating various data science concepts:

Employee dataset

In this example, we will create a synthetic employee dataset using the following details:

- **`Employee ID`**
- **`Name`**
- **`Age`**
- **`Salary`**
- **`Hire Date`**
- **`Department`**

This kind of data can be used for HR analytics or as a practice dataset for data science projects.

Here is the step-by-step process:

1. **Create column headers**:

   - **`A1: Employee ID`**
   - **`B1: Employee Name`**
   - **`C1: Age`**

- `D1: Salary`
- `E1: Hire Date`
- `F1: Department`

2. **Generate employee IDs**:

   a. In cell `A2`, type `1`, and in `A3`, type `2`.

   b. Select both cells, then drag the fill handle down to generate a list of employee IDs.

3. **Generate random employee names**:

   a. In cell `B2`, enter:

```
=CHOOSE(RANDBETWEEN(1,5), "John Smith", "Jane Doe", "Alex Johnson",
"Maria Garcia", "David Lee")
```

   b. Drag the fill handle down to generate names for all employees.

4. **Generate random ages**:

   a. In cell `C2`, enter the formula for random ages between `18` and `60`:

```
=RANDBETWEEN(18,60)
```

   b. Drag the fill handle down to generate ages for all employees.

5. **Generate random salaries**:

   a. In cell `D2`, enter:

```
=RANDBETWEEN(30000,120000)
```

   b. Drag the fill handle down to generate random salaries.

6. **Generate random hire dates**:

   a. In cell `E2`, enter the formula to generate random hire dates between January 1, 2010, and December 31, 2020:

```
=RANDBETWEEN(DATE(2010,1,1), DATE(2020,12,31))
```

   b. Drag the fill handle down to generate hire dates for all employees.

7. **Assign random departments**:

   a. In cell `F2`, enter:

```
=CHOOSE(RANDBETWEEN(1,3), "Sales", "Marketing", "Engineering")
```

   b. Drag the fill handle down to assign departments.

Final employee dataset example:

Employee ID	Employee name	Age	Salary	Hire date	Department
1	John Smith	32	55000	04/12/2015	Sales
2	Maria Garcia	28	70000	09/23/2017	Marketing
3	Alex Johnson	45	80000	03/15/2011	Engineering
4	Jane Doe	34	60000	06/18/2019	Sales
5	David Lee	52	95000	01/05/2016	Engineering

***Table 6.3**: Employee dataset*

This synthetic data can be used for HR analytics, testing algorithms, or practicing data manipulation in Excel.

Limitations of synthetic data

Synthetic data is artificially generated data that mimics the characteristics and structure of real-world data without containing any actual sensitive or personal information. While it is widely used in data science, machine learning, and analytics, it has its advantages and limitations. Understanding these can help you determine when to use synthetic data effectively.

Here are the limitations of synthetic data:

- **Lack of real-world nuances**: Synthetic data is an approximation of real-world data, but it may not capture all the subtle nuances and correlations that naturally occur in real datasets.
- **Overfitting risk in models**: When training machine learning models using synthetic data, there is a risk that the model could overfit to the synthetic data patterns and fail to generalize well to real-world data.
- **Quality and accuracy depend on generation methods**: The quality of synthetic data heavily depends on the methods used to generate it. If the generation process does not capture the key relationships, distributions, and outliers present in the real-world data, the synthetic dataset may not be useful for training or validating models.
- **Limited applicability in some domains**: While synthetic data can work well in many domains (e.g., finance, healthcare, retail), it may not always be suitable for all types of data. For example, generating high quality synthetic data for highly complex and dynamic environments, such as natural language understanding or real-time sensor data, can be difficult.
- **Ethical and legal concerns**: Despite its benefits in privacy, synthetic data can also be misused. For example, synthetic data could be created to mislead or manipulate decisions, such as in fraudulent research or financial reporting.

Benefits for training models

Synthetic data offers numerous advantages for training ML models, enabling more efficient and robust model development. Here are the key benefits that synthetic data provides for training models in various domains:

- **Expanding data availability**: Synthetic data enables the generation of large amounts of data when real-world data is limited, ensuring sufficient information for effective model training.
- **Privacy and security**: Protection of sensitive data: synthetic data does not contain accurate personal or sensitive information. This allows models to be trained without the risk of exposing confidential data.
- **Control over data distribution and structure**: One of the advantages of synthetic data is that it can be generated according to specific requirements, such as class balance, data distribution, and feature correlations. This allows you to control for potential biases or ensure that the data is structured in a way that optimizes model performance.
- **Accelerating model training**: Creating synthetic data can be much faster than collecting, cleaning, and labelling real-world data. This can drastically reduce the time it takes to develop and train ML models, allowing data scientists and developers to iterate quickly.
- **Ensuring model robustness and generalization**: Training models on synthetic data can help improve generalization by exposing the model to a variety of conditions, edge cases, and potential scenarios that it may not have encountered during training with real-world data.
- **Cost efficiency**: Collecting large amounts of real-world data, especially labeled data, can be expensive. Synthetic data offers an affordable alternative, enabling organizations to generate large datasets at a minimal cost, thereby reducing their reliance on purchasing or gathering proprietary data.
- **Testing and model validation**: Synthetic data is useful for testing models under various conditions that may not be well-represented in real data. It enables you to evaluate how well models perform across various scenarios without incurring errors or unethical implications.

Limitations and potential issues

While synthetic data offers several benefits for ML, model training, and data privacy, it also presents limitations and potential issues that must be carefully considered. Understanding these drawbacks helps ensure that synthetic data is used appropriately and effectively in various applications.

Here are the primary limitations and challenges:

- **Lack of real-world nuances**: Synthetic data may not capture all the intricacies and complexities found in actual data. Real-world data contains nuances, unexpected events, and rare occurrences that can be challenging to simulate accurately.
- **Risk of overfitting to synthetic patterns**: ML models trained solely on synthetic data might overfit the specific patterns and characteristics of the synthetic dataset. This occurs when the model becomes too tailored to the artificial data and fails to generalize well to real-world data. Since synthetic data is often generated under controlled conditions, it may lack the noise and variations present in real data, resulting in poor performance when deployed in the real-world.
- **Data quality and accuracy concerns**: Poorly designed synthetic data generation processes can result in inaccurate or unrealistic data, which could negatively affect the performance of the trained models.
- **Limited applicability for complex or high-dimensional data**: In complex datasets, such as natural language or high-resolution images, generating realistic synthetic data can be challenging. For example, generating synthetic text data that accurately reflects the richness of language, idiomatic expressions, or context can be difficult. Similarly, in the case of images or videos, generating synthetic data that includes fine-grained details may be complex and resource-intensive.
- **Risk of misleading or manipulative use**: Although synthetic data is often created for privacy protection and to avoid ethical concerns, it can also be misused. For example, synthetic data could be intentionally generated to manipulate models or results, especially in research or financial applications. Without proper oversight, synthetic data could lead to misleading conclusions or unethical applications.
- **Potential legal and ethical concerns**: While synthetic data is often considered privacy-preserving, generating synthetic data that mimics real individuals or real-world events too closely could still raise legal concerns. For example, if synthetic data resembles actual individuals' personal data or specific events, it could be viewed as an attempt to breach privacy regulations or mislead stakeholders.
- **Performance and reliability in real-world scenarios**: Even though synthetic data can be highly useful for model training, there is always a possibility that the model trained on synthetic data may underperform in real-world scenarios if the synthetic data does not account for the full range of variability and complexity found in actual data.

Practical applications

Synthetic data has become a powerful tool across various industries, enabling data scientists and machine learning engineers to develop models more efficiently and safely.

Here are several practical applications of synthetic data across different fields:

- **Healthcare and medical research**: Synthetic medical images (e.g., CT scans, MRIs, x-rays) are widely used to train ML models for medical image analysis. Generating synthetic images that include diverse conditions or rare diseases allows researchers to train more robust diagnostic models without needing to rely on a limited dataset of real medical images.
- **Autonomous vehicles and transportation**: Synthetic data plays a critical role in training autonomous vehicles. Self-driving car systems require large amounts of labelled data from diverse driving scenarios, including rare or dangerous situations that are difficult or expensive to capture using real-world data.
- **Finance and fraud detection**: Financial institutions use synthetic data to train fraud detection algorithms without using actual customer transaction data, ensuring that privacy is protected while still creating models capable of detecting fraudulent activities.
- **Retail and e-commerce**: In retail, synthetic data can be used to simulate customer purchasing patterns, behavior, and interactions with online stores. This helps retailers improve their recommendation systems, customer segmentation, and targeted marketing strategies.
- **Cybersecurity and threat detection**: In cybersecurity, synthetic data is used to simulate network traffic, attack patterns, and system vulnerabilities. By generating synthetic attack data (e.g., simulated hacking attempts, malware, phishing attacks), security systems can be trained to recognize and defend against real-world threats without compromising sensitive information.
- **NLP and text generation**: Synthetic text data can be generated for various NLP tasks, such as text classification, sentiment analysis, and language translation. This enables the training of models across a wide range of topics and domains without requiring access to sensitive textual data.
- **Manufacturing and product development**: In industries such as aerospace, automotive, and electronics, synthetic data is utilized to simulate various materials, design choices, and product behaviors under different conditions. This accelerates the product development cycle and allows companies to test different prototypes without physically building them.
- **Government and smart cities**: Synthetic data is used in urban planning and traffic management to simulate city infrastructure, traffic flow, and pedestrian movement. This helps governments and city planners optimize urban designs, reduce congestion, and improve traffic safety.
- **Gaming and virtual environments**: In the gaming industry, synthetic data is used to create virtual worlds, test gameplay mechanics, and simulate player interactions. By generating synthetic player data, game developers can test AI behavior and adjust game difficulty levels.

Example projects

Synthetic data has proven to be an invaluable resource in various industries, allowing developers, data scientists, and researchers to build robust models, test systems, and simulate real-world scenarios without relying on sensitive or expensive datasets.

Here are some example projects that showcase the diverse uses of synthetic data.

Autonomous vehicle simulation for traffic safety

Project overview: Synthetic data is used to simulate traffic scenarios for testing autonomous vehicle systems, such as collision avoidance, pedestrian detection, and traffic signal recognition.

Steps:

1. **Data generation**: Generate synthetic data of various driving environments, including road types (urban, rural, highways), weather conditions (rain, snow, fog), and various traffic scenarios (pedestrians crossing, vehicles changing lanes, accidents).
2. **Model training**: Train autonomous vehicle models to recognize traffic signals, pedestrians, other vehicles, and obstacles.
3. **Testing**: Test how the autonomous vehicle system responds to rare or extreme driving conditions (e.g., a car running a red light or a child running across the road).
4. **Outcome**: The autonomous vehicle system becomes better prepared for real-world traffic situations, improving safety and decision-making in the vehicle's environment.

Smart city traffic optimization system

Project overview: In a smart city project, synthetic data is used to simulate traffic patterns, road usage, and vehicle movement. This data is utilized to optimize traffic flow and reduce congestion in urban areas.

Steps:

1. **Data generation**: Generate synthetic traffic data, including vehicle speeds, traffic signal states, traffic volumes, and pedestrian activity.
2. **Model training**: Utilize machine learning or optimization algorithms to predict traffic congestion points, determine optimal traffic signal timings, and identify routes that minimize delays.
3. **Testing**: Simulate various scenarios (e.g., accidents, road closures, or rush-hour traffic) and assess the effectiveness of the traffic management system.
4. **Outcome**: A smart traffic optimization system that reduces congestion, improves travel time, and enhances safety on city roads.

Case studies

In this subsection, we will examine two case studies. The first case study deals with Synthetic data in healthcare. The second case study focuses on fraud detection and financial transactions.

Synthetic data in healthcare

A research institution utilized synthetic medical image generation to create diverse MRI scans to detect brain tumors. The actual data had insufficiently labeled MRI scans, especially for rare or underrepresented tumor types. Following are the challenges, solutions and outcomes:

- **Challenge**: Medical datasets, such as MRI scans, are often limited in quantity and may not include rare cases of tumors. Real data is also challenging to obtain due to privacy concerns, ethical issues, and the complexity of gathering labeled data for all possible cases.
- **Solution**: GANs may be used to generate realistic synthetic MRI images of brains with varying tumor sizes, locations, and types. The synthetic dataset may include benign and malignant tumors of different stages, allowing the model to generalize better.
- **Outcome**: The synthetic data was used to train a deep learning model for detecting tumors in MRI scans.

The model achieved comparable accuracy in detecting tumors on real-world data, even outperforming human radiologists in some instances.

Fraud detection and financial transactions

A financial institution faced challenges in detecting fraudulent transactions, as real-world fraud data was sparse, with most instances being rare and often involving small fraudulent amounts:

- **Challenge**: Fraudulent transactions occur infrequently, making it challenging for machine learning models to detect fraud using actual transaction datasets. Using real-world data would lead to imbalanced datasets, which are prone to overfitting and poor model generalization.
- **Solution**: A synthetic dataset can be created using a data augmentation technique to simulate normal customer behavior and various types of fraud, including credit card fraud, account takeover, and transaction laundering.
- **Outcome**: The synthetic data was used to train a fraud detection model, which improved the system's ability to recognize fraudulent activities even when they occurred in rare or hidden patterns.

  The model achieved high precision and recall when tested on both synthetic and real data, enabling better real-time fraud detection.

Synthetic data can help to prevent overfitting and bias towards the more frequent, non-fraudulent transactions.

Conclusion

This chapter explored the concept of synthetic data, its importance, creation methods, and practical applications in data science, as well as its advantages, limitations, and ethical considerations. The use of synthetic data is very important for model training in domains where real data is unavailable or sensitive. Also, it plays a crucial role in addressing issues such as data bias, ensuring privacy, and enabling secure data sharing.

There are several methods for generating synthetic data, including random data generation and data augmentation techniques. We can generate synthetic data in MS Excel using functions like RAND() and RANDBETWEEN(). The chapter includes advantages and limitations of Synthetic data. Synthetic data has a wide range of applications across industries such as healthcare, finance, and autonomous vehicles, where real data might be expensive, sparse, or sensitive. It aids in model testing, performance evaluation, and improving fairness and accuracy. Synthetic data is a powerful tool in data science, offering practical solutions for overcoming the limitations of real-world data.

In the next chapter, we will study Installing Python and IDEs, Python syntax and basics in variables and data types.

Exercises

1. How does synthetic data help in overcoming data scarcity issues? Provide an example.
2. Discuss the role of synthetic data in training ML models.
3. What are the key differences between random data generation and data augmentation techniques for creating synthetic data?
4. What are the basic Excel functions and formulas that can be used to generate synthetic data? Provide an example.
5. Explain how Excel's random number generation functions (e.g., RAND, RANDBETWEEN) can be used to create synthetic datasets.
6. Create a practical example using Excel to generate synthetic data for a simple linear regression model.
7. How can you apply conditional logic and formulas in Excel to generate specific types of synthetic data (e.g., categorical, continuous)?
8. Discuss the main advantages of using synthetic data in the context of training machine learning models.

9. What are some limitations and potential issues when using synthetic data in place of real data? How can these be mitigated?
10. Explain how synthetic data can reduce biases in machine learning models, especially in imbalanced datasets.
11. Discuss a case study where synthetic data was effectively used to solve a real-world problem. What was the impact on the overall project outcome?
12. Describe a practical project example where synthetic data was used to overcome the challenges of data privacy, availability, or quality.
13. What are the key challenges in using real-world data, and how does synthetic data help mitigate these challenges?
14. How can synthetic data help organizations in industries like healthcare, finance, and autonomous vehicles where real data may be difficult or costly to acquire?
15. Describe a method to handle missing data in synthetic datasets generated in Excel. How would you use Excel functions to fill in the gaps?
16. How can Excel be used to simulate categorical variables in synthetic data, and what considerations should be made for realistic representation?
17. Give an example of how synthetic data can be used in a research project for predicting future trends in business analytics.
18. Discuss how synthetic data could help in creating virtual environments for testing autonomous vehicles or drones.
19. How do you evaluate the effectiveness of synthetic data generation methods, and what metrics can be used to assess their quality?
20. Discuss the potential risks of relying on synthetic data in machine learning, particularly in terms of model performance and accuracy.

CHAPTER 7
Basics of Python Programming

Introduction

There has been a huge advancement in the field of data science in recent years. The field of data science involves complex tasks to be performed. Python is commonly used to perform data science tasks efficiently due to its simplicity, readability, and its set of libraries. Python has a rich set of libraries, such as NumPy for numerical computations, Pandas is used for data manipulation, Matplotlib and Seaborn is used for data visualization, and scikit-learn for ML. Python can easily be used with big data platforms like *Hadoop* and *Spark*, cloud services, and APIs, making it highly versatile for a wide range of data science applications. Its strong community support ensures that users have access to extensive documentation, tutorials, and community-driven solutions. All the previously-mentioned features of Python make it an ideal choice for data analysis, machine learning, and artificial intelligence tasks.

This chapter discusses the installation of Python, IDEs, understanding basics and syntax of Python, variables and data types in Python, control structures, etc.

Structure

This chapter covers the following topics:

- Installing Python and IDEs
- Python syntax and basics
- Variables and data types
- Control structures
- Functions and modules
- Error handling in Python
- Python Framework

Objectives

This chapter provides foundation in Python programming, beginning with the installation of Python and an introduction to popular **integrated development environments** (**IDEs**) such as Jupyter Notebook and PyCharm. The chapter then delves into the basics of Python syntax, define, and use of variables, key data types such as integers, floats, strings, lists, tuples, and dictionaries. This chapter also covers control structures, enabling readers to implement conditional logic using **`if`**, **`elif`**, and **`else`** statements, as well as iteration using for and while loops. It also discusses functions and modules, guiding readers on how to create reusable code blocks with functions and how to enhance code organization and reusability. By the end of this chapter, readers will have a thorough understanding of basics of python, its syntax, variables, data types used, control structures, using functions and libraries.

Installing Python and IDEs

Before we begin to write Python programs, it is essential to setup the programming environment. This involves two key steps:

1. Installing the Python interpreter.
2. Selecting an appropriate IDE.

Steps to install Python

Python is an open-source, high-level programming language that can be downloaded freely from the official website: **https://www.python.org/**. It is available for all major operating systems including Windows, macOS, and Linux.

Installing Python on Windows

Following are the steps of installing Python on Windows:

1. Visit the official Python downloads page: **https://www.python.org/downloads/**
2. Click on the latest stable version compatible with Windows.
3. Once the installer is downloaded, run it.

    Note: **Before clicking "Install Now," make sure to check the box that says "Add Python to PATH". This ensures that Python commands can be run from the command prompt.**

4. Click **Install Now** and wait for the installation to complete.

After installation, you can verify it by opening command prompt and typing **`python --version`**. If installed correctly, it will display the installed version number.

Installing Python on macOS

macOS often comes with a version of Python pre-installed, but it might be outdated. It is recommended to install the latest version manually.

The easiest way is to use Homebrew (a package manager for macOS) is as follows:

1. First, install Homebrew from **https://brew.sh/**
2. Open the Terminal and run: `brew install python`
3. Once installed, confirm the installation with: `python3 --version`

Installing Python on Linux

Most Linux distributions come with Python pre-installed. To update or install Python, use the package manager:

- **For Debian/Ubuntu**: `sudo apt install python3`
- **For Fedora**: `sudo dnf install python3`
- **For Arch Linux**: `sudo pacman -S python`

After installation, Python can be run in the terminal or command prompt using python or python3, depending on the system.

Overview of popular IDEs

An IDE is a software application that provides tools to make the process of writing code more efficient. It typically includes a code editor, debugger, compiler/interpreter, and other features such as code completion, syntax highlighting, and project management.

Popular Python IDEs includes the following:

- **Jupyter Notebook**: It is a web-based IDE that is widely used in data science, education, and research. It allows users to create and share documents that contain live code, equations, visualizations, and narrative text. Jupyter is especially useful for experimenting with code in an interactive way.

  Installation: The easiest way to install Jupyter Notebook is through the Anaconda distribution (**https://www.anaconda.com/**), which also includes many useful Python libraries.

  Alternatively, Jupyter can be installed via pip: `pip install notebook` to launch, type `jupyter notebook` in the terminal or command prompt.

- **PyCharm**: It is a powerful IDE developed by *JetBrains*, specifically designed for Python. It includes intelligent code completion, error detection, a built-in terminal, version control, and support for web development frameworks.

Download: PyCharm is available in two editions:

- o Community edition (Free and open-source).
- o Professional edition (Paid, with additional features).

Download from the following link: **https://www.jetbrains.com/pycharm/**

After installation, you can create new Python projects, manage virtual environments, and install packages easily.

- **Visual Studio Code (VS Code)**: It is a lightweight, cross platform code editor developed by *Microsoft*. It supports Python via extensions and offers a wide range of customizable features including themes, keyboard shortcuts, and integrations with Git.

  Download: **https://code.visualstudio.com/**

  After installation, install the Python extension by Microsoft from the Extensions Marketplace.

  Once configured, VS Code offers code linting, IntelliSense (auto-completion), debugging, and integration with Jupyter Notebooks.

  - **Other IDEs**:
    - o **Thonny**: It is deal for beginners. It comes with Python pre-installed and has a very simple interface.
    - o **Spyder**: It is often used in scientific computing. It also included in the Anaconda distribution.
    - o **IDLE**: It comes bundled with Python installation. This basic editor is suitable for small scripts.
    - o **Cursor IDE**: An AI-powered IDE built on a fork of VS Code, developed by *Anysphere*. It offers features like natural language code edits, smart multi line completions, codebase aware queries, and inline editing with AI assistance.
    - o **Kiro**: It is an AI based IDE developed by *AWS* using Code OSS (a VS Code base). It emphasizes structured development with built-in specifications, agent hooks, leadership steering, and integration into formal workflows.

Python syntax and basics

Understanding Python syntax and basic programming constructs is the foundation for anyone starting their journey in Python. Python is widely known for its simple and readable syntax, which makes it an ideal language for beginners and professionals alike. This section covers how to write and execute Python scripts, along with key syntax rules that form the foundation of all Python programs.

Writing and running Python scripts

A Python script is simply a file containing Python code, usually with a **.py** extension. These scripts can be written using any text editor or IDE like Jupyter Notebook, PyCharm, or VS Code.

The following are the steps for creating a script:

1. Open a text editor or IDE.
2. Write your Python code, for example:

   ```
   print("Hello, world!")
   ```

3. Save the file with a **.py** extension, e.g., **hello.py**.

The following are the steps for running a Script:

1. Open the command line or terminal.
2. Navigate to the directory where the file is saved.
3. Run the script using:

   python hello.py or **python3 hello.py**

In Jupyter Notebook, Python code can be run directly in cells. This is especially useful for step-by-step coding, data visualization, and documentation.

Basic syntax rules

Python uses a unique syntax that enhances readability and simplicity. Some key rules include:

- **Indentation**: Unlike many other programming languages that use braces **{}** to define blocks of code, Python uses indentation to mark blocks. Indentation must be consistent within a block, usually using four spaces.

  Example: If true, **print(This is indented correctly)**

  Incorrect indentation will result in an **IndentationError**.

- **Comments**: Comments are used to annotate code and are ignored during execution. In Python, single-line comments begin with a **#** symbol.

  ```
  # This is a comment
  print("Hello, world!")  # This is an inline comment
  ```

  For multi-line comments or documentation, triple quotes (**'''** or **"""**) can be used.

- **Case sensitivity**: Python is case sensitive. For example, **Variable**, **variable**, and **VARIABLE** are treated as different identifiers.

- **Statement termination**: Unlike many languages that require semicolons to terminate statements, Python uses line breaks. However, semicolons can be used to write multiple statements on a single line (though it is not recommended for readability).

```
x = 10; y = 20;
print(x + y)
```

- **Variable assignment**: Variables are created when a value is assigned to them. Python does not require explicit declaration of variable types.

  Example:

```
name = "Alice"
age = 25
height = 5.6
```

- **Printing output**: The **`print()`** function is used to display output.

```
print("Welcome to Python!")
print("Age:", age)
```

- **Taking user input**: The **`input()`** function is used to receive input from the user.

```
user_name = input("Enter your name: ")
print("Hello, " + user_name)
```

- Note that **`input()`** always returns a string. If you need an integer, use type casting:

```
age = int(input("Enter your age: "))
```

- **Python identifiers and keywords**: Identifiers are names used for variables, functions, classes, etc. They must begin with a letter (A-Z or a-z) or an underscore _, followed by letters, digits, or underscores.

  Example:

```
my_var = 10
_total = 50
name1 = "Python"
```

Python has reserved keywords that cannot be used as identifiers which are as follows:

`False`, **`True`**, **`None`**, **`and`**, **`or`**, **`not`**, **`if`**, **`else`**, **`elif`**, **`for`**, **`while`**, **`break`**, **`continue`**, **`def`**, **`return`**, **`import`**, **`from`**, **`class`**, **`try`**, **`except`**, etc.

Use the following keyword module to list all keywords:

```
import keywordprint(keyword.kwlist)
```

Variables and data types

Variables and data types form the core of any programming language. In Python, variables are used to store data, and each variable can hold a value of a specific type. Python is dynamically typed, meaning we do not declare the data type explicitly. Python automatically determines it based on the value assigned.

Defining variables

A variable is a symbolic name that refers to a value. You can think of it as a labeled box that stores data for later use.

Syntax:

```
variable_name = value
```

Examples:

```
x = 10
name = "Alice"
price = 99.99
```

Rules for naming variables include the following:

- Must begin with a letter (a–z, A–Z) or underscore (_).
- Can contain letters, digits (0–9), and underscores.
- Cannot be a Python keyword (like `if`, `for`, `def`, etc.).
- Python is case-sensitive: `Name` and `name` are different variables.

Common data types

Python supports a wide variety of built-in data types, which can be broadly categorized, as follows:

- **Numeric types**:
  - **Integer (int)**: Represents whole numbers, positive or negative, without decimals.

    ```
    a = 5
    b = -100
    ```

  - **Floating-point (float)**: Represents numbers with decimal points or in exponential form.

    ```
    pi = 3.14
    scientific = 2.5e3  # 2500.0
    ```

- **Complex (complex)**: Numbers with real and imaginary parts.

```
c = 3 + 4j
```

- **Text type**:
  - **String (str)**: A sequence of characters enclosed in single, double, or triple quotes.

    Example:

```
message = 'Hello'
name = "Alice"
multiline = """This is
a multiline string."""
```

Strings support indexing and slicing, e.g., **`name[0] returns 'A'`**.

- **Sequence types**:
  - **List (list)**: An ordered, mutable (changeable) collection of items. Can hold mixed data types.

    Example:

```
numbers = [1, 2, 3, 4]
mixed = [1, "apple", 3.14]
```

Lists support indexing, slicing, appending, removing, and looping.

  - **Tuple (tuple)**: An ordered, immutable (unchangeable) collection.

    Example:

```
coordinates = (10, 20)
```

Tuples are often used when data should not be modified.

- **Mapping type**:
  - **Dictionary (dict)**: An unordered collection of key-value pairs.

    Example:

```
student = {"name": "John", "age": 21, "grade": "A"}
```

Dictionaries allow quick access to values using keys, e.g., **`student["name"]`**.

- **Boolean type**:
  - **Boolean (bool)**: Represents truth values: **`True`** or **`False`**.

    Example:

```
is_active = True
is_logged_in = False
```

Boolean values are often the result of comparison or logical operations.

- **None type**:
    - **NoneType (None)**: It represents the absence of a value or a null value.

      ```
      result = None
      ```

      It is useful in default return values or placeholders.

- **Type conversion (type casting)**: Python allows explicit type conversion (casting) using built-in functions:

  ```
  x = int("5")        # Converts string to integer
  y = float("3.14")   # Converts string to float
  z = str(100)        # Converts integer to string
  ```

  To check the type of a variable, use the `type()` function:

  ```
  print(type(x))   # Output: <class 'int'>
  ```

Control structures

Control structures are essential elements in any programming language that allow you to control the flow of execution based on conditions or repetitive tasks. In Python, the most common control structures include if statements for decision-making and loops for iteration. These structures make programs dynamic, intelligent, and capable of solving real-world problems by reacting to various conditions and data patterns.

Conditional statements

Conditional statements are used to execute specific blocks of code only when certain conditions are met.

Syntax:

if condition:

```
    # code block executed if condition is Trueelif another_condition:
    # code block executed if another_condition is Trueelse:
    # code block executed if none of the above conditions are True
```

Example:

```
age = 20
if age >= 18:
    print("You are eligible to vote.")elif age > 0:
    print("You are too young to vote.")else:
    print("Invalid age entered.")
```

Key points:

- Conditions must be expressions that evaluate to true or false.
- Python uses indentation to define blocks instead of curly braces.
- You can nest if statements within one another for more complex logic.

For and while loop

Loops are used to repeat a block of code multiple times. Python provides two main types of loops: for loops and while loops, as follows:

- **For loops**: A for loop is used to iterate over a sequence like a list, tuple, string, or range.

  Syntax:

  ```
  for variable in sequence:
  ```

  Example 1:

  ```
  for i in range(5):
      print("Iteration", i)
  ```

  Output:

  ```
  Iteration 0
  Iteration 1
  Iteration 2
  Iteration 3
  Iteration 4
  ```

  You can also use a for loop to iterate over strings or lists:

  Example 2:

  ```
  for char in "Python":
      print(char)
  ```

- **While loops**: A while loop continues to execute as long as a specified condition is true.

  Syntax:

  ```
  while condition:
      # code block
  ```

  Example:

  ```
  count = 1
  while count <= 5:
      print("Count:", count)
      count += 1
  ```

Loop control statements

Python provides control statements to manage the behavior of loops:

- **break**: Exits the loop entirely.
- **continue**: Skips the current iteration and moves to the next.
- **pass**: Does nothing; used as a placeholder.

  Examples:

```
# Using breakfor i in range(10):
    if i == 5:
        break
    print(i
# Using continuefor i in range(5):
    if i == 2:
        continue
    print(i)
# Using passfor i in range(3):
    pass  # useful as a placeholder when a block is required
syntactically
```

Functions and modules

In Python, functions and modules are powerful tools that help organize code into manageable, reusable parts. They promote clean programming practices such as modularity, reusability, and abstraction, making your programs more efficient and easier to maintain.

Functions in Python

A function is a block of reusable code that performs a specific task. Functions help break programs into smaller, manageable chunks and allow the same code to be reused without rewriting it.

Types of functions are as follows:

- **Built-in functions**: Already provided by Python (e.g., `print()`, `len()`, `range()`)
- **User-defined functions**: Created by the programmer

Defining and calling functions

We can define a function using the def keyword.

Syntax:

```
def function_name(parameters):
    # code block
    return value  # (optional)
```

Example:

```
def greet(name):
    print("Hello,", name)
greet("Alice")  # Output: Hello, Alice
```

Returning values from function

Functions in Python can return values to the caller using the return statement, allowing the result of a computation to be reused or stored for further processing. When a return statement is executed, the function terminates and sends the specified value back to the point where it was called. This makes functions highly useful for modular and reusable code design.

Example:

```
def add(x, y):
    return x + y
result = add(5, 3)
print(result)  # Output: 8
```

Function parameters and arguments

The Function parameters and arguments used in Python are as follows:

- **Positional arguments**: Passed in order.
- **Keyword arguments**: Passed by name.
- **Default arguments**: Have default values if not provided.
- **Variable-length arguments**: Use **`*args`** or **`**kwargs`** to accept multiple arguments.

  Example:

  ```
  def display_info(name, age=18):
      print("Name:", name)
      print("Age:", age)
  display_info("John")  # Age defaults to 18
  ```

The following are the scope of variables:

- **Local variables**: Defined inside a function, accessible only within it.
- **Global variables**: Defined outside any function, accessible throughout the program.

Importing and using modules

A module is a file containing Python code (functions, classes, variables) that can be imported and used in other Python files. Python has many built-in modules and also allows you to create your own.

Creating module

Suppose you have a file named **mymodule.py**, as follows:

```
def square(x):
    return x * x
```

You can import and use it in another file:

```
import mymodule
print(mymodule.square(5))  # Output: 25
```

Importing modules

There are multiple ways to import a module. The following are the ways:

- **Import the whole module**:

  ```
  import math
  print(math.sqrt(16))  # Output: 4.0
  ```

- **Import a specific function**:

  ```
  from math import sqrt
  print(sqrt(25))  # Output: 5.0
  ```

- **Rename a module (aliasing)**:

  ```
  import math as mprint(m.pi)
  ```

Standard library modules

Python comes with a rich set of standard modules.

The following are some examples:

- **math**: Mathematical functions
- **random**: Random number generation
- **datetime**: Date and time manipulation
- **os**: Interacting with the operating system
- **sys**: Access to system-specific parameters

Functions and modules are critical building blocks in Python programming. Functions enable code reusability and logical organization, while modules help in organizing and sharing code across different programs.

Error handling in Python

In Python, error handling is done primarily using the try-except block, along with else, finally, and custom exceptions if needed. This allows your program to catch and respond to runtime errors instead of crashing.

Consider the following example that shows error handling in Python:

```
try:
    # Code that may raise an exception
    risky_code = 10 / 0
except ZeroDivisionError:
    # Code that runs if the exception occurs
    print("Error: Division by zero is not allowed.")
```

Consider the following code that uses finally, in which code runs regardless of error:

```
try:
    result = 10 / 2
except ZeroDivisionError:
    print("Cannot divide by zero.")
else:
    print(f"Result is {result}")
finally:
    print("Execution completed.")
```

Python framework

A framework in Python is a pre-built collection of modules, packages, and tools that provides a structured foundation for building applications.

Instead of writing everything from scratch, you use a framework to save time, enforce best practices, and focus on your application's logic.

Python frameworks can be broadly classified into:

- **Web development frameworks**: Used for building web applications (both front-end and back-end logic). these include:
    - **Django**: A high-level full-stack framework with ORM, authentication, admin panel, and scalability.

- **Flask**: A lightweight micro-framework, minimal but highly flexible.
- **FastAPI**: Modern, fast framework for building APIs with async support.
- **Pyramid**: Flexible, suitable for both small and large apps.

```
from flask import Flask
app = Flask(__name__)
@app.route('/')def hello():
    return "Hello, World!"
if __name__ == '__main__':
    app.run()
```

- **ML and data science frameworks:** Provide tools for AI, ML, and scientific computing. These include:
  - **TensorFlow**: Deep learning, neural networks.
  - **PyTorch**: Popular in research, dynamic computation graphs.
  - **Scikit-learn**: Classical ML algorithms (regression, classification, clustering).
  - **Pandas**: Data manipulation and analysis.
  - **NumPy**: Numerical computing.

```
from sklearn.linear_model import LinearRegression:

X = [[1], [2], [3], [4]]
y = [2, 4, 6, 8]

model = LinearRegression()
model.fit(X, y)print(model.predict([[5]]))  # Output ~ [10]
```

- **GUI (desktop app) frameworks**: Used to build desktop applications with graphical interfaces. It includes:
  - **Tkinter**: Built-in with Python, simple GUIs.
  - **PyQt/PySide**: Rich GUI features, cross-platform.
  - **Kivy**: For multi-touch apps, mobile + desktop.

```
import tkinter as tk

root = tk.Tk()
root.title("Simple GUI")
```

```
label = tk.Label(root, text="Hello, Python Frameworks!")
label.pack()

root.mainloop()
```

- **Testing frameworks:** Used for writing automated tests. These include:
    - **PyTest**: Simple and powerful testing.
    - **Unittest**: Built-in testing framework.
    - **Behave**: **Behavior-driven development** (**BDD**).
- **Other specialized frameworks:**
    - **Scrapy**: Web scraping.
    - **Beautiful Soup (library)**: Parsing HTML/XML.
    - **Celery**: Distributed task queue (asynchronous jobs).
    - **Odoo**: Business apps (ERP, CRM).

Conclusion

This chapter introduced the foundational elements of Python programming, beginning with installation of Python and setup a suitable development environment using popular IDEs such as Jupyter Notebook and PyCharm.

The chapter discussed the Python's basic syntax, demonstrating how to write and run scripts, follow indentation rules, and understand Python's straightforward, readable structure. It introduced variables and data types such as integers, floats, strings, lists, tuples, and dictionaries, explaining how data is stored, accessed, and manipulated in Python.

Further, it explained control structures, including conditional statements (if, elif, else) and loops (for, while), which enable decision-making and repetition in code. These constructs are essential for creating dynamic, responsive programs. It explained in detail the functions and modules. Functions allow code reuse and modular design, while modules promote code organization and scalability and laid a foundation in Python programming, preparing readers to write structured, logical, and reusable code using essential programming constructs. This chapter also discussed about error handling in Python and Python Frameworks.

In the next chapter, list, tuple, dictionaries, sets, frozen sets will be discussed along with the practical implementation.

Exercises

1. What are the steps involved in installing Python on a Windows system?
2. How can you verify that Python is successfully installed on your computer?
3. What is the purpose of setting the PATH variable during Python installation?
4. Compare Jupyter Notebook and PyCharm in terms of features and use cases.
5. What are the benefits of using an IDE for Python programming?
6. How do you write and execute a simple Python script?
7. What are the basic rules of Python syntax regarding indentation and line breaks?
8. What is the difference between a statement and an expression in Python?
9. How is a comment written in Python, and why are comments important?
10. What happens if you do not follow the correct indentation in Python code?
11. How do you define a variable in Python, and how is it different from statically typed languages?
12. What are the common data types supported by Python?
13. Give an example of a list and a tuple in Python and highlight the difference between them.
14. How do you convert a string to an integer in Python?
15. What is the syntax for declaring a dictionary, and how do you access its elements?
16. How is an if, elif, else statement structured in Python?
17. What is the difference between a for loop and a while loop in Python?
18. Write a Python loop that prints all even numbers from 1 to 20.
19. What are break and continue statements used for in loops?
20. How do you define and call a function in Python, and what is the significance of the return statement?

Join our Discord space

Join our Discord workspace for latest updates, offers, tech happenings around the world, new releases, and sessions with the authors:

https://discord.bpbonline.com

CHAPTER 8

Working with Python Data Structures

Introduction

Python provides efficient data structures for managing and organizing a collection of data in an effective way, which forms the backbone of most programs. Among these, lists, tuples, dictionaries, sets, and frozensets are fundamental for organizing data in expressive ways. Understanding how to create, manipulate, and utilize these structures is essential for writing clean, fast, and readable Python code.

This chapter introduces these core data structures. We will explore how to create lists, modify them, and use list comprehensions for elegant and concise transformations. We will discuss tuples, which are immutable sequences often used to represent fixed collections of related data. This chapter also discusses about dictionaries, which store data in key-value pairs and offer fast lookups. This chapter discusses sets and frozensets, which are unordered collections of unique elements. Sets are particularly useful for membership testing and eliminating duplicates, while frozensets offer immutability for use in certain contexts like dictionary keys.

This chapter also includes practical examples and hands-on exercises. These will help solidify your grasp of Python's core data structures.

Structure

This chapter covers the following topics:

- Lists
- Tuples
- Dictionaries
- Sets and frozensets
- Practical example and exercises

Objectives

This chapter aims to equip readers with Python's core data structures, including lists, tuples, dictionaries, sets, and frozensets. Readers will learn how to create and manipulate lists, access their elements, and apply list comprehensions for efficient data transformations. The chapter will highlight the characteristics of tuples, emphasizing their immutability and typical usage scenarios. It will guide readers on how to create and manipulate dictionaries using key-value pairs. It will also discuss the application of common dictionary methods and iteration techniques. Additionally, the chapter will introduce sets and frozensets, focusing on their uniqueness property, set operations such as union and intersection, and the differences between mutable and immutable collections. By the end of this chapter, readers will be able to choose the appropriate data structure for a given task and apply their knowledge through hands-on exercises and practical programming examples.

Lists

A list is one of the most versatile and commonly used built-in data structures in Python. It is an ordered, mutable collection of elements, which means that the items in a list maintain their order and can be changed after creation. Lists can contain elements of any data type, including other lists (nested lists), and can be easily modified, making them ideal for storing sequences of data in a wide range of applications.

Creating and manipulating lists

There are various ways to create a list. These include the following:

- You can create a list in Python by placing elements within square brackets `[]`, separated by commas.

  For example:

  ```
  fruits = ['apple', 'banana', 'mango']
  numbers = [1, 2, 3, 4, 5]
  mixed = [1, 'apple', 3.14, True]
  ```

- An empty list can be created using:

  ```
  empty_list = []
  ```

- Lists can also be created using the built-in **`list()`** function:

  ```
  letters = list('abc')  # ['a', 'b', 'c']
  ```

Manipulating lists

Python provides a wide range of methods and operations to work with lists:

- **Accessing elements**: List elements can be accessed by their index, with indexing starting at 0.

For example:

```
fruits = ['apple', 'banana', 'mango']
fruits[1]  # 'banana'
```

- **Modifying elements**: List is mutable. It means we can modify the elements of a list.

  For example:

```
fruits = ['apple', 'banana', 'mango']
fruits[0] = 'orange'  # Now fruits = ['orange', 'banana', 'mango']
```

- **Adding elements**: We can use **`insert()`**, **`append()`**, and **`extend()`** to add new elements to an existing list. **`append()`** adds an element to the end:

  For example:

```
fruits = ['apple', 'banana', 'mango']
fruits.append('grape')  # adds grape at the end
```

  `insert()` adds an element at a specific position:

  For example:

```
fruits = ['apple', 'banana', 'mango']
fruits.insert(1, 'kiwi') # adds Kiwi at first position
```

  `extend()` adds elements from another list:

  For example:

```
fruits = ['apple', 'banana', 'mango']
fruits.extend(['papaya', 'pear'])
```

- **Removing elements**: **`pop()`** and **`remove()`** is used to delete element from list. **`remove()`** deletes the first occurrence of a value:

  For example:

```
fruits = ['apple', 'banana', 'mango']
fruits.remove('banana') // This removes the element
```

  `pop()` removes an item by index (or the last item by default):

  For example:

```
fruits = ['apple', 'banana', 'mango']
fruits.pop(2) // This removes banana which is at 2 position in list.
```

  `clear()` removes all elements:

  For example:

```
fruits = ['apple', 'banana', 'mango']
fruits.clear() // makes list empty
```

- **Other useful methods**:
  - **`len(list)`** returns the number of elements.
  - **`list.index(value)`** finds the index of a value.
  - **`list.count(value)`** counts how many times a value appears.
  - **`list.sort()`** and **`list.reverse()`** sort and reverse the list respectively.
- **Slicing**: Python also supports slicing, i.e., to extract a sublist:

  For example:

```
numbers = [0, 1, 2, 3, 4, 5]
subset = numbers[1:4]  # [1, 2, 3]
```

Lists comprehensions

List comprehensions provide a concise and elegant way to create new lists by performing an operation on each element of an existing **`iterable`**, often replacing the need for **`for`** loops.

Basic syntax:

```
new_list = [expression for item in iterable]
```

- **Example 1**: Create a list of squares of numbers from 1 to 5:

```
squares = [x**2 for x in range(1, 6)]  # [1, 4, 9, 16, 25]
```

- **Example 2**: Filter even numbers from a list:

```
even_numbers = [x for x in range(10) if x % 2 == 0]  # [0, 2, 4, 6, 8]
```

- **Example 3**: Convert all words in a list to uppercase:

```
words = ['python', 'data', 'science']
upper_words = [word.upper() for word in words]  # ['PYTHON', 'DATA',
'SCIENCE']
```

List comprehensions can also be nested, though readability should be considered:

For example:

```
matrix = [[i * j for j in range(1, 4)] for i in range(1, 4)] # [[1, 2, 3], [2,
4, 6], [3, 6, 9]]
```

Tuples

A tuple is a built-in data structure in Python used to store an ordered sequence of elements. Tuples are very similar to lists, but with one key difference: tuples are immutable, meaning once they are created, their contents cannot be modified. This immutability makes tuples suitable for storing fixed collections of data and can also make programs more predictable and faster.

Creating tuples

Tuples can be created in the following ways:

- Tuples are created by placing elements within parentheses `()` separated by commas:

  For example:

  ```
  coordinates = (10, 20)
  person = ('Alice', 30, 'Engineer')
  ```

- Tuples can also be created without parentheses using just commas:

  For example:

  ```
  numbers = 1, 2, 3  # This is also a tuple
  ```

- To create a single-element tuple, a trailing comma is required:

  For example:

  ```
  single = (5,)  # This is a tuple
  not_a_tuple = (5)  # This is an integer
  ```

- Tuples can also be created using the **`tuple()`** constructor:

  For example:

  ```
  my_tuple = tuple(['a', 'b', 'c'])  # ('a', 'b', 'c')
  ```

Characteristics of tuples

Tuples have certain characteristics. These include the following:

- **Immutable**: Once a tuple is created, its contents cannot be changed. You cannot add, remove, or modify elements in a tuple.
- **Ordered**: Like lists, tuples maintain the order of elements. This means you can access elements using an index.
- **Heterogeneous**: Tuples can contain elements of different types: integers, strings, lists, etc.
- **Allow duplicates**: Like lists, tuples can contain duplicate values.
- **Can be nested**: Tuples can contain other tuples or lists as elements.
- **Faster than lists**: Due to their immutability, operations on tuples can be more performance efficient compared to lists.
- **Hashable**: Tuples can be used as keys in dictionaries and as elements in sets (only if all elements in the tuple are also immutable).

Operations with tuples

Even though tuples are immutable, we can still perform several operations:

- **Indexing and slicing**: Same as in the list; we can access an element using its position in a tuple. We can also perform slicing, i.e, extracting a string or selected elements given the range.

  For example:

```
data = ('apple', 'banana', 'cherry')
print(data[1])        # 'banana'
print(data[0:2])      # ('apple', 'banana')
```

- **Iteration**: Using loops, we can iterate through each element in the tuple.

  For example:

```
data = ('apple', 'banana', 'cherry')
for item in data:
print(item)
```

- **Membership testing**: We can test if the element is a part of a tuple; then it returns true, else false.

  For example:

```
data = ('apple', 'banana', 'cherry')
'banana' in data  # True
'grape' not in data  # True
```

- **Concatenation and repetition**: We can combine two tuples. Also, we can perform repetition of tuples.

  For example:

```
t1 = (1, 2)
t2 = (3, 4)
print(t1 + t2)      # (1, 2, 3, 4)
print(t1 * 3)       # (1, 2, 1, 2, 1, 2)
```

- **Tuple unpacking**: You can assign each element of a tuple to a variable:

  For example:

```
person = ('John', 25, 'Developer')
name, age, profession = person
print(name)       # 'John'
print(profession) # 'Developer'
```

- **Built-in functions**: Some built-in functions in a tuple include the following:
    - **len(tuple)**: Returns the number of elements.
    - **max(tuple) / min(tuple)**: Returns the maximum or minimum value.
    - **sum(tuple)**: Returns the total of numeric elements.
    - **tuple.count(value)**: Returns the number of times a value appears.
    - **tuple.index(value)**: Returns the first index of the specified value.

Use cases of tuples:

- Storing fixed data (e.g., days of the week).
- Returning multiple values from a function.
- Using tuples as dictionary keys or set elements.
- Representing coordinates (x, y), RGB color values, etc.

Dictionaries

A dictionary is a powerful built-in data structure in Python that stores data as key-value pairs. Unlike lists or tuples, where values are accessed by index, dictionary values are accessed using unique keys. Dictionaries are unordered (before Python 3.7) but maintain insertion order from Python 3.7 onwards. They are mutable, meaning their contents can be changed after creation.

Key-value pairs

A Key-value pair in a dictionary consists of two linked elements: a key, which acts as a unique identifier, and a value, which is the data associated with that key.

In this section, we will discuss the creation of a dictionary and accessing values using keys:

- **Creating a dictionary**: You can create a dictionary using curly braces `{}` or the `dict()` constructor:

  For example:

  ```
  student = {
      'name': 'Alice',
      'age': 22,
      'course': 'Computer Science'
  }
  ```

  Or using the `dict()` function:

  ```
  student = dict(name='Alice', age=22, course='Computer Science')
  ```

- **Accessing values by key**: Keys must be immutable types (like strings, numbers, or tuples), and must be unique, whereas values can be of any type and can repeat.

  For example:

```
student = dict(name='Alice', age=22, course='Computer Science')
print(student['name'])  # Alice
You can also use the .get() method to avoid errors if the key doesn't
exist:
print(student.get('grade', 'N/A'))  # N/A
```

Common dictionary methods

Python provides a wide range of useful methods to manipulate and interact with dictionaries:

- **keys()**: Returns a view object of all the keys in the dictionary.

  For example:

```
student = dict(name='Alice', age=22, course='Computer Science')
student.keys()  # dict_keys(['name', 'age', 'course'])
```

- **values()**: Returns a view object of all the values in the dictionary.

  For example:

```
student = dict(name='Alice', age=22, course='Computer Science')
student.values()  # dict_values(['Alice', 22, 'Computer Science'])
```

- **items()**: Returns a view object of all key-value pairs as tuples.

  For example:

```
student = dict(name='Alice', age=22, course='Computer Science')
student.items()  # dict_items([('name', 'Alice'), ('age', 22),
('course', 'Computer Science')])
```

- **update()**: Updates the dictionary with key-value pairs from another dictionary or iterable.

  For example:

```
student = dict(name='Alice', age=22, course='Computer Science',
grade='B')
student.update({'age': 23, 'grade': 'A'})
```

- **pop(key)**: Removes a key and returns its value. Raises an error if the key is not found.

  For example:

```
student = dict(name='Alice', age=22, course='Computer Science',
```

```
grade='A')
student.pop('grade')  # 'A'
```

- **popitem()**: Removes and returns the last inserted key-value pair (Python 3.7+).

  For example:

  ```
  student = dict(name='Alice', age=22, course='Computer Science')
  student.popitem()
  ```

- **clear()**: Removes all elements from the dictionary.

  For example:

  ```
  student.clear()
  ```

- **setdefault()**: Returns the value of a key if it exists; otherwise, inserts the key with a default value.

  For example:

  ```
  student.setdefault('gender', 'female')  # 'female'
  ```

Iterating over dictionary

You can loop through keys, values, or key-value pairs:

For example:

```
for key in student:
    print(key, student[key])
# OR
for key, value in student.items():
    print(f"{key}: {value}")
```

Use cases of dictionaries:

- Storing structured data like user profiles, product catalogs, or configuration settings.
- Fast lookup of values using keys.
- Representing JSON-like data structures.
- Counting frequencies of elements in a list (using `collections.Counter`).

Dictionaries are essential in Python programming due to their speed and flexibility, and are used in real-world tasks such as data processing, APIs, and object modeling.

Sets and frozensets

Sets and frozensets are built-in data structures in Python that store unordered collections of unique elements. They are especially useful for eliminating duplicates, performing mathematical set operations (like union and intersection), and checking for membership. While sets are mutable, meaning they can be changed after creation, frozensets are immutable and cannot be modified once created.

Creating sets

You can create a set using curly braces **{}** or the **set()** constructor:

- **Using curly braces**:
```
fruits = {'apple', 'banana', 'mango'}
```
- **Using set() function**:
```
numbers = set([1, 2, 3, 4, 4, 5])  # Duplicates will be removed
```
- An empty set must be created with **set()**, not **{}**, which creates an empty dictionary:
```
empty_set = set()
```

Note: All elements in a set must be hashable (i.e., immutable types like numbers, strings, or tuples).

Creating frozensets

A frozenset is created using the **frozenset()** function:

```
fset = frozenset([1, 2, 3, 3, 4])
```

Frozensets behave like sets, but they are immutable. You cannot add or remove elements after creation. They are useful when you need a set that can be used as a dictionary key or added to another set.

The frozenset type is built-in and is commonly used when you need a set-like object that is hashable and can be used as a dictionary key or as an element of another set.

We can create a frozenset using the built-in **frozenset()** constructor.

Consider the following example of the creation of frozensets in Python:

```
# From a list
fs = frozenset([1, 2, 3, 2])
print(fs) # Output: frozenset({1, 2, 3})
# From a set
s = set([4, 5, 6])
fs2 = frozenset(s)
```

```
# From a string (creates a frozenset of characters)
fs3 = frozenset("data")
print(fs3)  # Output: frozenset({'d', 'a', 't'})
```

Sets operations

Python provides many powerful operations to work with sets:

- Adding and removing elements (only for sets):

  For example:

```
myset = {1, 2, 3}
myset.add(4)              # {1, 2, 3, 4}
myset.remove(2)           # {1, 3, 4}
myset.discard(10)         # No error if element not found
myset.pop()               # Removes and returns a random element
myset.clear()             # Empties the set
```

Mathematical set operations

Let us assume the following two sets:

```
A = {1, 2, 3, 4}
B = {3, 4, 5, 6}
```

- **Union**: Combines elements from both sets (no duplicates):

```
A.union(B)           # {1, 2, 3, 4, 5, 6}
A | B                # Alternative syntax
```

- **Intersection**: Returns common elements:

```
A.intersection(B)    # {3, 4}
A & B     # Alternative syntax
```

- **Difference**: Returns elements in **A** but not in **B**:

```
A.difference(B)      # {1, 2}
A - B   # Alternative syntax
```

- **Symmetric difference**: Returns elements in **A** or **B** but not in both:

```
A.symmetric_difference(B)  # {1, 2, 5, 6}
A ^ B  # Alternative syntax
```

- **Set membership and comparison**: It is used in keyword checks membership:

  For example:

```
3 in A         # True
5 not in A     # True
```

- **Subset and superset relationships:**

```
{1, 2}.issubset(A)          # True
A.issuperset({1, 2})        # True
A.isdisjoint(B)             # False (they share 3 and 4)
```

Use cases of sets and frozensets:

- Removing duplicates from lists.

  For example:

```
unique_items = list(set([1, 2, 2, 3, 3, 3, 4]))
```

This removes duplicate elements from the list.

- Membership testing (fast lookups).
- Performing set theory operations (union, intersection).
- Using frozensets as dictionary keys or elements of other sets.
- Modeling relations, permissions, tags, and other group-based data.

Practical example and exercises

It is through practice that we can get through the gist of the data structures of Python. This section provides real-world examples and hands-on exercises that apply the concepts of lists, tuples, dictionaries, sets, and frozensets.

Hands-on exercise

Following is the list of exercises on data structures in Python that the readers can practice:

- Create a list of strings and sort them alphabetically.
- Write a tuple containing five elements. Access the third element.
- Create a dictionary of three students with their scores. Find the student with the highest score.
- Use a set to find the common elements between two lists.
- Write a program to count the frequency of each word in a sentence using a dictionary.

The above exercise provides practical exposure to how Python's data structures work in real applications. Practical examples are real-life coding situations that demonstrate how a particular data structure can be used to simplify a task or model a real-world problem. For instance:

- A list might be used to track items in a shopping cart.
- A tuple could represent a GPS coordinate.
- A dictionary is ideal for storing employee records using unique IDs.
- A set can eliminate duplicate entries from a dataset.
- A frozenset might be used as a constant reference group in a permissions system.

Solutions and explanations

In this section, we will discuss solutions and explanations to the exercise on data structures in Python. In this section, we will discuss the solutions and detailed explanations to the exercises on data structures in Python. Readers will gain clarity on how various data structures, such as lists, tuples, sets, and dictionaries are used to solve specific problems efficiently

Exercise 1: Working with lists

Problem: Create a list of numbers from 1 to 10. Remove all even numbers from the list and print the remaining list.

Solution:

```
numbers = list(range(1, 11))
filtered = [num for num in numbers if num % 2 != 0]print(filtered)
```

Explanation: We used **`range()`** to create a list of numbers from 1 to 10 and a list comprehension to filter out even numbers.

Exercise 2: Tuple unpacking

Problem: You have a tuple: **`student = ("Ravi", 21, "Physics")`**. Unpack it into individual variables and print them.

Solution:

```
student = ("Ravi", 21, "Physics")
name, age, course = student
print(f"Name: {name}, Age: {age}, Course: {course}")
```

Explanation: Tuple unpacking assigns each element of the tuple to a variable in order.

Exercise 3: Dictionary lookup and update

Problem: Create a dictionary of employee names and their salaries. Increase the salary of a specific employee by 10% and print the updated dictionary.

Solution:

```
salaries = {'Anita': 50000, 'Rahul': 60000, 'Neha': 55000}
salaries['Rahul'] = int(salaries['Rahul'] * 1.10)
print(salaries)
```

Explanation: We accessed and updated the dictionary value using the employee's name as a key.

Exercise 4: Removing duplicates with sets

Problem: Given a list of items with duplicates:

```
items = ['pen', 'book', 'pen', 'pencil', 'book', 'eraser']
```

Remove duplicates and print the unique items.

Solution:

```
items = ['pen', 'book', 'pen', 'pencil', 'book', 'eraser']
unique_items = list(set(items))
print(unique_items)
```

Explanation: Converting a list to a set removes duplicates. We then convert it back to a list.

Exercise 5: Frozenset as a dictionary key

Problem: Use a frozenset as a key in a dictionary to represent a group and assign it a value.

Solution:

```
group = frozenset(['Amit', 'Bhavna', 'Chetan'])
group_scores = {group: 85}
print(group_scores)
```

Explanation: Since frozensets are immutable and hashable, they can be used as dictionary keys.

Conclusion

In this chapter, we explored Python's data structures: lists, tuples, dictionaries, sets, and frozensets, which are the foundation for storing and managing data efficiently in Python programs. We discussed lists, which have mutable collections of elements. We learnt how to create and manipulate lists using indexing, slicing, built-in methods, and list comprehensions for concise data processing. Next, we covered tuples, which are immutable and typically used for fixed collections of values.

We discussed dictionaries, which store data as key-value pairs and allow fast data retrieval using keys. We learnt how to create, update, and access dictionary elements and explored useful dictionary methods for iteration and manipulation. We also discussed sets, which are unordered collections of unique items, and frozensets, which are immutable sets. Set operations such as union, intersection, difference, and membership testing were discussed, along with use cases for eliminating duplicates or checking overlaps. At last, we discussed practical examples and exercises on data structures in Python.

In the next chapter, we will discuss data analysis and the process involved in it. The process involved in data analysis includes: data collection, data cleaning, data exploration, and data modeling. Readers will also learn how to gather or generate datasets, import and export data using common tools, and derive basic insights through exploratory data analysis and visualizations.

Exercises

1. How do you create a list in Python, and how is it different from an array?
2. Write a Python statement to append an element to an existing list.
3. What is list slicing? Provide an example.
4. How can you remove all occurrences of a specific value from a list?
5. Explain list comprehensions with a syntax example that squares all numbers in a list.
6. What are the key characteristics of tuples in Python?
7. How is a tuple different from a list in terms of mutability?
8. Write a Python statement to unpack the values of a tuple into separate variables.
9. Can a tuple contain mutable elements like lists? Justify your answer with an example.
10. Describe how and when tuples are typically used in real-world Python programming.
11. How do you define a dictionary in Python with at least three key-value pairs?
12. What will dict.get('key') return if the key is not present in the dictionary?
13. Write a Python snippet to update the value of a specific key in a dictionary.
14. How can you loop through both keys and values of a dictionary?
15. Mention three common dictionary methods and their uses.
16. What is the main difference between a set and a list?
17. How do you perform union, intersection, and difference operations on two sets in Python?
18. What is a frozenset? When would you use it instead of a set?
19. Write a Python code example that removes duplicates from a list using a set.
20. Can sets contain duplicate values? What happens when you try to add one?

CHAPTER 9
Data Analysis Process

Introduction

In today's data-driven world, data analysis plays a pivotal role in guiding decisions, identifying trends, and solving complex problems. Data analysis involves the use of statistical and logical techniques to describe, illustrate, and evaluate data.

This chapter discusses data analysis and the process involved in data analysis in detail. The process involved in data analysis includes: data collection, data cleaning, data exploration, and data modeling. Readers will also learn how to gather or generate datasets, import and export data using common tools, and derive basic insights through exploratory data analysis and visualizations. The chapter discusses dataset generation and collection, and discusses various data sources such as open datasets, APIs, and the creation of custom datasets according to specific problems. We have discussed saving data in different formats, e.g., Excel, CSV, JSON, SQL database, and Parquet. This chapter provided a comprehensive overview of the data analysis process. It describes the steps involved in data analysis. The steps involved in data analysis are: data collection, data cleaning, data exploration, data modeling, interpretation, and reporting. This chapter also discusses Visualization. Visualization techniques include: histogram, box plot, scatter plot, bar chart, and correlation heatmap. This chapter introduced readers to **exploratory data analysis** (**EDA**), covering key concepts like descriptive statistics and visualization techniques.

By the end of this chapter, readers will have a comprehensive overview of the data analysis workflow, practical knowledge of working with different data formats, and an appreciation for the importance of clean, well-understood data before diving into advanced analytical techniques.

Structure

This chapter covers the following topics:

- Introduction to data analysis
- Steps in data analysis
- Dataset generation and collection
- Importing and exporting data
- Basic insights and exploratory data analysis

Objectives

The primary objective of this chapter is to give fundamental concepts and steps involved in the data analysis process. By the end of the chapter, readers will be able to understand data analysis and its importance in real-world applications. The chapter describes the key phases of data analysis, such as data collection, data cleaning, exploration, and modeling. This chapter describes various data sources, the creation of custom datasets, and applying techniques for importing and exporting data using popular formats such as CSV, Excel, and SQL. This chapter gives an introduction to EDA and gives insight into basic descriptive statistics and visualizations to extract initial insights from data.

Introduction to data analysis

In today's era, data is being generated at a faster pace through smartphones, online transactions, social media, sensors, and digital platforms. However, raw data alone holds little value unless it is properly analyzed and interpreted. Data analysis involves organizing, examining, and interpreting data to obtain meaningful patterns, detect trends, solve problems, or support decision-making. Whether it is a healthcare professional using patient data to predict disease risk, or a business analyst evaluating customer behavior to optimize marketing strategies, data analysis empowers users to make informed, evidence-based decisions.

This chapter introduces the foundational concepts of data analysis, explores its significance in various fields, and presents a structured view of how data flows through the analysis pipeline from its collection to interpretation. Through hands-on practices, real-world examples, and step-by-step breakdowns of the process, readers will gain both conceptual understanding and practical exposure to the essential components of effective data analysis.

Definition and importance

Data analysis may be defined as the systematic application of statistical, computational, and logical techniques to describe, evaluate, and interpret data. It involves transforming raw data into useful information to support decision-making, uncover hidden patterns, test hypotheses, and generate insights. Data analysis helps in converting data into a form that is understandable and actionable.

In the digital era, where vast amounts of data are generated every second from sources like social media, sensors, transactions, and devices, data analysis has become a necessity. Data analysis is used in the field of business to analyze customer behavior to improve services, doctors use data to diagnose diseases, governments monitor trends for policy making, and researchers study data to validate scientific theories.

The importance of data analysis lies in its potential to reduce uncertainty, improve operational efficiency, and guide strategic decisions. Organizations that leverage data analysis gain a competitive edge by responding faster to market trends, optimizing processes, and identifying opportunities or risks earlier than their competitors.

Overview of data analysis process

The data analysis process involves a series of structured steps that ensure data is collected, prepared, examined, and interpreted properly. These steps help in achieving consistency, reliability, and accuracy throughout the analytical workflow. The stages in the data analysis process are as follows:

1. **Problem definition**: Identify the business or research question and define goals and objectives
2. **Data collection**: Gathering data from various sources such as databases, APIs, surveys, experiments, sensors, or online platforms.
3. **Data preparation**: Removing or correcting inaccuracies, handling missing values, eliminating duplicates, and converting data into a usable format.
4. **Data exploration**: Performing initial investigations using descriptive statistics and visualizations to understand the structure, patterns, and distributions in the dataset.
5. **Data modeling**: Applying statistical models, algorithms, or **machine learning** (**ML**) techniques to make predictions, classify data, or identify relationships.
6. **Interpretation and reporting**: Drawing conclusions based on the results of analysis and communicating insights clearly through reports, dashboards, or visualizations.

Each step is interdependent and often iterative. For example, exploration might reveal data quality issues requiring additional cleaning, or modeling might require the collection of more relevant data.

Steps in data analysis

The process of data analysis is a structured sequence of stages that transform raw data into meaningful insights. Each step plays a crucial role in ensuring the accuracy, reliability, and relevance of the final results. The major steps involved in data analysis include: data collection, data cleaning, data exploration, and data modeling. These steps are as follows:

1. **Problem definition**: It is the process of clearly identifying the business or research question to be addressed. It involves understanding the context, stakeholders' needs, and the purpose of the analysis. Clear goals and objectives are set to guide the analysis.
2. **Data collection**: Data collection is the first and foundational step in the data analysis process. It involves gathering relevant data from various sources depending on the problem or objective. Data can be collected through the following ways:
   - **Primary sources**: Surveys, interviews, experiments, or sensors.
   - **Secondary sources**: Online repositories, databases, APIs, web scraping, or existing reports.

- The quality and relevance of the data collected greatly impact the success of the analysis. Hence, it is important to clearly define what data is needed, how it will be collected, and how it aligns with the objectives of the analysis.

3. **Data preparation**: Once data is collected, it often contains inconsistencies, noisy data, missing values, duplicate entries, or incorrect formatting. Data cleaning (also known as **data preprocessing**) is the step where such issues are identified and resolved to improve the data's quality and usability. Key tasks involved in data cleaning include:

   - Handling missing or null values.
   - Removing duplicate or irrelevant entries.
   - Correcting data types and formats.
   - Filtering out outliers or noise.
   - Normalizing or standardizing values.

   Clean data ensures that the analysis is trustworthy and the insights derived are accurate and actionable.

   Example: Replacing missing values in a medical dataset with the column mean or removing outliers in a financial dataset that may skew results.

4. **Data exploration**: Data exploration, often referred to as **EDA**, is the step where analysts begin to understand the dataset's structure and find initial patterns or anomalies. This step combines statistical methods and visual tools to examine relationships, distributions, and trends. Common techniques used in EDA include:

   - Generating summary statistics (mean, median, standard deviation).
   - Visualizing data using histograms, box plots, scatter plots, and correlation matrices.
   - Identifying variable distributions and outliers.
   - Exploring relationships between variables.

   EDA provides direction for further analysis and helps identify data features that may be important for modeling.

5. **Data modeling**: In this step, the cleaned and explored data are used to build statistical or ML models. Data modeling involves selecting appropriate algorithms to uncover relationships, make predictions, or classify information based on the data. Types of modeling techniques include:

   - **Descriptive models**: summarize data characteristics (e.g., clustering).
   - **Predictive models**: forecast future outcomes (e.g., regression, classification).
   - **Prescriptive models**: recommend actions based on predictions (e.g., optimization models).

Model evaluation is a key part of this step, where models are tested using validation data to ensure they generalize well. Metrics such as accuracy, precision, recall, RMSE, or F1 Score are used to assess performance.

Dataset generation and collection

The foundation of any meaningful data analysis lies in the quality and relevance of the dataset used. This section covers how datasets are obtained, the common sources of publicly available datasets, and how to create custom datasets according to specific needs.

Sources of datasets

There are numerous platforms and resources that offer datasets for academic, professional, and research purposes. These datasets are used in a wide range of domains such as healthcare, finance, education, social media, and e-commerce. Some of the major sources include:

- Open data repositories:
    - **Kaggle**: Offers thousands of datasets across various topics with built-in tools for analysis.
    - **UCI ML repository**: A classic source for structured datasets used in ML.
    - **Data.gov (USA), data.gov.in (India)**: Government-hosted portals providing datasets on demographics, economy, agriculture, and more.
    - **Google dataset search**: A search engine specifically for locating datasets across the web.
- **APIs**: Many modern applications and platforms offer APIs that allow users to collect real-time or historical data programmatically. Examples include:
    - Twitter API for social media data.
    - OpenWeatherMap API for weather data.
    - World Bank API for economic indicators.
- **Academic and research institutions**: Universities and research organizations often share data from studies and experiments for public use, especially in fields like medicine, psychology, and environmental science.
- **Public datasets from tech companies**: *Google*, *Microsoft*, *Amazon*, and *Facebook* have released datasets related to search, vision, language, and recommendation systems for research purposes.

Creating custom datasets

In many real-world scenarios, predefined datasets may not exist or may not fully meet the analytical requirements. In such cases, analysts need to generate their own custom datasets. This involves designing and executing data collection methods aligned with the objectives of the study. Common methods to create custom datasets include:

- **Surveys and questionnaires**: Used in social sciences, marketing, and healthcare to gather structured information from target groups. Tools like *Google Forms*, *SurveyMonkey*, or *Typeform* can be used for digital distribution.
- **Web scraping**: Extracting data from websites using tools like *Beautiful Soup*, *Scrapy*, or browser automation frameworks like *Selenium*. Often used for collecting news articles, e-commerce pricing data, or job listings.
- **Sensor data and IoT devices**: Used in fields such as environmental monitoring, agriculture, and smart cities. Devices record physical conditions like temperature, air quality, or motion.
- **Manual data entry and observation**: In specific cases such as lab experiments, small business records, or observational studies, data may be collected and entered manually.
- **Simulation and synthetic data**: Tools like *Faker* (for generating fake personal data), scikit-learn's `make_classification()`, or **generative adversarial network** (**GAN**) can be used to simulate realistic data when privacy or data availability is a concern.
- Creating custom datasets provides flexibility and control over the attributes and structure of the data, but also requires attention to data quality, ethical considerations, and reproducibility.

Importing and exporting data

In the data analysis process, one of the most essential technical skills is the ability to import data from various sources and export processed data into desired formats. This step ensures that analysts can access raw data for analysis and share cleaned or summarized results with other systems or stakeholders. With the help of tools like Python and libraries such as pandas, this task becomes both efficient and flexible.

Reading data from files in Excel, CSV, SQL

Data can be stored in a variety of file formats or databases, and analysts must be able to read from these sources into a working environment such as Python. In this section, we will discuss reading from CSV files, reading from Excel files, and reading from SQL databases, as follows:

- **Reading from CSV files**: CSV is one of the most commonly used formats for storing tabular data due to its simplicity and compatibility.

```
import pandas as pd
df = pd.read_csv("data.csv")
```

CSV files are lightweight and easy to handle, but they lack support for advanced features like formatting or multiple sheets.

- **Reading from Excel files**: Excel files (**.xls** or **.xlsx**) are widely used in business environments and can contain multiple sheets, cell formatting, and formulas.

  ```
  import pandas as pd
  df = pd.read_excel("data.xlsx", sheet_name="Sheet1")
  ```

  Reading Excel files often requires additional packages like **openpyxl** or **xlrd**, depending on the Excel version.

- **Reading from SQL databases**: Structured data is often stored in relational databases like MySQL, PostgreSQL, or SQLite. Python can connect to these databases using appropriate connectors.

  ```
  import sqlite3
  conn = sqlite3.connect("example.db")
  df = pd.read_sql_query("SELECT * FROM users", conn)
  ```

  With SQL integration, analysts can perform powerful queries, joins, and aggregations before loading the data into memory.

Saving data into different formats

After processing or analyzing data, it is important to be able to save or export results for sharing, reporting, or further analysis, as follows:

- **Saving as CSV**: `df.to_csv (cleaned_data.csv, index=False)`

  CSV is ideal for lightweight data sharing and interoperability.

- **Saving as Excel**: `df.to_excel("results.xlsx", sheet_name="Summary", index=False)`

  Excel is better suited for reporting or when data needs to be reviewed or edited manually.

- **Saving to SQL database**: `df.to_sql("table_name", conn, if_exists="replace", index=False)`

  This is useful for integrating results into a larger data pipeline or dashboarding system.

Some other supported formats:

- **JSON**: Used for semi-structured data or APIs:

  ```
  df.to_json("data.json", orient="records")
  ```

- **Parquet**: Efficient for large-scale data processing and storage in big data platforms.

```
df.to_parquet("data.parquet")
```

Basic insights and exploratory data analysis

Once data is collected and cleaned, the next essential step is to understand the structure and underlying patterns within it. This is achieved through EDA. It is a crucial phase in the data analysis process that involves summarizing and visualizing data to gain basic insights before applying advanced modeling techniques.

EDA helps analysts detect trends, spot anomalies, test assumptions, and determine relationships between variables. It provides both a quantitative and visual summary of the dataset, allowing for more informed and focused decision-making in subsequent analysis stages.

Descriptive statistics

Descriptive statistics are numerical measures that summarize and describe the main features of a dataset. They provide a simple yet powerful way to understand the central tendency, spread, and shape of the data distribution.

Key descriptive statistics include:

- **Measures of central tendency**:
  - **Mean**: The average value.
  - **Median**: The middle value when the data is sorted.
  - **Mode**: The most frequently occurring value.
- **Measures of dispersion**:
  - **Standard deviation**: Indicates how much values deviate from the mean.
  - **Variance**: The square of the standard deviation.
  - **Range**: Difference between the maximum and minimum values.
  - **Interquartile range (IQR)**: Measures the spread of the middle 50% of the data.
- **Shape and distribution**:
  - **Skewness**: Indicates asymmetry in the data distribution.
  - **Kurtosis**: Measures the tailedness of the data.

Using Python's **pandas** and **numpy**, descriptive statistics can be easily generated:

```
import pandas as pd
df = pd.read_csv("data.csv")
df.describe()
```

This command provides a summary including count, mean, std, min, 25%, 50%, 75%, and max for each numerical column.

Diagnostic analytics

Diagnostic analytics focuses on understanding why something happened in the data. Key methods and techniques in diagnostic analytics include the following:

- Drill down and slice and dice analysis
- Correlation analysis
- Hypothesis testing (t-tests, chi-square tests, **analysis of variance** (**ANOVA**))
- Root cause analysis

This type of analysis helps identify factors responsible for trends, anomalies, or performance changes observed during EDA.

Predictive analytics

Predictive analytics forecast the future outcomes based on historical data. It uses statistical and ML models to identify patterns and predict what is likely to happen next.

Common methods and techniques include:

- Regression analysis (linear, logistic).
- Time series forecasting.
- Classification algorithms (decision trees, random forests, SVM).
- ML models.

Predictive analytics is widely used in areas such as demand forecasting, risk assessment, and customer behavior prediction.

Prescriptive analytics

Prescriptive analytics recommends actions to take based on predictive insights.

Key methods and techniques include:

- Optimization models
- Simulation techniques
- Decision trees and rule-based systems
- Reinforcement learning

This type of analysis supports decision-making by evaluating possible outcomes and suggesting the best course of action.

Visualization techniques

While descriptive statistics provide a summary, visualization techniques offer a graphical representation that often reveals insights not immediately obvious through numbers alone. Visualizations help in identifying trends, clusters, gaps, and outliers, and are essential for communicating findings effectively. Some widely used Visualization tool include the following:

- **Power BI**: Power BI is a business intelligence tool developed by Microsoft. It helps users to create interactive dashboards and reports. It integrates easily with various data sources such as Excel, SQL databases, and cloud services. It offers drag and drop features, real-time data updates, and integrates with Microsoft products. This makes it suitable for business users and organizations.
- **Tableau**: Tableau is a powerful and widely used data visualization tool known for its ability to handle large datasets and create visually rich, interactive dashboards. It allows users to explore data through simple drag and drop actions and supports advanced analytics, geospatial mapping, and storytelling features.
- **ggplot2**: ggplot2 is a data visualization package in R based on the *grammar of graphics*. It allows users to build complex and highly customizable plots layer by layer. ggplot2 is especially popular in academic research and statistical analysis as it produces clear, consistent, and publication quality visualizations.

Common EDA visualization techniques include:

- **Histogram**: Displays the frequency distribution of a variable. It helps in understanding data distribution and skewness.

```
import matplotlib.pyplot as plt
df['Age'].hist(bins=10)
plt.title("Age Distribution")
plt.xlabel("Age")
plt.ylabel("Frequency")
```

- **Box plot**: It highlights the spread, median, and outliers in the data. It is useful for comparing distributions across groups.

```
import seaborn as sns
sns.boxplot(x='Gender', y='Salary', data=df)
```

- **Scatter plot**: It shows the relationship between two continuous variables. It is useful for identifying correlations or clusters.

```
plt.scatter(df['Experience'], df['Salary'])
```

```
plt.xlabel('Years of Experience')
plt.ylabel('Salary')
```

- **Bar chart**: It is ideal for comparing categorical data.

  ```
  df['Department'].value_counts().plot(kind='bar')
  ```

- **Correlation heatmap**: It visualizes the correlation coefficients between numeric variables. It helps in feature selection for modeling.

  ```
  sns.heatmap(df.corr(), annot=True, cmap='coolwarm')
  ```

Conclusion

This chapter provided a comprehensive overview of the data analysis process. It describes the steps involved in data analysis. The core steps of the process: data collection, cleaning, exploration, and modeling were discussed. The chapter delved into dataset generation and collection, discussed various data sources such as open datasets, APIs, and the creation of custom datasets according to specific problems. Techniques for importing and exporting data from common formats like CSV, Excel, and SQL were discussed to ensure smooth data handling and sharing. We also discussed saving data in different formats, e.g., Excel, CSV, JSON, SQL database, and Parquet. The steps involved in data analysis are: data collection, data cleaning, data exploration, data modeling, interpretation, and reporting.

Finally, the chapter introduced readers to EDA, covering key concepts like descriptive statistics and visualization techniques. Visualization techniques include: histogram, box plot, scatter plot, bar chart, and correlation heatmap. All the contents in this chapter have provided the foundation of effective data analysis, enabling readers to deal with real-world data problems efficiently. In the next chapter, we will discuss the core Python libraries: NumPy, Pandas, Matplotlib, and SciPy that are used for efficient numerical computations, data visualizations, and scientific problem-solving. It also introduces practical examples and exercises that aim to equip readers with both conceptual understanding and applied skills.

Exercises

1. Define data analysis. Why is it important in today's world?
2. List and briefly describe the main steps involved in the data analysis process.
3. What are the key differences between data cleaning and data exploration?
4. Identify three common sources of datasets. Provide examples for each.
5. Explain the process of creating a custom dataset. What factors should be considered?
6. Describe how to import a CSV file into Python using pandas. Provide a sample code snippet.
7. How can you export a DataFrame from Python to an Excel file? Show with code.

8. Differentiate between structured and unstructured data. Which one is easier to analyze and why?
9. What are the missing values in a dataset? List two ways to handle them.
10. Explain the importance of data visualization in exploratory data analysis.
11. What is the purpose of descriptive statistics? Name four commonly used descriptive statistics.
12. Give an example where data analysis led to an impactful decision in business or healthcare.
13. Write a Python script to read a dataset and display its first five rows.
14. What challenges might arise during the data collection phase? How can they be addressed?
15. How would you deal with outliers in a dataset during data cleaning?
16. Name and explain two visualization tools or libraries used in Python.
17. Why is it important to understand the context of the data before modeling it?
18. Describe the difference between correlation and causation with an example.
19. How can SQL be used in the data analysis process? Give a real-world use case.
20. Perform a basic exploratory data analysis on a sample dataset of your choice. Include at least one graph and a summary of your findings

Chapter 10
Essential Python Libraries for Data Science

Introduction

In the field of data science, Python has rapidly become one of the most efficient and popular programming languages. Its widespread use is largely due to its simplicity, readability, and versatility, which make it accessible for beginners and powerful for experts. More importantly, Python offers a rich ecosystem of specialized libraries that are specifically designed to handle various aspects of data analysis. Among the most notable are NumPy, Pandas, Matplotlib, and SciPy. These libraries provide data scientists and analysts with the tools necessary to perform complex data manipulation, numerical computations, visualization, and scientific problem-solving with ease.

This chapter focuses on introducing these core Python libraries and demonstrating their capabilities in the context of data science. NumPy serves as the foundation for numerical computing, offering efficient array operations and mathematical functions. Pandas builds on this by providing flexible data structures such as DataFrames, which simplify data manipulation and analysis. Matplotlib is a powerful library for creating detailed and customizable visualizations, allowing users to explore data patterns graphically. SciPy complements these libraries by delivering advanced scientific computing tools, including optimization, integration, and statistical functions.

To help readers gain both conceptual understanding and practical proficiency, this chapter includes a variety of examples and hands-on exercises. These activities are designed to reinforce the application of each library in real-world scenarios, ensuring that learners can confidently use Python's data science tools to analyze, visualize, and solve complex problems effectively. By mastering these libraries, readers will be well equipped to tackle diverse challenges in data-driven fields such as finance, healthcare, and technology. The skills acquired here will serve as a strong foundation for further exploration into advanced data science techniques and **machine learning** (**ML**).

Structure

This chapter covers the following topics:

- Introduction to NumPy
- Working with Pandas DataFrames

- Data visualization with Matplotlib
- Scientific computing with SciPy
- Practical examples and exercises

Objectives

The primary objective of this chapter is to equip readers with the essential Python libraries used in data analysis and scientific computing: NumPy, Pandas, Matplotlib, and SciPy. By the end of the chapter, readers will be able to make use of these libraries efficiently for numerical computation, data manipulation, and data visualization. Using examples and exercises, this chapter aims to reinforce practical skills and problem-solving techniques. Learners will be able to apply these tools in real-world scenarios. Reading data from *CSV*, Excel and *JSON* may be performed using Pandas library. Pandas is used for data cleaning, filtering and merging.

NumPy can be used for Efficient numerical data handling. NumPy is used for mathematical operations and transformations. Beautiful Soup is used for web scraping. SQLAlchemy is used for database connectivity (SQL-based data sources). Scikit- learn is used for scaling, encoding and normalization. The libraries used for visualization are: Matplotlib, Plotly, Seaborn, Bokeh and Altair. The libraries used for performing **natural language processing** (**NLP**) tasks are: **Natural Language Toolkit** (**NLTK**) (used for text preprocessing and linguistic analysis), spaCy (used for text preprocessing, **Name Entity Recognition** (**NER**), **point of sale** (**POS**) tagging, information extraction and text classification). Transformer library is given by *Hugging Face*. It is based on transformer architectures such as *BERT*, *GPT*, *RoBERTa*, and *T5*. It is used for: text classification, sentiment analysis, question answering systems, text summarization, translation, language modeling, text generation and context aware semantic understanding.

Introduction to NumPy

NumPy is a powerful open-source library that forms the foundation of scientific computing in Python. It is designed for efficient numerical operations on large datasets and provides support for multidimensional arrays (ndarrays), mathematical functions, linear algebra operations, and more. Compared to traditional Python lists, NumPy arrays offer faster performance and greater flexibility, making them essential for data analysis, ML, and scientific simulations.

Creating and manipulating arrays

The core feature of NumPy is the ndarray, a multi-dimensional array object that can store elements of the same data type. Arrays can be created from lists or tuples, or generated using built-in functions, as follows:

- **Creating arrays**:

```
import numpy as np
# From a list
```

```
arr = np.array([1, 2, 3, 4])
# 2D Array
matrix = np.array([[1, 2], [3, 4]])
# Using functions
zeros = np.zeros((2, 3))      # 2x3 array of zeros
ones = np.ones((3, 2))        # 3x2 array of ones
range_array = np.arange(0, 10, 2)  # Array: [0, 2, 4, 6, 8]
linspace_array = np.linspace(0, 1, 5)  # 5 evenly spaced values between
0 and 1
```

- **Array attributes and indexing**: NumPy arrays support powerful slicing, indexing, and reshaping:

```
arr.shape          # Returns the shape of the array
arr.ndim           # Number of dimensions
arr.size           # Total number of elements
arr.dtype          # Data type of elements
# Indexing and slicingprint(arr[1])         # Access second
elementprint(arr[1:3])        # Elements from index 1 to 2
```

- **Reshaping and modifying arrays**:

```
reshaped = arr.reshape(2, 2)          # Change shape to 2x2
matrix = np.array([[1, 2], [3, 4]])
transposed = matrix.T                 # Transpose a matrix
concatenated = np.concatenate([arr, arr])  # Combine arrays
```

  Array manipulation makes it easy to transform data into the required formats for analysis or modeling.

Mathematical operations

NumPy supports fast and vectorized element-wise mathematical operations on arrays. These operations are optimized for performance and do not require explicit loops. The mathematical operations performed in NumPy are as follows:

- **Element-wise operations**:

```
a = np.array([1, 2, 3])
b = np.array([4, 5, 6])
# Addition, subtraction, multiplication, division
print(a + b)   # [5, 7, 9]
print(a * b)   # [4, 10, 18]
print(a / b)   # [0.25, 0.4, 0.5]
```

- **Aggregate functions**:

```
NumPy provides functions to compute summary statistics:
a.sum()          # Sum of elements
a.mean()         # Mean value
a.std()          # Standard deviation
a.max(), a.min()# Maximum and minimum
```

- **Linear algebra and matrix operations**: For scientific and engineering applications, NumPy also includes a set of linear algebra functions:

```
from numpy.linalg import inv, det
matrix = np.array([[1, 2], [3, 4]])
inverse = inv(matrix)           # Inverse of matrix
determinant = det(matrix)       # Determinant
dot_product = np.dot(a, b)      # Dot product of two arrays
```

NumPy offers a highly efficient and flexible platform for handling numerical data. Its array-centric architecture and powerful mathematical tools make it ideal for building more advanced analytical and computational systems. With the help of NumPy, users can work effectively with large datasets and other scientific libraries in the Python ecosystem.

Working with Pandas DataFrames

Pandas is a powerful open-source Python library designed for data manipulation and analysis. It provides two core data structures, series (one-dimensional) and DataFrame (2D), that allow users to handle labeled and structured data with ease. While NumPy is optimized for numerical operations on arrays, Pandas builds on top of NumPy to offer a more intuitive and flexible approach for working with tabular data, making it indispensable in data science, business analytics, and machine learning workflows.

DataFrame creation

A DataFrame is a 2d, mutable, heterogeneous tabular data structure with labeled axes (rows and columns), similar to a spreadsheet or SQL table. A Dataframe may be created using following ways:

- **Creating a DataFrame from a dictionary**:

```
import pandas as pd

data = {
    'Name': ['Alice', 'Bob', 'Charlie'],
    'Age': [25, 30, 35],
```

```
    'City': ['New York', 'London', 'Paris']
}

df = pd.DataFrame(data)print(df)
```

- **Creating from a list of lists or tuples**:

```
data = [
    ['Alice', 25, 'New York'],
    ['Bob', 30, 'London'],
    ['Charlie', 35, 'Paris']
]

df = pd.DataFrame(data, columns=['Name', 'Age', 'City'])
```

- **Reading from external files**: Pandas makes it easy to import data from external sources:

```
df_csv = pd.read_csv("data.csv")
df_excel = pd.read_excel("data.xlsx")
```

- **Creating an empty DataFrame**:

```
df_empty = pd.DataFrame(columns=['Name', 'Age', 'City'])
```

Data manipulation techniques

Pandas offers a rich set of operations to clean, filter, modify, and analyze data efficiently. Manipulation of data may be performed using following ways:

- **Inspecting data**:

```
df.head()       # First 5 rows
df.tail()       # Last 5 rows
df.shape        # Rows and columns count
df.info()       # Summary of DataFrame
df.describe()   # Descriptive statistics for numerical columns
```

- **Accessing data**:

```
df['Age']                # Access a single column (returns a Series)
df[['Name', 'City']]     # Access multiple columns
df.iloc[0]               # Row by index
df.loc[0, 'Name']        # Specific cell by label
```

- **Filtering rows**:

```
df[df['Age'] > 30]                    # Filter rows where age > 30
df[df['City'] == 'London']           # Filter rows with a specific
condition
```

- **Adding and modifying columns**:

```
df['Salary'] = [50000, 60000, 70000]  # Add new column
df['Age'] = df['Age'] + 1             # Modify existing column
```

- **Deleting columns and rows**:

```
df.drop('Salary', axis=1, inplace=True)    # Drop column
df.drop(1, axis=0, inplace=True)           # Drop row by index
```

- **Handling missing data**:

```
df.fillna(0)              # Replace missing values with 0
df.dropna()                # Drop rows with missing values
```

- **Sorting and grouping**:

```
df.sort_values(by='Age')                  # Sort by column
df.groupby('City')['Age'].mean()          # Group by City and get
average age
```

- **Merging and joining DataFrames**:

```
df1 = pd.DataFrame({'ID': [1, 2], 'Name': ['A', 'B']})
df2 = pd.DataFrame({'ID': [1, 2], 'Score': [85, 90]})
df_merged = pd.merge(df1, df2, on='ID')
```

Pandas DataFrames offer an intuitive and high-performance structure for managing and analyzing structured data. With capabilities for easy data import, flexible indexing, powerful grouping and aggregation, and seamless integration with NumPy and Matplotlib, Pandas has become an essential tool for data professionals. Mastery of DataFrame operations is essential for tasks ranging from data cleaning and transformation to exploratory analysis and reporting.

Data visualization with Matplotlib

Data visualization is a key component of data analysis, enabling analysts to explore data visually, detect trends, and communicate insights effectively. In Python, the most widely used library for visualization is Matplotlib. It provides a versatile and powerful platform for creating static, interactive, and animated plots.

Matplotlib supports a variety of plot types such as line plots, bar charts, scatter plots, histograms, and pie charts. It integrates well with NumPy and Pandas, making it ideal for visualizing numerical and tabular data during the exploratory data analysis process.

Basic plotting

To get started with Matplotlib, you typically use its **`pyplot`** module, which provides functions similar to MATLAB for creating and displaying plots. Following are the functions provided by **`pyplot`** module of **`matplotlib`**:

- **Line plot**:

```
import matplotlib.pyplot as plt
x = [1, 2, 3, 4, 5]
y = [2, 4, 6, 8, 10]
plt.plot(x, y)
plt.title("Line Plot")
plt.xlabel("X-axis")
plt.ylabel("Y-axis")
plt.show()
```

- **Bar chart**:

```
categories = ['A', 'B', 'C', 'D']
values = [10, 15, 7, 12]
plt.bar(categories, values)
plt.title("Bar Chart")
plt.show()
```

- **Scatter plot**:

```
x = [1, 2, 3, 4, 5]
y = [5, 7, 4, 9, 6]

plt.scatter(x, y)
plt.title("Scatter Plot")
plt.xlabel("X-axis")
plt.ylabel("Y-axis")
plt.show()
```

- **Histogram**:

```
data = [1, 2, 2, 3, 3, 3, 4, 4, 5]
plt.hist(data, bins=5)
plt.title("Histogram")
plt.xlabel("Value")
plt.ylabel("Frequency")
plt.show()
```

These basic plots provide an essential toolkit for visualizing distributions, relationships, and comparisons.

Customizing plots

Matplotlib allows extensive customization to make plots more readable, professional, and tailored to specific needs. We can perform customization to the plots provided by Matplotlib in the following ways:

- **Titles, labels, and legends**:

```
plt.plot(x, y, label='y = 2x')
plt.title("Customized Line Plot")
plt.xlabel("Input")
plt.ylabel("Output")
plt.legend()
plt.grid(True)
plt.show()
```

- **Changing line and marker styles**:

```
plt.plot(x, y, color='green', linestyle='--', marker='o', linewidth=2)
plt.title("Styled Line Plot")
plt.show()
```

- **Adjusting figure size**:

```
plt.figure(figsize=(8, 4))
plt.plot(x, y)
plt.title("Figure with Custom Size")
plt.show()
```

- **Subplots**:

```
plt.subplot(1, 2, 1)
plt.plot(x, y)
plt.title("Plot 1")
plt.subplot(1, 2, 2)
plt.bar(categories, values)
plt.title("Plot 2")
plt.tight_layout()
plt.show()
```

- **Saving plots**:

```
plt.plot(x, y)
```

```
plt.title("Save this Plot")
plt.savefig("plot.png")
```

These customizations make your plots not only visually appealing but also more informative and suitable for presentations or reports.

Matplotlib is a library for data visualization in Python, offering flexibility and control over every aspect of a plot. Mastering basic plotting and customization techniques allows analysts and scientists to visualize patterns, trends, and anomalies, and to communicate their findings clearly.

Scientific computing with SciPy

As data analysis evolves into more complex computations and modeling, the need for scientific tools becomes essential. **Scientific Python** (**SciPy**) is a powerful open-source library that provides advanced functionality for scientific and technical computing. It is widely used in domains like mathematics, engineering, biology, machine learning, and physics due to its ability to solve real-world computational problems.

While NumPy provides basic numerical tools, SciPy can be used for high-level operations such as optimization, interpolation, numerical integration, signal processing, linear algebra, and statistics.

Overview of SciPy modules

SciPy is organized into sub-packages, each focusing on a specific area of scientific computation. The following are some of the key modules:

- **scipy.linalg**: It is used in linear algebra:
  - Extends NumPy's linear algebra functions.
  - Supports matrix decompositions, solving linear systems, and eigenvalue problems.

    ```
    from scipy.linalg import inv
    import numpy as np
    A = np.array([[1, 2], [3, 4]])
    A_inv = inv(A)
    ```
- **scipy.optimize**: It is useful for optimization:
  - Useful for minimizing (or maximizing) functions, curve fitting, and root finding.

    ```
    from scipy.optimize import minimize
    f = lambda x: x**2 + 5*np.sin(x)
    result = minimize(f, x0=2)
    ```
- **scipy.integrate**: It is used for Integration. Performs definite and indefinite integration. It includes methods for solving **ordinary differential equations (ODEs).**

```
from scipy.integrate import quad
result, _ = quad(lambda x: x**2, 0, 3)
```

- **scipy.interpolate**: Interpolation:
  - It estimates values between known data points.
  - It is useful for smoothening noisy data or constructing missing values.

```
from scipy.interpolate import interp1d
x = [0, 1, 2]
y = [0, 1, 4]
f = interp1d(x, y)
print(f(1.5))  # Interpolated value
```

- **scipy.stats**: It is used for statistical functions. It offers probability distributions, statistical tests, and summary statistics.

```
from scipy import stats
data = [2, 4, 4, 4, 5, 5, 7, 9]
mean = stats.tmean(data)
mode = stats.mode(data)
```

- **scipy.signal**: It is used for signal processing; for filtering, spectral analysis, and signal transformation. It is used in audio processing, telecommunications, and image enhancement.
- **scipy.spatial**: It is used in spatial data structures. It provides tools for distance computation, clustering, and nearest neighbor searches.

Practical applications

SciPy is not just theoretical; it is extensively applied in real-world scenarios across disciplines:

- **Engineering simulations**: It is used in solving systems of equations in electrical circuits. It is used for modeling mechanical systems using differential equations.
- **ML and AI**: It may be used for curve fitting and parameter optimization in training models. It can be used for statistical analysis for feature selection and hypothesis testing.
- **Scientific research**: It may be used for data interpolation in experimental physics or chemistry. It is used in the integration of biological response curves or pharmacokinetic models.
- **Finance and economics**: It is used in optimization for portfolio balancing. It is used in statistical tests for stock price behavior analysis.

- **Signal and image processing**: It is used for filtering noise from audio or **electrocardiogram** (**ECG**) signals. It is used in analyzing frequency components in images or videos.

SciPy greatly enhances the capabilities of Python for scientific computing. By offering specialized modules tailored for complex computational tasks, it empowers researchers, analysts, and engineers to perform efficient, accurate, and scalable computations. Combined with NumPy, Pandas, and Matplotlib, SciPy completes the core scientific Python stack that underpins modern data science and research-based applications.

Practical examples and exercises

Practical application of theoretical knowledge is key to mastering data analysis and scientific computing. This section provides real-life examples and hands-on projects that may be solved using NumPy, Pandas, Matplotlib, and SciPy.

Hands-on projects

Consider the following projects that performs the task of Data Analysis:

- **Project 1**: Analyze student performance data:
  - **Objective**: Use Pandas and Matplotlib to explore and visualize a dataset of student grades.
  - **Tasks**:
    - Load a dataset containing student names, subjects, and marks.
    - Calculate the average score per student.
    - Identify the top 3 performing students.
    - Plot a bar chart of average scores.
    - Save the processed results into a new Excel file.
- **Project 2**: NumPy-based matrix computation:
  - **Objective**: Apply NumPy to perform linear algebra operations.
  - **Tasks**:
    - Create a 3x3 matrix and a 3x1 vector.
    - Perform matrix multiplication.
    - Calculate the determinant and inverse of the matrix.
    - Solve the equation $Ax = b$.

- **Project 3**: Weather data visualization:
  - **Objective**: Visualize weather trends using line plots and histograms.
  - **Tasks**:
    - Load a dataset containing daily temperatures for a month.
    - Plot the daily temperature as a line graph.
    - Plot a histogram showing the frequency of temperature ranges.
    - Highlight the hottest and coldest days.
- **Project 4**: SciPy optimization:
  - **Objective**: Use **`scipy.optimize`** to minimize a cost function.
  - **Tasks**:
    - Define a cost function (e.g., $f(x) = x^2 + 10*sin(x)$).
    - Use **`scipy.optimize.minimize()`** to find the value of **`x`** that minimizes the function.
    - Plot the cost function and mark the minimum

Some of the exercises related to Python libraries:

- Create a NumPy array of integers from 1 to 20. Reshape it into a 4×5 matrix
- Write a function using NumPy to normalize an array between 0 and 1.
- Load a CSV file using Pandas and list all unique values in a given column.
- Create a Pandas **`DataFrame`** with random sales data for 3 products over 7 days. Calculate total weekly sales.
- Plot a line graph showing product sales over a week using Matplotlib.
- Use **`scipy.stats`** to compute the mean, median, and mode of a numeric column in a dataset.
- Merge two DataFrames based on a common column and calculate group-wise averages.
- Use **`scipy.integrate.quad()`** to compute the integral of x^2 from 0 to 2.
- Plot a pie chart showing the percentage contribution of different departments in a company's workforce.
- Simulate 1000 normally distributed random values using NumPy and plot the histogram.

Solutions and explanations

This section considered some of the solved examples along with their explanations, as follows:

- **Example**: NumPy array reshape and statistics:

  ```
  import numpy as np
  arr = np.arange(1, 21).reshape(4, 5)
  print("Reshaped Array:\n", arr)
  mean = np.mean(arr)
  std = np.std(arr)
  print("Mean:", mean)
  print("Standard Deviation:", std)
  ```

  - **Explanation**:

    ```
    np.arange(1, 21) creates an array from 1 to 20.
    np.reshape(4,5) changes the shape to a 4x5 matrix.
    ```

  Mean and standard deviation are calculated directly using NumPy functions.

- **Example**: Student data analysis with Pandas:

  ```
  import pandas as pd
  data = {
      'Student': ['Alice', 'Bob', 'Charlie', 'David'],
      'Math': [85, 90, 95, 80],
      'Science': [88, 84, 91, 87]
  }

  df = pd.DataFrame(data)
  df['Average'] = df[['Math', 'Science']].mean(axis=1)
  top_students = df.sort_values('Average', ascending=False).head(3)
  print(top_students)
  ```

  - **Explanation**:
    - **`DataFrame`** created from a dictionary.
    - Average is computed row-wise.
    - Top three students are selected using **`sort_values()`**.

- **Example**: Plotting daily temperature:

  ```
  import matplotlib.pyplot as plt
  days = list(range(1, 11))
  ```

```
temps = [30, 32, 31, 29, 33, 35, 34, 30, 28, 32]
plt.plot(days, temps, marker='o', color='blue')
plt.title("Daily Temperature Over 10 Days")
plt.xlabel("Day")
plt.ylabel("Temperature (°C)")
plt.grid(True)
plt.show()
```

- **Explanation**:
  - A line chart is used to visualize trends.
  - Grid, markers, and labels enhance readability.

- **Example**: Optimization with SciPy:

```
from scipy.optimize import minimizeimport numpy as np
f = lambda x: x**2 + 10*np.sin(x)
result = minimize(f, x0=0)
print("Minimum at x =", result.x)
```

- **Explanation**:
  - Defines a nonlinear function.
  - **`minimize()`** is used to find the local minimum starting from **`x0=0`**.

Conclusion

This chapter gives insight into the essence of Python libraries such as NumPy, Pandas, Matplotlib, and SciPy. NumPy is used for fast numerical computing. It can be used to manipulate arrays, perform element-wise calculations, and carry out linear algebra tasks such as matrix multiplication and solving equations.

Pandas is used for working with structured data using a DataFrame. Pandas may be used for reading data from various sources, filtering, aggregating, transforming, and analyzing data using built-in Pandas functions. These skills are crucial for real-world data cleaning and preparation. Matplotlib may be used to generate line plots, bar charts, scatter plots, histograms, and more. Customization may be performed using labeling, styling, and subplots.

SciPy may be used for advanced scientific computing. It can be used for optimization, integration, interpolation, statistics, and signal processing. SciPy bridges the gap between numerical data and scientific applications. The next chapter covers how raw data is cleaned, organized, and transformed into meaningful information. It also explains how visualizations help reveal patterns, trends, and insights. By combining these techniques, readers will learn to turn complex datasets into a clear and actionable understanding.

Exercises

1. What is a NumPy array? How is it different from a Python list?
2. Write Python code to create a 1D NumPy array of numbers from 0 to 9.
3. How do you reshape a NumPy array into a 3x3 matrix?
4. Write code to perform element-wise multiplication between two NumPy arrays.
5. What is the output of the following code?

```
import numpy as np
a = np.array([10, 20, 30])
b = np.array([1, 2, 3])print(a / b)
```

6. What are a Pandas DataFrame? How does it differ from a NumPy array?
7. Create a DataFrame using a dictionary with columns: Name, Age, and City.
8. Write code to read data from a CSV file called sales.csv.
9. How do you filter rows in a DataFrame where the Age column is greater than 30?
10. Explain the difference between .loc[] and .iloc[] in Pandas with examples.
11. Write code to plot a simple line graph of x = [1, 2, 3, 4] and y = [10, 20, 25, 30].
12. How can you add a title, x-axis label, and y-axis label to a plot in Matplotlib?
13. What is the difference between a bar chart and a histogram?
14. Write a program to plot a pie chart showing the distribution of five categories.
15. What does plt.subplot (2,1,1) do in a Matplotlib script?
16. What is the purpose of the SciPy library in Python? How is it related to NumPy?
17. Which SciPy module is used for solving optimization problems?
18. Write code using scipy.integrate.quad() to calculate the integral of x^2 from 0 to 2.
19. What are the key differences between scipy.linalg and numpy.linalg?
20. Use scipy.stats to compute the mean, median, and mode of the following list: [5, 8, 6, 8, 10, 8].

CHAPTER 11
Data Processing and Visualization

Introduction

Today, the field of data science is very important in industry that involves handling large amounts of data and performing analysis on it. In the data science workflow, we start with collecting and storing data. In order to extract meaningful insights from data, raw data must undergo processing and transformation. After this step, analysis and visualization are performed. Data visualization is the way to communicate findings visually, as effective data visualization not only enhances understanding but also supports better decision-making.

This chapter begins by exploring the fundamentals of data processing, including essential techniques such as data cleaning and transformation. These steps help in handling missing values, removing duplicates, correcting inconsistencies, and converting raw data into a usable format.

The chapter then introduces a variety of data visualization tools, providing a comparative overview and guidance on how to choose the right tool based on the type of data, audience, and desired output. This chapter also discusses geospatial visualization, demonstrating how to create and plot maps using specialized tools and libraries.

Finally, the chapter covers interactive visualizations, which allow users to explore data dynamically rather than viewing static charts. With tools like Plotly, Bokeh, and Altair, interactive visualizations can be embedded in dashboards and web applications for achieving deeper insights.

Structure

This chapter covers the following topics:

- Basics of data processing
- Introduction to data visualization tools
- Advanced visualization with Seaborn
- Creating and plotting maps

- Interactive visualizations
- Performance optimization

Objectives

The primary objective of this chapter is to discuss data processing steps that involve data cleaning and data transformation. This chapter discusses various data visualization tools and also teaches how to select the most appropriate tool based on the type of data, audience, and desired insight. This chapter gives insight into data visualization created using Seaborn, which helps to create pleasing visualizations that may be customized according to the needs.

The chapter also aims to introduce the principles of geospatial data visualization, showing how to create and plot maps using Python libraries for mapping. Readers will explore real-world applications of mapping in fields like public health, transportation, and the environment.

This chapter also teaches the ability to build interactive visualizations that allow for dynamic data exploration. They will learn about popular libraries such as Plotly, Bokeh, and Altair, and how to use them to create engaging visual outputs for reports, dashboards, and web applications.

Basics of data processing

Data processing is a fundamental step in the field of data analysis. It involves converting raw data into a structured and usable format. Data Processing performed properly ensures that the insights derived from data analysis are reliable and accurate. Two critical sub-processes within data processing are data cleaning and data transformation.

Data cleaning

Data cleaning is the process of identifying and correcting (or removing) errors, inconsistencies, and inaccuracies from datasets. Real-world data is rarely clean; missing values, duplicate entries, incorrect formats, and outliers are common. Cleaning ensures that the data used for analysis is accurate, complete, and consistent.

Key tasks in data cleaning:

- **Handling missing values:** Missing data can be addressed by removing records, imputing values (mean, median, mode), or using model-based techniques.

- **Removing duplicates:** Duplicate records can bias results and must be identified and removed.

- **Correcting inconsistent formats:** Standardizing units (e.g., *kg* vs. *kilograms*) or date formats (e.g., *MM/DD/YYYY* vs. *DD-MM-YYYY*) is essential for uniformity.

- **Filtering outliers:** Outliers can distort statistical analyses; they can be removed or treated depending on the context.
- **Standardizing data:** Ensuring uniform case formatting, trimming whitespaces, and removing special characters, where unnecessary.

Consider the following python code that performs data cleaning:

```
import pandas as pd

df = pd.read_csv("sales_data.csv")

# Remove duplicate rows
df.drop_duplicates(inplace=True)

# Fill missing values with column mean
df['Revenue'].fillna(df['Revenue'].mean(), inplace=True)

# Standardize text data
df['Product_Name'] = df['Product_Name'].str.strip().str.lower()
```

Data transformation

Data transformation involves converting data into suitable formats or structures that can enhance analysis or model performance. Transformation techniques help reveal hidden patterns, normalize data distributions, and reduce complexity.

Key techniques in data transformation:

- **Normalization and scaling:** Used to bring data into a comparable scale, especially for machine learning algorithms.
- **Min-max scaling**: Transforms data to a [0, 1] range.
- **Standardization (Z-score):** Centers data around mean zero and standard deviation 1.
- **Encoding categorical variables:** Most ML algorithms require numerical input, so categorical (non-numeric) data must be converted into a numerical format. Encoding categorical variables is performed using the following methods:
  - **Label encoding:** Assigns a numeric label to each category.
  - **One-hot encoding:** Converts categories into binary vectors.
- **Log transformation:** Useful for skewed data to normalize the distribution.
- **Feature extraction:** Deriving new features from existing data (e.g., extracting day, month, year from a date).
- **Aggregation and grouping:** Summarizing data by groups to gain higher-level insights.

Introduction to data visualization tools

Data visualization may be defined as the process of representing data in graphical formats such as charts, graphs, and maps. It plays a vital role in uncovering patterns, trends, and insights that may not be immediately apparent in raw data. The selection of the right visualization tools significantly impacts the effectiveness, clarity, and interactivity of the visual output.

Overview of visualization tools

A variety of tools and libraries are available for creating data visualizations, ranging from simple charts for reports to complex, interactive dashboards for web applications. Visualization tools can broadly be categorized into programming libraries, **graphical user interface** (**GUI**)-based tools, and dashboard platforms.

Popular visualization tools include the following:

- **Matplotlib:** It is a Python library. It is used for static 2D plots.
- **Seaborn:** It is a Python library. It is built on Matplotlib, and it offers high-level interfaces and aesthetically pleasing statistical graphics.
- **Plotly:** It is used for creating interactive web-based visualizations.
- **Tableau:** It is a BI tool with drag-and-drop functionality for creating dashboards and sharing reports.
- **Power BI:** It is a GUI tool, developed by Microsoft. It integrates with Excel and enterprise databases.
- **D3.js:** It is a JavaScript-based library. It provides fine-grained control over visual elements for web-based interactive visualizations.
- **ggplot2:** It is a widely used R package for declarative, layered graphics based on the grammar of graphics.
- **Google Data Studio:** It is a free web tool to build interactive dashboards using Google ecosystem data.

Choosing right tool for the job

Choosing the right visualization tool depends on various factors such as the complexity of the data, the audience, the purpose of visualization, the interactivity needs, and the technical expertise. Factors considered to choose a tool are:

- **Complexity of visuals required:**
    - For simple plots (bar, line, pie), tools like *Excel*, *Matplotlib*, or *Tableau* may suffice.
    - For complex, layered statistical visualizations, Seaborn or ggplot2 is preferred.

    - For advanced custom visuals, especially on the web, D3.js or Plotly can be used.
- **Interactivity needs:** Use Plotly, Dash, Power BI, or Tableau if dynamic filters, tooltips, or zooming features are required.
- **Integration with other systems:**
    - We should choose tools that integrate well with our data pipeline.
    - For Python workflows, Matplotlib, Seaborn, and Plotly work well.
    - For enterprise settings with databases or Excel, Power BI, or Tableau is ideal.
- **Ease of use vs. customization:** GUI tools like Tableau and Power BI are user-friendly with minimal coding. Libraries like Matplotlib, Seaborn, and D3.js offer deeper customization with more technical input.
- **Audience and purpose:**
    - For executive dashboards, choose tools that support storytelling (e.g., Tableau, Power BI).
    - For academic or research visualizations, tools like Seaborn, ggplot2, and Matplotlib are more appropriate.

The following are the tools used for different use cases:

Use case	Tool used
Statistical data visualization	Seaborn, ggplot2
Interactive dashboards	Plotly Dash, Tableau, Power BI
Web-based custom visualizations	D3.js, Plotly.js
Report generation	Google Data Studio, Power BI
Real-time data updates	Power BI, Tableau with live connectors
Basic plots for analysis	Matplotlib, Excel

Table 11.1: Tools used for different use cases

Data visualization tools are essential instruments in the data analyst's toolkit. Selecting the right tool depends on the use case, data complexity, and the desired level of interactivity. By understanding the strengths and limitations of each tool, analysts can craft visuals that not only inform but also engage and inspire action.

Advanced visualization with Seaborn

Seaborn is a powerful Python data visualization library built on top of Matplotlib. It provides a high-level interface for drawing attractive and informative statistical graphics. Seaborn is particularly useful for complex plots and data exploration tasks, offering features for visualizations, relationships, and trends with minimal code. In this section, we will discuss plotting complex plots using Seaborn.

Creating complex plots

Seaborn allows users to create intricate plots that reveal deeper insights about data distributions, trends, and relationships across variables.

Common complex plots in Seaborn are:

- **Pair plot (sns.pairplot):** It is used for visualizing pairwise relationships between multiple numerical variables. It is helpful for quick exploration of correlations. The following code shows implementation of pair plot:

```
import pandas as pd
import seaborn as sns
df = pd.read_csv("sales_data.csv")
sns.pairplot(df, hue="species")
```

- **Heatmap (sns.heatmap):** It displays correlation matrices or frequency tables. It is useful for identifying relationships or missing values. The following code shows implementation of heatmap:

```
import pandas as pd
import seaborn as sns
df = pd.read_csv("sales_data.csv")

sns.heatmap(df.corr(), annot=True, cmap="coolwarm")
```

- **Violin plot (sns.violinplot):** It combines a boxplot and **kernel density estimation (KDE)** to show distribution and central tendency. It is useful for comparing multiple distributions. The following code shows the implementation of a violin plot:

```
import pandas as pd
import seaborn as sns
df = pd.read_csv("sales_data.csv")
sns.violinplot(x="day", y="total_bill", data=df)
```

- **Facet grid (sns.FacetGrid):** It is used for plotting multiple subplots based on categorical variables. It helps to visualize relationships within subsets of data. The following code shows the implementation of the facet grid:

```
import pandas as pd
import seaborn as sns
df = pd.read_csv("sales_data.csv")
```

```
g = sns.FacetGrid(df, col="sex", row="time")
g.map(sns.histplot, "total_bill")
```

- **Regression plot (sns.lmplot):** It combines a scatter plot with a regression line. It is useful for showing trends and linear relationships. The following code shows the implementation of a regression plot:

```
import pandas as pd
import seaborn as sns
df = pd.read_csv("sales_data.csv")
sns.lmplot(x="total_bill", y="tip", data=df)
```

Customizing visualizations

Customization in Seaborn enhances clarity in plots. Seaborn supports a wide range of customization options that help tailor the visualization to the intended audience.

Key customization techniques are:

- **Styling the plot:** Seaborn supports multiple themes: darkgrid, whitegrid, dark, white, and ticks. For example, in Python, it is shown as follows:

```
sns.set_style("whitegrid")
```

- **Color palettes:** Custom color palettes can be applied to suit thematic or branding needs:

```
sns.set_palette("pastel")
```

- **Plot size and aspect ratio:**

```
sns.set_context("talk")  # Options: paper, notebook, talk, poster
```

- **Annotations and labels:** Add axis labels, titles, legends, and annotations for better readability. Annotations and labels may be added in Python in the following ways:

```
plot = sns.boxplot(x="day", y="total_bill", data=df)
plot.set_title("Boxplot of Total Bill by Day")
plot.set_xlabel("Day of the Week")
plot.set_ylabel("Total Bill (in USD)")
```

- **Combining multiple plots:** Combine Seaborn plots with Matplotlib for more granular control. Seaborn plot may be combined with **`matplitlib`** in the following ways:

```
import matplotlib.pyplot as plt
sns.histplot(data=df, x="total_bill", hue="sex", multiple="stack")
plt.axvline(x=20, color='red', linestyle='--', label='Threshold')
plt.legend()
```

- **Controlling axes and ticks:** Tweak axis labels, ticks, and limits to improve presentation. It can be represented in Python as follows:

```
plt.xticks(rotation=45)
plt.xlim(0, 50)
```

Seaborn excels in creating sophisticated and visually pleasing statistical plots with minimal effort. Its integration with pandas DataFrames, complex visual structures, and rich customization options makes it an ideal tool for both exploratory data analysis and presentation-quality graphics.

Creating and plotting maps

Geospatial data visualization involves displaying data that has a spatial component, such as coordinates, regions, or boundaries, on a map. This type of visualization helps identify geographic patterns, trends, and distributions, making it especially valuable in fields like urban planning, public health, environmental monitoring, and logistics.

Geospatial data visualization

Geospatial data typically includes latitude and longitude coordinates or area-based identifiers like ZIP codes, districts, or country names. Plotting such data allows us to analyze:

- **Spatial distributions:** E.g., mapping population density across districts.
- **Movement and flow:** E.g., tracking delivery routes or migration paths.
- **Hotspots and anomalies:** E.g., identifying areas with high disease outbreaks or sales.

Types of map visualizations:

- **Choropleth maps:** Color-coded regions representing aggregated values (e.g., population, income, sales).
- **Point maps (Scatter maps):** Plotting locations using latitude and longitude is useful for marking incidents, landmarks, or data points.
- **Heatmaps (Density maps):** Displaying data density using color gradients is helpful for visualizing concentrations of events or entities.
- **Flow maps:** Visualize the movement of people, goods, or information between locations.

  Example (Using Python and Plotly):

```
import plotly.express as px
df = px.data.gapminder().query("year == 2007")
fig = px.choropleth(df, locations="iso_alpha",
```

```
                           color="lifeExp",
                           hover_name="country",
                           color_continuous_scale=px.colors.sequential.Plasma)
fig.show()
```

Tools for mapping data

A range of tools and libraries is available to create geospatial visualizations, catering to both coders and non-coders:

Popular geospatial visualization tools are:

- **Folium (Python):** It is a library. It is easy to use, integrates with Leaflet.js, and supports interactive maps.
- **Plotly (Python, JS):** It is a library. It allows interactive choropleths, scatter geo plots, and heatmaps.
- **Geopandas (Python):** It is a library. It extends pandas for geospatial operations and plotting.
- **Kepler.gl GUI/web tool:** High-performance web-based tool for large-scale geospatial analysis.
- **Tableau GUI tool:** Supports map charts and geospatial data layering with minimal coding.
- **QGIS desktop software:** Advanced **geographic information system** (**GIS**) analysis tool used for detailed spatial analysis and map creation.
- **Google Maps API:** API-Integrates geospatial visualizations into websites or apps with rich customization.

Choosing the right tool:

Requirement	Suggested tool
Basic interactive maps in Python	Folium, Plotly
Large-scale GIS data visualization	QGIS, Kepler.gl
Combining geospatial data with statistical plots	Geopandas
Business dashboards with maps	Tableau, Power BI
Web integration	Google Maps API, Leaflet.js

***Table 11.2**: Geospatial visualization tools*

The following example is used for generating interactive maps using Folium:

```
import folium
# Create a map centered at a location
m = folium.Map(location=[28.6139, 77.2090], zoom_start=6)

# Add a marker
folium.Marker([28.6139, 77.2090], popup='New Delhi').add_to(m)

# Display the map
m.save("india_map.html")
```

Interactive visualization

In the era of big data and user centric analytics, static visualizations often fall short in conveying complex, multi-dimensional insights. Interactive visualizations empower users to explore data dynamically, making analytics more intuitive, engaging, and actionable. This section introduces the concept of interactivity in data visualization, discusses how to create interactive plots, and explores tools and libraries that enable interactivity.

Creating interactive plots

Interactive plots go beyond static charts by allowing user actions such as zooming, filtering, hovering, panning, and clicking to reveal additional data insights. These features are crucial for:

- **Drill down analysis:** Explore deeper layers of data by clicking on chart elements.
- **Real-time feedback:** Update visuals based on user inputs or filters.
- **Enhanced storytelling:** Interactive dashboards guide users through a data narrative.
- **Creating interactive plots also involve the following:**
    - o Linking widgets (sliders, dropdowns) to data filters.
    - o Displaying tooltips that appear when hovering over data points.
    - o Enabling dynamic axes, legends, or series selection.

Interactive plots are commonly used in dashboards, reports, and web applications where user driven exploration is key.

Tools and libraries for interactivity

Several powerful tools and libraries support the development of interactive data visualizations in Python and other environments:

- **Plotly:**
  - **Language:** Python, R, JavaScript
  - **Key features:**
    - Drag and zoom functionality.
    - Hover tooltips and annotations.
    - Easy integration with Dash for dashboard creation.
    - **Use case example:** Plotly is ideal for 3D plots, interactive scatter plots, and maps.
- **Bokeh:**
  - **Language:** Python
  - **Key features:**
    - Rich set of widgets for interactivity (sliders, buttons).
    - Linked brushing between plots.
    - Server-based interactive visualizations.
    - **Use case example:** Ideal for building interactive web dashboards with real-time data streaming.
- **Altair:**
  - **Language:** Python
  - **Key features:**
    - Declarative grammar of graphics.
    - Simple syntax for adding interactivity.
    - Good for small to medium-sized datasets.
    - **Use case example:** Rapid development of interactive charts with minimal code.
- **Dash:**

  Language: Python (built on top of Flask and Plotly).

  Key features:
  - Full-stack web app framework for building interactive dashboards.
  - Allows integration of complex logic and callbacks.
  - **Use case example:** Enterprise-grade interactive dashboards with filters and controls.

- **Panel and Holoviews:**
    - **Language:** Python
    - **Key features:**
        - High-level abstraction for creating interactive plots.
        - Integrates well with Bokeh and Matplotlib.
        - Panel supports layout and widget management.
        - **Use case example:** Interactive scientific visualizations with large datasets.
- **D3.js:**
    - **Language:** JavaScript
    - **Key features:**
        - Highly customizable, data-driven document manipulation.
        - Full control over **Scalable Vector Graphics** (**SVG**) elements.
        - **Use case example:** Interactive visualizations on the web with custom styling and animations.

Performance optimization

Performance optimization is a crucial consideration in data science projects, particularly when data analysis work move into production systems such as dashboards, reports, and real-time applications. As datasets grow in size and complexity, inefficient processing or poorly designed visual outputs can lead to slow performance, increased resource consumption, and poor user experience.

One important aspect of optimization is resolution and DPI management. Choosing appropriate resolution settings ensures that visualizations are clear. High DPI is important for print and presentation quality graphics, while lower DPI is often sufficient for web-based dashboards. Managing these settings correctly helps balance visual quality with performance and storage efficiency.

Another key consideration is the choice between vector and raster formats. Vector formats such as SVG and PDF scale without loss of quality and are ideal for charts, diagrams, and publication ready figures. Raster formats such as PNG and JPEG are pixel based and better suited for images, but they are resolution dependent and can increase file size and rendering time if not optimized. Understanding when and where to use each format is essential for efficient visualization delivery.

Caching strategies play a significant role in improving system performance. By storing intermediate results, processed datasets, or rendered visualizations, caching reduces the need for repeated computations and database queries. This is particularly valuable in dashboards and reporting systems where the same analyses are accessed frequently. Effective caching improves response time and reduces computational load.

In interactive applications, debouncing and throttling are essential techniques. Debouncing ensures that a function is executed only after a specified period of inactivity, while throttling limits the number of times a function can be called within a given time interval. These techniques prevent excessive recalculations, resulting in better interactions and overall performance.

Best practices and practical tips

Best practices and practical tips provide guidance derived from real-world data science implementations, helping practitioners apply theoretical knowledge effectively. Maintaining clean, modular, and well documented code is essential for collaboration and long-term project sustainability. Clear documentation of assumptions, data sources, and methodologies improves transparency and reproducibility. Version control systems and standardized environments further support consistent and repeatable analyses.

Ensuring data quality through validation, consistency checks, and error handling is another critical best practice. Designing clear and interpretable visualizations helps avoid misinterpretation and supports effective decision-making.

Ethical considerations and lessons learned from real-world projects should be taken into consideration. Responsible data usage, awareness of bias, and clear communication with stakeholders are essential for building trustworthy data science solutions. By incorporating these best practices, readers are better prepared to deliver robust, scalable, and impactful data science projects in professional environments.

Conclusion

This chapter helps readers delve into data processing and visualization, which are foundational skills in the data science pipeline. Beginning with the basics of data processing, readers learned about data cleaning and transformation, which is required for preparing data for analysis.

The chapter provided an introduction to data visualization tools. Readers gained insights into how to choose the right tool for different data types, visualization goals, and audience requirements.

This chapter introduced advanced plotting with Seaborn, a Python library that simplifies the creation of complex statistical graphics. Readers explored how to create layered visualizations, enhance readability, and customize plot elements to suit specific analytical narratives.

The topic on geospatial data visualization equipped readers with the knowledge to create and plot maps in fields such as public health, environmental studies, and logistics. Finally, the chapter covered interactive visualizations, which allow users to engage with data dynamically. We also discussed performance optimization, best practices and practical tips.

In the next chapter, we will discuss the mathematical foundations necessary for data science, followed by a practical introduction to supervised and unsupervised learning techniques. The next chapter talks about decision-making techniques like decision trees and random forests, which play a pivotal role in predictive analytics and interpretable ML.

Exercises

1. What is the difference between data cleaning and data transformation?
2. Give two examples of data inconsistencies and how they can be corrected.
3. Write Python code using Pandas to remove missing values from a DataFrame.
4. Explain the importance of data transformation in preparing data for analysis.
5. What function in Pandas can be used to apply a transformation to multiple columns at once?
6. List three popular Python libraries used for data visualization and mention one use case for each.
7. What factors should you consider when choosing a data visualization tool?
8. Compare Matplotlib and Seaborn in terms of usability and output quality.
9. Why is it important to consider your audience when creating visualizations?
10. What is the role of interactive dashboards in modern data storytelling?
11. Write a Seaborn command to create a boxplot comparing scores across different subjects.
12. How does Seaborn simplify complex visualizations compared to Matplotlib?
13. What kind of plot would you use to explore the correlation between two numerical variables?
14. Name two customization options available in Seaborn to improve plot readability.
15. How can you visualize the distribution of a single variable using Seaborn?
16. What is geospatial data? Provide two examples.
17. Name two Python libraries used for geospatial data visualization.
18. Write a brief code snippet to plot latitude and longitude coordinates using folium or geopandas.
19. In which real-world domains is map visualization most commonly used?
20. What challenges might you face when visualizing geographic data?

CHAPTER 12
Mathematical and Scientific Applications

Introduction

In the field of data science, it is important to have a strong foundation in mathematics and scientific principles. Mathematical and scientific applications help in designing, training, and optimizing intelligent models. Mathematical foundations such as linear algebra and calculus enable machine learning algorithms in effective data transformation, model computation, and gradient-based optimization.

This chapter explores the mathematical foundations necessary for data science, followed by a practical introduction to supervised and unsupervised learning techniques. It helps in understanding how machines learn from data to make decisions or uncover hidden patterns. The chapter also discusses decision-making techniques like decision trees and random forests, which play a pivotal role in predictive analytics and interpretable **machine learning** (**ML**).

Structure

This chapter covers the following topics:

- Mathematical foundations in data science
- Basics of supervised learning
- Basics of unsupervised learning
- Decision-making techniques
- Trend and predictive mining using Python

Objectives

The primary objective of this chapter is to enable readers to delve into mathematical and scientific applications that act as foundations for data science. Readers will gain insights into core mathematical concepts such as linear algebra and calculus that help in the functioning of machine learning algorithms, enabling efficient data manipulation and optimization. The chapter aims to familiarize users with the basic principles of supervised learning, including widely used algorithms like linear regression and decision trees, helping them understand how models are trained to predict outcomes. It also introduces the fundamentals of unsupervised learning, covering key techniques such as k-means clustering and **principal component analysis** (**PCA**), which are used for discovering patterns and reducing data dimensions. The chapter also discusses decision-making techniques like decision trees and random forests. It also discusses trend analysis and predictive modeling using Python, allowing them to apply time series analysis and forecasting methods in real-world scenarios. Overall, the objective is to build a balanced foundation of theory and practice, preparing readers to apply mathematical reasoning and scientific methods to data-driven problem-solving.

Mathematical foundations in data science

Data science is the amalgamation of mathematics, programming, and domain knowledge. In mathematics, linear algebra and calculus play a fundamental role in understanding how data is structured, manipulated, and interpreted. These two areas in mathematics provide a theoretical framework for algorithms, enabling efficient data processing and optimization. A strong hold on these topics helps practitioners build, customize, and troubleshoot ML models more effectively.

Linear algebra

Linear algebra is the branch of mathematics concerned with vectors, matrices, and linear transformations. In data science, it provides the foundational tools to represent and manipulate structured data, especially high-dimensional data commonly encountered in machine learning tasks.

Key concepts and applications:

- **Vectors and matrices**: Data is often represented as vectors (1D arrays) and matrices (2D arrays). Each row in a dataset can be viewed as a vector of features, and the entire dataset as a matrix.
- **Matrix operations**: Operations such as matrix multiplication, transposition, and inversion are widely used in model training and transformation of data.
- **Systems of linear equations**: Many algorithms, including linear regression, are based on solving systems of equations, which is a central task in linear algebra.
- **Dot product and projections**: Concepts like the dot product and vector projections are used in similarity computations (e.g., cosine similarity in **natural language processing** (**NLP**) or clustering).
- **Eigenvalues and eigenvectors**: These are key to PCA, which reduces the dimensionality of datasets while retaining variance, a common step in data preprocessing.

Linear algebra is crucial for understanding the inner workings of models such as linear regression, support vector machines, and neural networks. Libraries like NumPy, SciPy, and TensorFlow use efficient linear algebra routines for performance optimization.

Calculus

Calculus, particularly differential calculus, is another cornerstone of data science. It provides the mathematical foundation for optimization, which is the process of minimizing (or maximizing) a function in machine learning; this usually means minimizing a loss function.

Key concepts and applications:

- **Derivatives and gradients**: A derivative represents the rate of change. In ML, gradients are used to update model parameters in algorithms like gradient descent.
- **Partial derivatives**: For functions with multiple variables (as in multivariate models), partial derivatives measure how the function changes with respect to each variable independently.
- **Gradient descent algorithm**: This iterative method updates parameters by moving in the direction of the negative gradient to minimize error. It is fundamental to training models like logistic regression and deep neural networks.
- **Chain rule**: Used extensively in backpropagation in neural networks, allowing for the calculation of gradients in complex models involving many layers.

Without calculus, it would be impossible to train models that adjust parameters based on feedback. In deep learning, for example, calculus enables neural networks to learn by minimizing the error between predicted and actual outputs through multiple iterations.

Probability theory and statistics

Probability theory and statistics form the base in the field of data science. Probability theory provides a framework to model randomness, uncertainty, and risk, which are inherent in real-world data. Statistics enables the analysis, interpretation, and validation of data and model outcomes.

Key concepts and applications:

- **Random variables and probability distributions**: Data is often modeled using distributions such as normal, binomial, and Poisson distributions to understand patterns, variability, and likelihood of events.
- **Descriptive statistics**: Measures such as mean, median, variance, and standard deviation summarize data characteristics and provide initial insights before modeling.

- **Inferential statistics**: Techniques like confidence intervals and hypothesis testing help determine whether observed patterns are statistically significant and generalizable.
- **Bayesian probability**: Bayesian methods allow models to update predictions as new data becomes available, widely used in recommendation systems and probabilistic models.
- **Statistical estimation**: Parameter estimation techniques such as **maximum likelihood estimation** (**MLE**) are used to fit models to data.
- **Model evaluation and uncertainty**: Statistical metrics help assess model performance, reliability, and confidence in predictions.

Probability and statistics are essential for tasks such as data exploration, feature selection, anomaly detection, predictive modeling, and Decision-making. They enable data scientists to not only build models but also interpret results responsibly and assess the validity.

Basics of supervised learning

Supervised learning is one of the most widely used approaches in ML and data science. As the name suggests, it involves learning from a *supervisor*, in this case, historical data that contains both input features and known output labels. The objective is to learn a mapping from inputs to outputs so that the model can predict outcomes for unseen data. Supervised learning is effective when past observations and outcomes are available, making it suitable for predictive tasks across domains such as healthcare, finance, education, marketing, and engineering.

Definition and types

Supervised learning is a machine learning paradigm where the model is trained using a labeled dataset, which means each training example consists of input variables (features) and a known output (target label). The model learns a function that best maps the input to the correct output by minimizing prediction errors.

There are two main types of supervised learning tasks:

- **Classification**: The goal is to predict a categorical label.
    - Examples include spam detection (spam or not), disease diagnosis (positive or negative), or handwriting recognition (digits 0–9).
    - **Algorithms**: Logistic regression, decision trees, random forest, support vector machines, k-nearest neighbors.
- **Regression**: The goal is to predict a continuous numeric value.
    - Examples include predicting house prices, temperature, or stock prices.

- **Algorithms**: Linear regression, ridge/lasso regression, decision trees (for regression), gradient boosting.

In both types, the algorithm learns patterns from the training data and uses that learning to make accurate predictions on new, unseen data.

Linear regression and decision trees

Linear regression and decision trees are the well-known supervised learning algorithms. Following section discusses about linear regression and decision trees:

- **Linear regression**: Linear regression is one of the simplest and most interpretable supervised learning algorithms used for regression tasks. It assumes a linear relationship between the input variables (independent variables) and the output variable (dependent variable).
  - **Model equation**:

    $$y=\beta 0+\beta 1x1+\beta 2x2+\cdots+\beta nxn+\epsilon y = \beta 0+\beta 1x1+\beta 2x2+\cdots+\beta nxn+\epsilon$$

    where $\beta 0$ is the intercept, $\beta 1,\ldots,\beta n/\beta 1,\ldots,\beta n$ are coefficients, and ϵ\epsilon ϵ is the error term.
  - **Applications**: Forecasting sales, estimating costs, predicting exam scores based on study hours, etc.
- **Decision trees**: A decision tree is a versatile algorithm used for both classification and regression tasks. It mimics human decision-making by learning simple decision rules inferred from the data features. The tree is constructed by splitting the dataset based on feature values that best separate the target variable.
  - Internal nodes represent decisions based on feature conditions.
  - Leaf nodes represent the output (class or value).
  - **Advantages**:
    - Easy to understand and interpret.
    - Requires little data preprocessing (no need for feature scaling).
    - Can handle both numerical and categorical data.
  - **Limitations**:
    - Prone to overfitting, especially on small datasets.
    - Sensitive to noisy data.

Decision trees serve as building blocks for more complex ensemble models like random forests and gradient boosting machines, which improve prediction accuracy by combining multiple trees.

Supervised learning forms the foundation of many real-world AI applications like fraud detection, medical diagnostics, etc. Understanding the types of tasks it handles, along with fundamental algorithms like linear regression and decision trees, gives learners the tools to begin building predictive models with labeled data.

Model evaluation in supervised learning

Model evaluation is a critical step in supervised learning that assesses how well a trained model performs on unseen data. The primary objectives of model evaluation are to:

- Measure the predictive performance of a model
- Compare different models or algorithms
- Detect issues such as overfitting and underfitting
- Select optimal model parameters
- Ensure generalization to new, unseen data

To evaluate a model fairly, the available labeled dataset is typically divided into multiple subsets:

- **Training set**: The training set is used to learn model parameters and patterns from the data.
- **Validation set**: The validation set is used to tune hyperparameters, select models, and prevent overfitting.
- **Test set**: The test set is used only once to evaluate the final performance of the selected model. It represents unseen data and provides an unbiased estimate of real-world performance. A common split ratio is 70% training, 15% validation, and 15% testing, though this may vary depending on dataset size.

Evaluation in supervised learning

Evaluation metrics for classification models include the following:

- **Confusion metrics**: A confusion matrix summarizes prediction results as:
    - **True positive (TP)**: Correctly predicted positive cases
    - **True negative (TN)**: Correctly predicted negative cases
    - **False positive (FP)**: Incorrectly predicted positive cases
    - **False negative (FN)**: Incorrectly predicted negative cases

- **Accuracy**: It measures the proportion of correct predictions.

$$Accuracy = (TP+TN)/ (TP+TN+FP+FN)$$

- **Precision**: Precision measures how many predicted positive cases are actually positive.

$$Precision= (TP/TP+FP)$$

- **Recall:** Recall measures how many actual positive cases were correctly identified.

$$Recall= TP/(TP+FN)$$

- **F1 Score**: The F1 Score is the harmonic mean of precision and recall.

Evaluation metrics for regression

Regression models predict continuous numeric values. Their evaluation focuses on measuring prediction error is as follows:

- **Mean absolute error (MAE)**:

$$MAE=1/n\sum|yi-y\wedge i|$$

It represents the average absolute difference between predicted and actual values and is easy to interpret.

- **Mean squared error (MSE)**:

$$MSE=1/n\sum(yi-y\wedge i)^2$$

MSE penalizes larger errors more strongly due to squaring.

- **Root mean squared error (RMSE)**:

$$RMSE=sqrt(MSE)$$

RMSE is expressed in the same units as the target variable, making it more interpretable.

- **R^2 Score (coefficient of determination)**:

$$R^2=1-[\sum(yi-y^-)^2/\sum(yi-y\wedge i)^2]$$

R^2 measures how well the model explains variance in the target variable. Values closer to **1** indicate better fit.

Basics of unsupervised learning

While supervised learning works with labeled data, unsupervised learning operates on unlabeled datasets, where the goal is to explore the underlying structure or patterns in the data without predefined outputs. It is particularly useful when the data lacks clear categories or labels but still contains meaningful relationships.

Unsupervised learning is widely used in exploratory data analysis, pattern recognition, customer segmentation, dimensionality reduction, and anomaly detection.

Definition and types

Unsupervised learning refers to a class of machine learning techniques that attempt to identify hidden patterns, groupings, or structures in data without using labeled outputs. The model is not provided with any guidance about what to predict. Instead, it tries to discover natural groupings or features that summarize the data effectively.

There are two major types of unsupervised learning tasks:

- **Clustering**: In clustering, we group data points into clusters such that items in the same group are more similar to each other than to those in other groups.

  Applications: Customer segmentation, document clustering, market research, and image segmentation.

- **Dimensionality reduction**: In Dimensionality Reduction, we reduce the number of input features while preserving the essential structure or variance in the data.

  Applications: Data compression, visualization, noise reduction, and speeding up machine learning models

K-means clustering and PCA

K-means is one of the most popular and intuitive clustering algorithms. It aims to partition a dataset into K clusters, where each data point belongs to the cluster with the nearest mean (centroid).

Steps involved in k-means clustering are:

1. Select the number of clusters KKK.
2. Randomly initialize KKK centroids.
3. Assign each data point to the nearest centroid.
4. Recompute centroids based on assigned points.
5. Repeat *steps 3* and *4* until convergence (centroids no longer change significantly).

Advantages:

- o Simple to implement and fast.
- o Works well on large datasets.

Limitations:

- o Requires predefining the number of clusters.

- Sensitive to initial centroid selection and outliers.
- Assumes spherical cluster shapes and equal variance.

- **PCA**: It is a statistical technique used for dimensionality reduction. It transforms the original features into a new set of uncorrelated variables called principal components, ordered by the amount of variance they capture.

  Steps involved in PCA are:

  1. Standardize the dataset (mean = 0, variance = 1).
  2. Compute the covariance matrix.
  3. Find the eigenvalues and eigenvectors.
  4. Project the data onto the top principal components that capture the most variance.

  Applications:

  - Simplifying datasets for visualization (e.g., reducing high-dimensional data to 2D or 3D).
  - Noise filtering and feature extraction.
  - Preprocessing step before applying supervised learning algorithms.

  Advantages:

  - Reduces computational complexity.
  - Removes multicollinearity among features.
  - Improves model performance by eliminating redundant variables.

  Limitations:

  - Linear technique may not capture complex, non-linear relationships.
  - Can make data less interpretable due to loss of original feature meanings.

Unsupervised learning provides powerful tools for discovering patterns and simplifying data without relying on labeled examples. Algorithms like k-means clustering enable automatic grouping of data, while PCA helps reduce the complexity of high-dimensional datasets. Mastering these techniques is essential for uncovering hidden insights in raw data and for preparing it effectively for further analysis or modeling.

Evaluation of unsupervised learning

Unsupervised learning evaluation focuses on measuring the quality, consistency, and usefulness of the discovered patterns or structures.

Evaluation metrics for unsupervised learning are categorized into internal, external, and relative metrics, as follows:

- **Internal evaluation metrics**: It is the clustering or structure using only the data itself, without any external labels. These metrics assess how well data points are grouped based on cohesion (within cluster similarity) and separation (between cluster dissimilarity).
    - **Silhouette coefficient**: The silhouette coefficient measures how similar a data point is to its own cluster compared to other clusters.

      $$Silhouette=(b-a)/max(a,b)$$

      Where:

      a = average distance to points in the same cluster.

      b = average distance to points in the nearest neighboring cluster.

      Range lies between –1 to +1. Values close to +1 indicate well separated clusters.

      Values near 0 indicate overlapping clusters.
    - **Davies Bouldin Index (DBI)**: The DBI measures the average similarity between each cluster and its most similar cluster. Lower DBI values indicate better clustering. Penalizes clusters that are close together or highly dispersed.
    - **Calinski Harabasz Index**: Also known as the **Variance Ratio Criterion**, it evaluates the ratio of between cluster variance to within cluster variance. Higher values indicate well defined and compact clusters. It works best for convex and well separated clusters.
- **External evaluation metrics**: External metrics are used only when compare the clustering result with known class labels (for validation or benchmarking).
    - **Adjusted Rand Index (ARI)**: Measures the similarity between predicted clusters and true labels while correcting for chance. Range lies from –1 to 1.Higher values indicate better agreement.
    - **Normalized Mutual Information (NMI)**: Measures the shared information between the clustering assignments and true labels. Range lies from 0 to 1. Higher values indicate better clustering quality.
    - **Purity**: Purity measures the extent to which clusters contain data points from a single class. It is easy to interpret. It does not penalize a large number of clusters.
- **Relative evaluation metrics**: Relative metrics compare clustering results across different parameter settings or models.

- **Elbow method**: It is used primarily with k-means clustering. It plots **within cluster sum of squares** (**WCSS**) against the number of clusters. The *elbow point* indicates the optimal number of clusters.

- **Stability based evaluation**: Evaluates how consistent clusters are when:
  - The algorithm is run multiple times.
  - The dataset is slightly modified.
  - Stable results suggest robust clustering.
- **Evaluation metrics for dimensionality reduction**: For unsupervised dimensionality reduction methods such as PCA:
  - Explained variance ratio.
  - Measures how much information (variance) is retained after dimensionality reduction.
  - Higher explained variance indicates better representation.
- **Reconstruction error**: Measures the difference between original data and reconstructed data from reduced dimensions. Lower error indicates minimal information loss.

Decision-making techniques

In data science and machine learning, decision-making techniques play a crucial role in modeling how systems and individuals make choices based on data. These techniques are especially useful for classification and regression tasks, where the goal is to predict an outcome based on multiple inputs. Two of the most widely used decision-making tools in ML are decision trees and random forests. These models are intuitive, versatile, and often provide interpretable results.

Decision trees

A decision tree is a tree like model that splits the dataset into branches to make decisions or predictions. It is structured with nodes representing features or conditions, branches representing decisions or outcomes of those conditions, and leaves representing final outputs (class labels or predicted values).

In a decision tree, the root node evaluates the feature that best splits the data-based on a certain criterion (e.g., Gini index, entropy, or MSE). The dataset is divided into subsets based on this split. The process continues recursively, forming a tree structure. The algorithm stops when it reaches a stopping condition (e.g., maximum depth, no more improvement).

Types of decision trees include the following:

- **Classification trees**: Output a categorical label (e.g., Yes/No, class A/B/C).
- **Regression trees**: Output a continuous value (e.g., price, temperature).

Advantages:

- Easy to understand and visualize.
- No need for feature scaling or normalization.
- Can handle both numerical and categorical data.

Limitations:

- Prone to overfitting, especially with deep trees.
- Sensitive to small changes in data (instability).
- Can become biased if classes are imbalanced.

Random forests

A random forest is an ensemble learning technique that builds multiple decision trees and combines their outputs to improve predictive accuracy and control overfitting. It is one of the most powerful and commonly used algorithms for both classification and regression tasks.

In a random forest, multiple decision trees are constructed using bootstrapped samples of the original dataset. At each split in a tree, a random subset of features is considered (not all features).

The predictions from all trees are combined using the following methods:

- **Classification**: Majority vote of all trees.
- **Regression**: Average of all tree outputs.

This randomness makes the model robust and less prone to overfitting compared to a single decision tree.

Advantages:

- Higher accuracy than individual trees.
- Reduces variance and avoids overfitting.
- Automatically handles missing values and maintains performance with unbalanced datasets.

Limitations:

- Less interpretable than a single decision tree.
- Requires more computational resources (training time and memory).
- Slower predictions compared to simpler models.

Applications:

- Customer churn prediction
- Fraud detection
- Loan default risk classification
- Disease diagnosis

Trend and predictive mining using Python

In many real-world applications, data is collected over time, such as stock prices, sales figures, weather data, website traffic, and more. Analyzing and forecasting trends in such data is a powerful asset in decision-making, strategic planning, and anomaly detection. Trend and predictive mining involve identifying patterns over time and using these patterns to make informed predictions about the future.

Python offers a robust ecosystem of libraries such as Pandas, NumPy, Statsmodels, scikit-learn, and Prophet that make time series analysis and predictive modeling both accessible and effective.

Time series analysis

Time series data consists of observations collected sequentially over time. Unlike typical datasets, time series data has a temporal component, which introduces dependencies that must be accounted for.

Key components of time series:

- **Trend**: Long-term upward or downward movement in the data.
- **Seasonality**: Repeating patterns or cycles over a specific time period (e.g., hourly, daily, monthly).
- **Cyclic patterns**: Irregular fluctuations due to economic or natural factors.
- **Noise**: Random variation that is not explained by trends or seasonality.

Common techniques:

- **Moving averages**: Smoothens the series to identify trends.
- **Decomposition**: Separates the series into trend, seasonal, and residual components.
- **Autocorrelation and partial autocorrelation**: Identify relationships between current and past values.

- **Autoregressive Integrated Moving Average (ARIMA)**: A powerful statistical model for forecasting that combines autoregression, differencing (to remove trend), and moving averages.
- **Exponential smoothing**: Gives more weight to recent observations for short-term forecasting.
- **Facebook Prophet**: An intuitive and robust Python library developed for forecasting with daily or seasonal data, handling missing values and holidays.

Example applications are as follows:

- Forecasting product demand in retail
- Predicting energy consumption
- Monitoring website visitor trends

Predictive modeling techniques

Predictive modeling refers to using historical data to train a model that can forecast future outcomes. While time series analysis deals specifically with time-ordered data, predictive modeling can use both temporal and non-temporal features.

Steps in predictive modeling include the following:

1. **Data preprocessing**: Handle missing values, normalize data, create lag features, etc.
2. **Feature engineering**: Create meaningful input features that capture trends, seasonality, or external variables (e.g., holidays, weather).
3. **Model selection**: Choose appropriate algorithms for forecasting or classification.
4. **Model evaluation**: Use metrics such as RMSE, MAE, or MAPE to assess model accuracy.
5. **Forecasting**: Generate predictions and visualize the results to inform decision-making.

Common predictive models are as follows:

- **Linear regression**: Useful for simple, linear trends.
- **Decision trees and random forests**: Handle complex, non-linear relationships.
- **Gradient boosting models (e.g., XGBoost, LightGBM)**: Often deliver high accuracy in structured data prediction tasks.
- **Long short-term memory (LSTM)**: A type of neural network especially effective for learning from long sequences in time series forecasting.

- **Facebook Prophet**: Combines statistical forecasting with the flexibility of machine learning, suited for business analysts and non-experts.

Python tools and libraries are:

- **Pandas and NumPy**: Data manipulation and preprocessing.
- **Matplotlib and Seaborn**: Visualization of time series and trends.
- **Statsmodels**: Statistical modeling and ARIMA implementation.
- **Scikit-learn**: Regression and ensemble models.
- **Prophet**: Easy-to-use forecasting with trend and seasonality components.
- **TensorFlow/Keras**: Deep learning-based forecasting models like LSTM.

Trend and predictive mining provide the foundation for understanding past behavior and forecasting future outcomes in a data-driven world. Whether through traditional time series models like ARIMA or advanced machine learning techniques like Random Forests and **Long-Term Short Memory** (**LSTMs**), Python offers a rich suite of tools for analysis and forecasting. Mastering these techniques enables data scientists to build robust predictive systems that are essential in business, finance, healthcare, and beyond.

Conclusion

This chapter provided a detailed discussion on mathematical and scientific principles that power modern data science solutions. It began with an introduction to essential mathematical tools: linear algebra and calculus, highlighting their significance in understanding data transformations and model optimization. The chapter then explored both supervised and unsupervised learning paradigms, including foundational algorithms like linear regression, decision trees, k-means clustering, and PCA.

Decision-making techniques, such as decision trees and random forests, were discussed that can be used for effective predictions. The final section discussed applied analytics, introducing Python-based methods for trend detection and predictive modeling, particularly in the context of time series data.

This chapter helps in bridging the gap between mathematical theory and practical data science applications, helping in solving problems in data-driven domains. In the next chapter, we will discuss about developing recommender systems and its types.

Exercises

1. What are the key applications of linear algebra in data science and ML?
2. How do vectors and matrices help represent and manipulate data?

3. Explain the concept of eigenvalues and eigenvectors in the context of dimensionality reduction.
4. How is calculus used in optimizing machine learning models?
5. What role does gradient descent play in training machine learning algorithms?
6. Define supervised learning and give two real-world examples of its applications.
7. Differentiate between classification and regression with suitable examples.
8. What is the principle behind linear regression, and how is it used for prediction?
9. How does a decision tree algorithm make decisions based on data features?
10. List two advantages and two disadvantages of using decision trees for supervised learning.
11. Define unsupervised learning and explain how it differs from supervised learning.
12. Describe the working mechanism of the k-means clustering algorithm.
13. What is the objective of PCA?
14. How does PCA help in reducing the dimensionality of data while preserving variance?
15. Give an example scenario where unsupervised learning would be more appropriate than supervised learning.
16. What is entropy, and how is it used in constructing decision trees?
17. How does a random forest improve the performance of a single decision tree?
18. Compare decision trees and random forests in terms of accuracy and interpretability.
19. What are the key parameters to tune when building a random forest model?
20. What is time series analysis, and how is it applied in predictive modeling?

CHAPTER 13
Developing Recommender Systems

Introduction

In today's digital world, where users are provided with enormous amounts of information, recommender systems play an important role in helping users choose the content, product, or service based on their specific needs and preferences. From suggesting movies on streaming platforms like *Netflix*, recommending products on *Amazon*, to suggesting personalized playlists on *Spotify*, recommender systems have become a part and parcel of modern applications.

Recommender systems are defined as intelligent information filtering tools that can be used to predict user preferences and deliver personalized suggestions. By analyzing patterns in user behavior, item characteristics, or a combination of both, these systems transform vast amounts of raw data into meaningful and relevant insights.

In this chapter, we will discuss recommender systems, their types, techniques, and practical implementations. We will also explore **collaborative filtering** (**CF**), content-based recommendations, and hybrid approaches. Recommender systems are not only important for user engagement but also for business growth across industries.

Structure

This chapter covers the following topics:

- Introduction to recommender systems
- CF techniques
- Content-based recommendation
- Knowledge-based recommender system
- Context Aware Recommender system
- Hybrid recommender systems
- Building simple recommender system in Python
- Advanced recommender system techniques
- Case studies and practical applications

Objectives

The primary objective of this chapter is to provide readers with a discussion about recommender systems, their importance, and their applications in real-world scenarios. By the end of this chapter, readers will be able to understand recommender systems, their role in enhancing user experience, and decision-making. They will be able to understand the differences between types of recommender systems - CF, content-based methods, and hybrid approaches. Implementation of a simple recommender system in Python will provide hands-on experience to the readers to translate theory into practice. Case studies from real-world examples, e.g., e-commerce and streaming services, are discussed, along with methods for evaluating recommender systems using appropriate metrics and strategies for performance tuning.

Introduction to recommender systems

In the digital era, we have a tremendous amount of information, products, and services. These enormous choices available create a challenge for users to decide the relevant items quickly and effectively. Recommender systems help in addressing this issue by providing personalized suggestions that match user interests and preferences.

As data is growing day by day, recommender systems have become indispensable across multiple domains, including e-commerce, streaming services, online education, healthcare, and social media. They represent one of the most impactful applications of data science and machine learning, blending techniques from statistics, information retrieval, and AI to deliver personalized experiences in real-time.

Definition and purpose

A recommender system is an intelligent software tool that analyzes patterns in user behavior, past interactions, and item characteristics to predict what a user may like or find useful. These systems improve user satisfaction, drive customer engagement, increase sales, and strengthen loyalty. For example, product recommendations on e-commerce platforms contribute significantly to revenue, while personalized playlists in music streaming services keep users engaged for longer periods.

The purpose of recommender systems is as follows:

- To help users choose items that align with their needs or tastes.
- To support businesses and platforms in improving engagement, retention, and decision-making.

Types of recommender systems

Recommender systems are generally categorized into three major types, each based on how they generate recommendations:

- CF, which makes predictions based on user-item interaction patterns (e.g., *users who liked this also liked that*).
- Content-based filtering, which relies on item attributes or user profiles (e.g., *recommending a book with a similar genre to one the user already liked*).
- Hybrid approaches, which combine collaborative and content-based methods to overcome limitations and improve accuracy.

CF techniques

CF is one of the most popular and effective approaches for building recommender systems. The main idea of CF is that users who behaved similarly in the past will likely have similar preferences in the future. Instead of relying on item features, CF leverages the collective wisdom of the crowd by analyzing user-item interaction patterns such as ratings, purchases, or clicks.

For example, if User A and User B both liked the same set of movies, and User A also enjoyed another movie that User B has not yet watched, the system can recommend that movie to User B. This principle, that *people with similar tastes will prefer similar items*, forms the basis of CF.

CF techniques are broadly classified into two types: User-based CF and Item-based CF.

User-based CF

User-based CF focuses on identifying similar users and recommending items based on what those similar users liked.

User-based CF performs the following:

- Represent users and their interactions (ratings, clicks, purchases) in a user-item matrix.
- Compute similarity between users (commonly using cosine similarity or Pearson correlation).
- Find the top N most similar users (neighbors) to the target user.
- Recommend items that those neighbors liked but the target user has not yet interacted with.
- **Example**: Suppose *Alice* and *Bob* have both rated several movies similarly. Alice rated *Inception* highly, but Bob has not seen it yet. The system recommends *Inception* to Bob because Alice, his *similar user*, liked it.

Advantages are as follows:

- Easy to implement and interpret.
- Works well when user preferences are rich and there are many overlapping ratings.

Disadvantages are as follows:

- Struggles with scalability when the number of users is very large.
- Suffers from data sparsity because most users interact with only a small fraction of items.

Item-based CF

Item-based CF, instead of comparing users, focuses on finding similar items based on user ratings or interactions.

Item-based CF works as follows:

- Build an item similarity matrix by analyzing how users rated pairs of items.
- For a given user, find items similar to the ones they already liked.
- Recommend those similar items to the user.
- **Example**: If many users who liked *The Lord of the Rings* also liked *The Hobbit*, then *The Hobbit* will be recommended to a user who rated The Lord of the Rings highly.

Advantages are as follows:

- More scalable than user-based filtering since the number of items is usually smaller than the number of users.
- Stable recommendations because item similarities do not change as frequently as user preferences.

Disadvantages are as follows:

- Requires a sufficient number of co-ratings between items.
- Cannot recommend entirely new or rarely rated items (cold start problem).

Content-based recommendation

Content-based recommendation is another well-known approach for building recommender systems. Unlike CF, which includes user-item interactions, content-based methods make recommendations by analyzing the attributes or features of items and matching them with user preferences.

The central idea is that if a user liked an item in the past, they are more likely to like similar items with similar characteristics in the future. For example, if a reader enjoyed a science fiction novel, the system might recommend other science fiction books or works by the same author.

Content-based recommendation is particularly useful when user-item interaction data is sparse or when the system needs to recommend entirely new items (which CF cannot easily handle).

Content representation

In order to make recommendations, items must first be represented in a form that a computer can understand and compare. This process is called content representation. Content representation may be done as follows:

- **Item profiles**: Each item is described using a set of attributes or features.
    - **Example:** For movies: genre, director, actors, keywords, year of release.
    - **For books:** Author, genre, keywords, publisher.
    - **For songs:** Artist, album, tempo, lyrics.
- **User profiles**: The system builds a profile of the user-based on their interactions with items.
    - **Example**: If a user frequently watches action movies, their profile will show a preference for the action genre.
- **Feature extraction**: In text-based domains (like articles, books, or movie descriptions), features can be extracted using techniques such as **term frequency inverse document frequency** (**TF-IDF**) or word embeddings.
    - **Example**: In images, features may come from color histograms or deep learning models.

By representing both users and items in terms of features, the system can establish a meaningful basis for comparison

Similarity measures

Once items and users are represented as feature vectors, the next step is to measure how similar they are. This similarity score determines the recommendations. The similarities are as follows:

- **Common similarity**: Measures the cosine of the angle between two vectors. It works well for high-dimensional data like text features.

- **Euclidean distance**: Calculates the straight-line distance between two vectors in feature space. A smaller distance means greater similarity.
- **Pearson correlation**: Measures the linear relationship between feature values. It is useful when data has rating based attributes.
- **Jaccard similarity**: Compares similarity between two sets (e.g., genres, tags). It is defined as the ratio of common features to total features.

Advantages of content-based recommendation:

- Can recommend new items (no need for many user interactions).
- Highly personalized, as recommendations are directly tied to the user's preferences.
- Transparent, easy to explain recommendations (e.g., *Recommended because you liked Sci-Fi movies*).

Limitations are as follows:

- Limited to the features used (if item descriptions are poor, recommendations suffer).
- Struggles to suggest items outside the user's established preferences (called the *overspecialization problem*).
- Feature engineering can be complex, especially in domains like music or images.

Knowledge-based recommender system

A knowledge-based recommender system recommends items using explicit domain knowledge, rules, constraints, and user requirements rather than relying on past ratings.

Types of knowledge-based recommender system includes the following:

- **Rule-based recommender systems**: It uses IF–THEN rules:

  Example: `IF user_budget < ₹50,000 AND usage = "office"`

  `THEN recommend "Laptop with i5, 8GB RAM"`

- **Case-based recommender systems**: It uses past cases and solutions. It finds similar previous problems and adapts solutions.
- **Constraint-based recommender systems**: It uses hard and soft constraints. It eliminates items that violate user constraints.

  Examples: Travel planning systems (dates, budget, destination type).

Advantages are as follows:

- High transparency and explainability

- Works well for complex and high-involvement products
- Suitable when user preferences are explicit

Limitations are as follows:

- Knowledge acquisition is time consuming
- Requires expert defined rules
- Limited adaptability without manual `updatesNot` ideal for highly dynamic or entertainment domains

Context Aware Recommender System

A **Context Aware Recommender System** (**CARS**) is an advanced recommender system that improves recommendation accuracy by incorporating contextual information such as time, location, device, user activity, or environment along with traditional user and item data.

Approaches to CARS:

- **Contextual pre-filtering**: Filters data-based on current context before applying recommendation.

  Example: Recommend movies watched on weekends only

- **Contextual post filtering**: Generates recommendations first, then adjusts or filters them using context.

  Example: Remove long movies late at night

- **Contextual modeling**: Context is directly integrated into the recommendation model.

  Example: Tensor factorization, deep learning models

Hybrid recommender system

While CF and content-based recommendation methods have their own set of limitations. CF struggles with the cold start problem (difficulty recommending new items or to new users), while content-based methods often face overspecialization (recommending only items similar to what the user has already seen). To overcome these issues, hybrid recommender systems combine the strengths of both approaches to provide more efficient and accurate recommendations.

Hybrid systems are widely used in real-world applications that provide recommendations even in challenging scenarios where one method alone might fail.

Combining CF and content-based methods

Hybrid recommender systems can be designed in different ways depending on how collaborative and content-based techniques are integrated. Some common strategies include:

- **Weighted hybrid**: Both CF and content-based methods are applied separately, and their outputs are combined using a weighted score.

  Example: If CF suggests Movie A with 0.8 confidence and CBF suggests it with 0.6, the system may compute a final weighted score (say, 0.7) to recommend it.

- **Switching hybrid**: The system dynamically switches between CF and content-based approaches depending on the situation.

  Example: Use content-based methods for new users (cold start) and CF once enough user data is available.

- **Cascade hybrid**: One recommender refines the results of the other.

  Example: CF generates a list of possible movies, and then CBF re-ranks them based on item features for better personalization.

- **Feature augmentation hybrid**: Output from one method is used as input features for the other.

  Example: A user's content-based profile is used as an additional feature in CF.

- **Mixed hybrid**: Recommendations from both methods are presented together.

  Example: An e-commerce site might display a row of *Similar to what you viewed* (content-based) alongside *People who bought this also bought* (collaborative).

By combining these approaches, hybrid systems can provide more efficient and effective recommendations than single method systems.

Advantages and use cases

Advantages of hybrid recommender systems include the following:

- **Addresses cold start problem**: New items can be recommended using content-based features, while CF improves as more user data accumulates.
- **Improved accuracy**: Combining different signals often results in better predictions than relying on one method alone.
- **Increased diversity**: Recommendations are not limited to narrow item categories, avoiding overspecialization.
- **Flexibility**: Hybrid designs can be tailored to specific domains and data availability.

Building simple recommender system in Python

Understanding the practical implementation provides deeper insight into how the techniques to build a recommender system work in real-world scenarios. In this section, we will discuss the process of building a basic recommender system in Python.

Step-by-step implementation

To build a recommender system, we follow these steps:

1. **Install and import required libraries**: Python provides excellent libraries for building recommender systems, including Pandas, NumPy, Surpirse, LIghtFM, PyTorch, TensorFlow, Implicit, SparkMLib and scikit-learn. The libraries for recommender systems need to be imported. Consider the following example for importing libraries:

```
import pandas as pd
import numpy as np
from sklearn.metrics.pairwise
import cosine_similarity
```

2. **Load the dataset**: We will use a `MovieLens` dataset (a widely used dataset for movie recommendations). It contains user ratings for different movies:

```
# Load ratings data (userId, movieId, rating)
ratings = pd.read_csv("ratings.csv")
# Load movie titles
movies = pd.read_csv("movies.csv")
# Merge datasets
data = pd.merge(ratings, movies, on="movieId")
data.head()
```

3. **Create a user item matrix**: This matrix represents users as rows and movies as columns, with ratings as entries:

```
# Create pivot table: rows -> users, columns -> movies, values ->
ratings
user_movie_matrix = data.pivot_table(index="userId", columns="title",
values="rating")
user_movie_matrix.fillna(0, inplace=True)
user_movie_matrix.head()
```

4. **Compute similarity between items**: We will use cosine similarity to calculate similarity between movies:

```
# Transpose matrix to get movie-user representation
movie_user_matrix = user_movie_matrix.T
```

```
# Compute similarity between movies
similarity_matrix = cosine_similarity(movie_user_matrix)
similarity_df = pd.DataFrame(similarity_matrix, index=movie_user_matrix.
index, columns=movie_user_matrix.index)
```

5. **Make recommendations**: To recommend movies, we find the most similar movies to a given movie:

```
def recommend_movies(movie_name, n=5):
    # Get similarity scores for the given movie
    scores = similarity_df[movie_name].sort_values(ascending=False)

    # Return top n similar movies (excluding the movie itself)
    recommendations = scores.iloc[1:n+1].index.tolist()
    return recommendations
    # Example: Recommend movies similar to "Toy Story
    (1995)"print(recommend_movies("Toy Story (1995)", n=5))
```

Practical example

Let us test the system with a few movies:

```
print("Recommendations for 'Jumanji (1995)':")
print(recommend_movies("Jumanji (1995)", 5))
print("\nRecommendations for 'Pulp Fiction (1994)':")
print(recommend_movies("Pulp Fiction (1994)", 5))

Sample Output (will vary depending on dataset):

Recommendations for Jumanji (1995):
The Mask (1994)
Ace Ventura: Pet Detective (1994)
Batman Forever (1995)
Casper (1995)
Dumb & Dumber (1994)
Recommendations for Pulp Fiction (1994):
Reservoir Dogs (1992)
Fight Club (1999)
Goodfellas (1990)
Usual Suspects, The (1995)
Trainspotting (1996)
```

Advanced recommender system technique

The recommender systems built using CF and content-based filtering face issues such as scalability, sparsity, and the complexity of modern user-item interactions. To overcome these limitations, researchers and practitioners have developed more advanced methods that leverage mathematical modeling and machine learning. Two of the most impactful techniques are matrix factorization and deep learning-based recommenders. These approaches have revolutionized the field and are widely used in large-scale commercial applications such as *Netflix*, *Amazon*, and *Spotify*.

Matrix factorization

Matrix factorization is a powerful technique for handling large, sparse user-item rating matrices. Instead of directly analyzing the huge rating matrix, it decomposes the matrix into the product of two smaller matrices:

- User latent factor matrix
- Item latent factor matrix

Each user and item is represented in a latent feature space (hidden dimensions), where similarity patterns can be captured more effectively.

Mathematically, the user item rating matrix R is approximated as:

$$R \approx P \times QT$$

Where:

- P = user feature matrix
- Q = item feature matrix
- T = number of latent features (typically much smaller than the number of users/items)

Example: If a user likes action and comedy movies, the latent factors may capture these preferences even if the user never explicitly rated a particular movie. The recommender can then predict missing ratings by multiplying the user and item latent vectors.

Algorithms: Different algorithms for matrix factorization include the following:

- **Singular value decomposition (SVD)**: A foundational method for matrix factorization.
- **Stochastic gradient descent (SGD)**: Optimizes latent matrices by minimizing error between predicted and actual ratings.
- **Alternating least squares (ALS)**: Alternates between optimizing user and item matrices for faster convergence, commonly used in large-scale systems.

Advantages are as follows:

- Handles sparsity effectively.
- Captures hidden patterns in user item interactions.
- Provides higher accuracy compared to basic CF.

Applications are as follows:

- Netflix's early recommendation algorithm (Netflix Prize winner).
- Large-scale retail platforms to uncover hidden associations between users and products.

Deep learning approaches

With the growth of big data and neural networks, deep learning has become mandatory for building a modern recommender system. Unlike traditional methods that rely on explicit ratings alone, deep learning approaches can incorporate multiple data sources such as user interactions, content features, contextual signals, and even sequential behavior (clicks, watch history, browsing sessions).

Types of deep learning models in recommender systems include the following:

- **Neural CF** (NCF):
    - o Uses deep neural networks to model user item interactions instead of simple dot products.
    - o Can learn complex, nonlinear relationships between users and items.
- **Autoencoders**: Ussseful for dimensionality reduction and reconstructing missing ratings.

  Example: A denoising autoencoder can learn latent representations of users/items and handle sparse data effectively.
- **Recurrent neural networks (RNNs)**: Capture sequential behavior, such as predicting the next song a user will listen to based on their playlist. They are widely applied in music and video streaming platforms.
- **Convolutional neural networks (CNNs)**: Extract content-based features from images, videos, or text descriptions.

  Example: Fashion recommenders analyzing product images to suggest similar styles.
- **Hybrid deep models**: Combine collaborative signals with content and contextual data.

  Example: YouTube's recommender system, which uses deep neural networks for both candidate generation and ranking.

Advantages are as follows:

- Ability to model complex, nonlinear patterns.
- Can integrate heterogeneous data (ratings, reviews, images, text, clicks).
- Scalable for large datasets with millions of users and items.

Challenges are as follows:

- High computational cost.
- Requires large amounts of training data.
- Risk of reduced interpretability compared to traditional methods.
- Bias and fairness

Case studies and practical examples

Recommender systems are no longer confined to just academic research. They are used as the core functionality of some of the world's most popular platforms. From online shopping to entertainment, education, and healthcare, these systems have transformed the way users interact with digital services. In this section, we explore real-world case studies.

Examples from e-commerce, streaming services, etc.

Amazon's recommender systems make use of item-based CF for recommending products. When a user views or purchases an item, Amazon recommends related products under the familiar banner: *Customers who bought this also bought....* Amazon has also integrated content-based features (product descriptions, categories) and contextual data (location, time, device) to improve personalization.

Netflix uses a hybrid approach combining CF, matrix factorization, and deep learning. It makes use of user viewing history, ratings, and contextual factors like time of day to recommend movies or shows. Netflix famously offered a $1 million prize for improving its recommendation accuracy.

Spotify employs CF for playlist generation (based on the listening behavior of similar users) and content-based methods for analyzing audio features such as tempo, rhythm, and lyrics. The popular *Discover Weekly* playlist is powered by these hybrid techniques.

YouTube and *TikTok* use deep learning-based hybrid recommenders. They track user clicks, watch time, likes, and shares to train neural networks that predict what content will keep users engaged. These systems not only rank items but also generate personalized feeds in real-time.

Learning platforms such as *Coursera* and *Udemy* recommend courses based on what similar learners studied (CF) and the textual content of courses (content-based). Hybrid systems also consider user skill levels and career goals to improve relevance.

Evaluation metrices and performance tuning

To ensure recommender systems provide meaningful and accurate suggestions, it is important to evaluate their performance. Some common metrics include:

- **Accuracy based metrics**:
  - **Root mean squared error** (**RMSE**) and **mean absolute error** (**MAE**) measure prediction accuracy for rating-based systems.
  - Precision, recall, and F1 Score evaluate how well recommended items match the user's true preferences.
- **Ranking metrics**:
  - **Mean Average Precision (MAP)** and **normalized discounted cumulative gain** (**NDCG**) assess the quality of ranked recommendation lists. These are especially relevant in domains like search engines and streaming platforms.
  - **Diversity and novelty**: A good system balances accuracy with diversity, ensuring recommendations are not overly repetitive. Novelty measures how well the system introduces users to new, unexplored items.
- **Performance tuning**:
  - Adjusting similarity measures (cosine, Pearson correlation).
  - Hyperparameter tuning for matrix factorization (latent dimensions, learning rate, regularization).
  - Using A/B testing on live platforms to validate improvements
- **Business metrics**:
  - User engagement (click through rate, conversion rate)
  - Diversity (catalog coverage, recommendation diversity)
  - Business impact (revenue, user retention)

Conclusion

In this chapter, we discussed recommender systems, which are essential tools for providing personalized suggestions in today's data-driven world. We discussed different recommender systems, CF, content-based methods, and hybrid approaches. CF techniques, including user-based and item-based models, were discussed along with content-based recommendations that rely on feature representation and similarity measures. We then examined hybrid recommender systems that integrate multiple approaches to overcome individual limitations and enhance accuracy. This chapter also discussed the implementation of a simple recommender system using Python. Advanced techniques such as matrix factorization and deep learning methods were introduced to show how modern systems achieve scalability and improved performance. Case studies from e-commerce and streaming services illustrated the real-world impact of recommender systems.

In the next chapter, various real-world applications of data science through detailed case studies will be discussed, highlighting the practical use of data science techniques in different industries.

Exercises

1. Define a recommender system. Why are recommender systems important in modern applications?
2. Differentiate between CF and content-based recommendation. Provide one real-world example of each.
3. Explain the main advantages and disadvantages of CF systems.
4. What is the difference between user-based and item-based CF? Which one is more scalable for large datasets?
5. Discuss how similarity measures (e.g., cosine similarity, Pearson correlation) are used in recommender systems.
6. What challenges do recommender systems face when dealing with sparse data?
7. Describe the cold start problem in recommender systems. How can hybrid methods help address this issue?
8. What role does content representation play in content-based recommendation? Give an example with movies or books.
9. Explain how matrix factorization improves the performance of CF.
10. What are the main advantages of hybrid recommender systems compared to using a single method?
11. Give two examples of industries where recommender systems are widely used and explain their impact.
12. Write Python code to compute the cosine similarity between two vectors representing user preferences.

13. Implement a simple user-based CF recommender in Python using a small dataset.
14. Create a content-based recommender in Python using item features (e.g., recommending movies based on genre).
15. What are the benefits of using deep learning in recommender systems compared to traditional methods?
16. List at least three evaluation metrics used in recommender systems and explain when each is appropriate.
17. Suppose a streaming platform wants to recommend new songs to users. Which recommender system approach would you choose and why?
18. Compare the scalability of memory based and model based CF techniques.
19. Discuss how contextual information (time, location, device) can enhance recommendations.
20. Write the steps involved in building a simple recommender system using Python.

CHAPTER 14
Real-world Applications and Case Studies

Introduction

There are numerous applications of predictive analytics and **machine learning** (**ML**) across diverse industries. By analyzing data from healthcare, finance, retail, and social media, we can observe how predictive insights provide improved outcomes, smarter decision-making, and sustainable business growth.

This chapter presents a series of case studies that demonstrate the impact of predictive analytics and machine learning across various sectors. In healthcare, predictive modeling supports prognosis and better patient diagnosis, while electronic health records serve as rich data sources for analysis. In the financial domain, time series modeling helps in stock price forecasting, and machine learning techniques strengthen fraud detection and risk assessment. In the retail sector, customer segmentation and market basket analysis provide conducive insights into consumer behavior and purchasing patterns. In social media analytics, **natural language processing** (**NLP**) and text mining techniques reveal customer sentiment, enabling effective brand monitoring and reputation management.

The chapter also includes lessons learned and best practices, offering readers a roadmap for overcoming common hurdles and maximizing the impact of predictive analytics across industries.

Structure

The chapter covers the following topics:

- Case study: Healthcare data analysis
- Case study: Financial market predictions
- Case study: Retail and customer analytics
- Case study: Social media sentiment analysis
- Lessons learned from case studies

Objectives

The objective of this chapter is to demonstrate how predictive analytics and ML can be effectively applied across multiple domains through real-world case studies. It showcases the practical applications in healthcare, finance, retail, and social media, emphasizing the role of techniques such as predictive modeling, time series forecasting, anomaly detection, market basket analysis, and sentiment analysis. The chapter also aims to provide the importance of diverse data sources such as electronic health records, financial transaction logs, retail purchase histories, and social media streams and how they help in meaningful insights. This chapter addresses the practical strategies for applying analytics in real-world contexts.

Case study: Healthcare data analysis

Healthcare is considered as one of the most data rich industries, with hospitals, clinics, and research institutions generating enormous volumes of information on a daily basis. From medical imaging and laboratory reports to prescriptions and sensor readings from wearable devices, the healthcare data analytics presents numerous opportunities to enhance patient care and improve clinical decision-making. By conversion of raw medical data into actionable insights, healthcare organizations can move from reactive treatment toward proactive, personalized, and preventive care.

Data science enables extraction of meaningful information from complex datasets to improve patient care quality, reduce costs, and guide clinical decision-making. Let us consider a case study, that discusses about challenge faced by hospitals, predicting patient readmissions within 30 days of discharge, especially for patients with chronic conditions like diabetes. High readmission rates are costly and indicate gaps in care continuity. To address this issue, we have performed analysis on publicly available readmission datasets to build machine learning models that identify patients at high risk for readmission.

One publicly available dataset is Kaggle's *Hospital Readmissions* dataset, which contains demographic, clinical, and visit-related information for more than 100,000 diabetic patient encounters, including features like age group, number of lab procedures, medications, emergency visits, diagnoses, and readmitted status. This dataset is widely used for healthcare analytics and ML practice. There are synthetic datasets structured similarly to real clinical data such as those available on data cataloging sites, containing hospital admission records with demographics, diagnoses, procedures, and readmission outcomes that support predictive analytics. The **Healthcare Cost and Utilization Project** (**HCUP**) , **Nationwide Readmissions Database** (**NRD**) is one of the most comprehensive sources of hospital discharge and readmission information. We will use the following python code that performs analysis on Hospital dataset:

```
import pandas as pd
```

Example: Load the Kaggle Hospital Readmissions dataset:

```
data = pd.read_csv("diabetic_data.csv")
print(data.shape)
print(data.head())
```

Healthcare data often has missing values, categorical variables, and inconsistent formats. Preprocessing steps typically include filling missing values, encoding categorical features (e.g., age groups, admission types), normalizing numerical variables like time in hospital or lab counts, and handling class imbalance. Feature engineering, such as computing total prior visits or converting categories to binary indicators, improves model performance. For text variables like clinical notes (if present), natural language processing approaches such as TF-IDF can extract features that complement structured data.

```
from sklearn.preprocessing import StandardScaler

# Simple imputation example
data['time_in_hospital'] = data['time_in_hospital'].fillna(data['time_in_
hospital'].median())

# One-hot encode categorical features
data = pd.get_dummies(data, columns=['race', 'gender', 'admission_type_id'],
drop_first=True)

# Normalize continuous columns
scaler = StandardScaler()
continuous_cols = ['time_in_hospital', 'num_lab_procedures', 'num_
medications']
data[continuous_cols] = scaler.fit_transform(data[continuous_cols])
```

Exploratory data analysis (**EDA**) helps reveal patterns such as readmission frequency across age groups, the association between multiple emergency visits and readmission, and the role of chronic conditions or lab outcomes in risk. Correlation matrices and distribution plots can guide feature selection.

Next, we can split the data and build a predictive model. A common baseline is a random forest classifier due to its robustness with mixed data types:

```
from sklearn.model_selection import train_test_split
from sklearn.ensemble import RandomForestClassifier
from sklearn.metrics import classification_report, roc_auc_score

X = data.drop('readmitted', axis=1)
y = data['readmitted'].apply(lambda x: 1 if x == '<30' else 0)
```

```
X_train, X_test, y_train, y_test = train_test_split(X, y, test_size=0.2,
random_state=42)

rf = RandomForestClassifier(n_estimators=200, random_state=42)
rf.fit(X_train, y_train)

y_pred = rf.predict(X_test)
y_prob = rf.predict_proba(X_test)[:, 1]

print(classification_report(y_test, y_pred))
print("AUC:", roc_auc_score(y_test, y_prob))
```

The preceding code performs performance evaluation using AUC-ROC, precision, recall, and F1 Score and are especially important for healthcare datasets where class imbalance is common.

Predictive modeling for patient outcomes

One of the most transformative applications of ML in healthcare is the development of predictive models for patient outcomes. These models use historical patient data, such as demographics, medical history, lab results, and treatment plans, to estimate the likelihood of future health events. For example, predictive modeling can identify patients at high risk of hospital readmission, leading to reduced treatment costs and improved outcomes. Similarly, predictive tools can be applied in chronic disease management, forecasting the progression of conditions like diabetes or heart disease and enabling timely interventions.

ML algorithms such as logistic regression, random forests, support vector machines, and deep learning models are widely used in healthcare domain. For instance, neural networks can process complex medical images to predict disease severity, while ensemble methods can combine multiple predictors to improve diagnostic accuracy. The key advantage of predictive modeling lies in its ability to provide clinicians with data-driven support, helping them make more informed and timely decisions. However, challenges remain, particularly regarding interpretability, as medical professionals must trust and understand model predictions before incorporating them into patient care.

Analyzing electronic health records

Electronic health records (**EHRs**) have become crucial in modern healthcare systems, offering a comprehensive digital repository of patient information. They include structured data such as lab test results, medication histories, and billing codes, as well as unstructured data like physician notes and clinical narratives. Analyzing EHRs through ML techniques offers immense potential to improve and provide better analysis in the healthcare industry.

Predictive analytics on EHRs can uncover patterns that might otherwise go unnoticed. For example, NLP can extract valuable insights from unstructured physician notes, identifying early warning signs of disease or potential adverse drug reactions. Time series models can track patient data over time, predicting disease progression or treatment response. Clustering techniques applied to EHRs enable patient stratification, helping clinicians group patients with similar health profiles and design personalized treatment pathways.

Despite the advantages of EHRs, there lie huge challenges as well. Data is often incomplete and inconsistent across different institutions. Privacy and security concerns also remain paramount, as healthcare data is highly sensitive. Overcoming these challenges requires robust preprocessing methods, secure data sharing frameworks, and ethical guidelines to ensure patient confidentiality while maximizing the utility of data.

Case study: Financial market predictions

The financial sector has long been at the forefront of adopting advanced analytical techniques due to the dynamic, data-driven nature of markets. Every second, vast volumes of data are generated from stock exchanges, trading platforms, and digital transactions. Extracting actionable insights from this data is crucial for investors, financial institutions, and regulators to make informed decisions, reduce risks, and safeguard against fraud. Predictive analytics and machine learning have become essential tools in this environment, enabling both short-term market forecasting and long-term risk management.

Time series analysis for stock prices

Stock prices are inherently volatile and influenced by multiple factors such as economic conditions, company performance, investor sentiment, and geopolitical events. Traditional statistical models, such as **Autoregressive Integrated Moving Average** (**ARIMA**), have been widely used to capture patterns in stock market time series. However, the increasing complexity of financial data has led to the adoption of machine learning and deep learning methods, which can model nonlinear relationships and capture hidden patterns.

Techniques such as **recurrent neural networks** (**RNNs**) and **long short-term memory** (**LSTM**) networks are particularly effective in analyzing sequential financial data, as they can account for dependencies across time. Hybrid models combining statistical approaches with machine learning are also gaining popularity, offering improved forecasting accuracy. For example, predictive models can forecast short-term price movements, assisting traders in making profitable decisions, or predict long-term market trends to guide institutional investors in portfolio management.

Despite these advancements, stock price prediction remains challenging due to market volatility, sudden shocks, and the influence of external factors that are difficult to quantify. As such, predictive analytics is often used as a decision support tool rather than a foolproof forecasting mechanism.

Risk assessment and fraud detection

Apart from forecasting prices, predictive analytics plays a critical role in risk assessment and fraud detection in financial systems. Risk assessment models analyze customer profiles, credit histories, and transaction behaviors to evaluate the likelihood of default, enabling banks to make more reliable lending decisions. By incorporating machine learning, these models can adapt to new risk patterns, improving accuracy over traditional methods.

Fraud detection is another area where machine learning has a transformative impact. Financial fraud can occur in many forms, including credit card fraud, identity theft, insider trading, and money laundering. Detecting such activities requires analyzing millions of transactions in real-time to identify anomalies. ML models, such as random forests, gradient boosting, and neural networks, can recognize unusual patterns that may indicate fraudulent activity. Techniques like unsupervised anomaly detection and clustering are particularly useful for identifying novel fraud schemes that were not present in historical data.

The key challenge in fraud detection lies in maintaining a balance between accuracy and false positives. Overly sensitive systems may flag legitimate transactions as fraud, leading to customer dissatisfaction, while less sensitive systems may fail to detect actual fraudulent activity. As fraudsters continually evolve their methods, financial institutions must regularly update and retrain their models to stay ahead.

Case study: Retail and customer analytics

The retail sector has undergone a massive transformation with the rise of e-commerce, omnichannel strategies, and data-driven decision-making. Every customer interaction, from browsing online catalogs to in-store purchases, generates valuable data. Harnessing this information through predictive analytics and machine learning enables retailers to better understand consumer behavior, optimize operations, and enhance customer satisfaction. Two widely adopted applications in this field are customer segmentation and market basket analysis, both of which have become essential tools for modern retail strategies.

Customer segmentation

Customer segmentation involves dividing a retailer's customer base into distinct groups based on shared characteristics, such as demographics, purchasing behavior, or preferences. Traditional segmentation often relied on simple attributes like age or income, but ML has expanded this approach by enabling data-driven clustering based on complex patterns in customer behavior.

Algorithms such as k-means clustering, hierarchical clustering, and Gaussian mixture models are commonly used for segmentation. By analyzing purchase history, browsing data, and engagement with promotions, retailers can identify meaningful groups; for example, price-sensitive customers, brand-loyal buyers, or seasonal shoppers. This allows businesses to tailor marketing campaigns, personalize product recommendations, and design loyalty programs that resonate with specific customer groups.

Segmentation not only improves sales and customer satisfaction but also helps in resource allocation. For instance, high-value customers can be targeted with premium offers, while churn-prone customers can be engaged with retention strategies. However, effective segmentation requires clean, comprehensive data and continuous model updates as customer behaviors evolve.

Market basket analysis

Market basket analysis (**MBA**) is another cornerstone of retail analytics, focusing on identifying associations between items that customers frequently purchase together. The goal is to uncover patterns, such as *customers who buy bread and butter are also likely to buy jam*. These insights enable retailers to optimize store layouts, recommend complementary products, and design cross-selling strategies.

Association rule learning algorithms, particularly the Apriori and FP-Growth algorithms, are widely used for MBA. For example, supermarkets use MBA to decide product placement, ensuring that frequently co-purchased items are located near each other. E-commerce platforms leverage the same concept to provide *Frequently Bought Together* recommendations, significantly increasing average order value.

Beyond sales, an MBA can also enhance inventory management by helping retailers anticipate demand for product bundles and reduce stockouts. However, challenges arise when analyzing sparse or noisy transaction data, requiring careful preprocessing and validation to ensure meaningful results.

Case study: Social media sentiment analysis

In today's time, social media platforms such as *Twitter* (*X*), *Facebook*, *Instagram*, and *LinkedIn* serve as rich sources of unstructured data, providing public opinions, emotions, and discussions. Businesses and organizations increasingly rely on sentiment analysis to capture consumer perceptions, monitor brand reputation, and gain actionable insights from vast amounts of online interactions. Social media sentiment analysis integrates text mining and NLP techniques to transform raw, unstructured posts into meaningful indicators of public sentiment.

Text mining and NLP

Text mining involves extracting patterns, keywords, and contextual meaning from textual data, while NLP provides the computational framework to understand semantics, syntax, and sentiment. Techniques such as tokenization, part-of-speech tagging, and sentiment lexicons help classify text into categories like positive, negative, or neutral. More advanced models use deep learning architectures such as RNNs, transformers (**Bidirectional Encoder Representations from Transformers** (**BERT**)), GPT, and attention mechanisms to capture elements such as sarcasm, irony, or context-dependent meaning.

Social media data is often noisy, containing slang, abbreviations, emojis, and misspellings. Preprocessing tasks such as stop word removal, lemmatization, and emoji interpretation are essential to improve accuracy. Once processed, machine learning classifiers like logistic regression, **support vector machine** (**SVM**), or deep neural networks can be trained to detect sentiment trends in real-time.

Brand monitoring and reputation management

For businesses, social media sentiment analysis provides a powerful tool for brand monitoring and reputation management. By tracking mentions of a brand, product, or service, companies can quickly identify emerging issues, customer dissatisfaction, or viral trends. For example, spikes in negative sentiment following a product launch may indicate quality issues that require immediate attention, while positive sentiment can validate marketing strategies.

Organizations also use sentiment dashboards to benchmark themselves against competitors, track the effectiveness of campaigns, and predict market responses. Reputation management extends beyond crisis detection. It also enables proactive engagement. Companies can address customer complaints in real-time, strengthen trust through transparency, and amplify positive feedback to reinforce brand loyalty.

The key challenge lies in ensuring accuracy across diverse languages, cultures, and platforms, where sentiment expressions may vary. Nonetheless, social media sentiment analysis has become an indispensable strategy for businesses aiming to remain agile, customer-centric, and competitive in the digital era.

Lessons learned from case studies

The diverse case studies presented across healthcare, finance, retail, and social media emphasize both the vast potential of data analytics and the practical challenges encountered in real-world implementations. While each domain has unique characteristics, several common themes emerge regarding challenges, solutions, and best practices.

Common challenges and solutions

One of the most significant challenges across domains is data quality. Missing values in healthcare records, noisy social media posts, incomplete financial transactions, or inconsistent retail data can all undermine model accuracy. Addressing these issues requires robust preprocessing techniques such as data cleaning, normalization, and imputation strategies.

Another recurring difficulty is data privacy and security. Healthcare systems must comply with regulations like HIPAA, financial markets are tightly regulated, and customer analytics must respect consumer data rights. Solutions include adopting anonymization, encryption, and compliance frameworks to ensure ethical use of data.

Model generalization also poses a challenge. Predictive models trained on limited or biased data often fail in dynamic environments, such as rapidly changing stock markets or evolving customer preferences. Regular retraining, cross-validation, and the use of adaptive learning algorithms help reduce these risks.

Finally, interpretability remains critical. In healthcare and finance, especially, stakeholders must understand how predictions are made. **Explainable AI** (**XAI**) techniques such as **SHapley Additive exPlanations** (**SHAP**) values, LIME, or rule-based models provide transparency, ensuring trust and accountability.

Key takeaways and best practices

From these challenges emerge valuable lessons. First, data-driven projects must begin with clear objectives and domain knowledge. Understanding patient care pathways, financial risk indicators, customer behavior, or public sentiment is as important as technical skill.

Second, iterative model development is essential. Starting with simple models for baseline insights and progressively moving toward advanced methods like deep learning allows organizations to balance accuracy, interpretability, and resource constraints.

Third, integrating MLOps practices such as continuous monitoring, automated retraining, and deployment pipelines ensures that models remain relevant and effective over time.

Finally, these case studies highlight the importance of human-machine collaboration. Analytics tools provide insights, but actionable outcomes require expert interpretation, ethical considerations, and strategic decision-making.

Together, these lessons emphasize that successful analytics projects are not just technical exercises but holistic endeavors requiring alignment of data, tools, people, and processes.

Conclusion

This chapter explored how predictive analytics and ML can be applied across multiple domains through real-world case studies. In healthcare, predictive modeling and EHR analysis demonstrated the potential of data-driven methods to improve patient outcomes, though challenges such as bias and interpretability remain critical. The financial sector case highlighted how time series modeling supports stock price forecasting, while risk assessment and fraud detection showcase the role of machine learning in enhancing trust and stability in markets. In retail, customer segmentation and MBA revealed the value of understanding consumer behavior to drive targeted marketing and optimize sales strategies. The social media sentiment analysis case illustrated how text mining and NLP techniques provide actionable insights into brand reputation and customer sentiment.

The chapter concluded with key lessons learned: data quality, domain knowledge, ethical considerations, and scalability are essential for success. Collectively, these case studies emphasize that while challenges exist, predictive analytics offers powerful tools for decision-making, innovation, and competitive advantage across industries. In the next chapter, we will discuss practical problems in the field of data science.

Exercises

1. What types of predictive models are commonly used for forecasting patient outcomes?
2. How can EHRs be preprocessed to improve model accuracy?
3. Identify two potential biases that may occur when analyzing healthcare data.
4. Why is interpretability especially important in predictive modeling for healthcare?
5. What are the key characteristics of time series data in stock price analysis?
6. Explain the role of feature engineering in financial market prediction models.
7. How can machine learning aid in detecting fraudulent transactions?
8. What challenges arise when applying risk assessment models to volatile markets?
9. How does customer segmentation benefit the targeted marketing campaigns?
10. Explain the concept of market basket analysis and give one real-world application.
11. What data sources are typically used to perform customer behavior analysis?
12. Why is data privacy a concern in retail analytics?
13. What is sentiment analysis, and how is it applied in brand monitoring?
14. Describe one method of text preprocessing in NLP.
15. How can social media sentiment analysis influence business decision-making?
16. Identify one challenge in analyzing multilingual social media data.
17. What are two common challenges faced across different case studies in data analytics?
18. Suggest one best practice for ensuring data quality in real-world projects.
19. Why is domain knowledge critical when interpreting predictive model outputs?
20. Summarize one key takeaway from the application of ML across industries.

Chapter 15
Practical Examples and Exercises

Introduction

In the previous chapters, we have explored theoretical foundations and technical skills essential to data science; it is time to put that knowledge into practice. This chapter is designed to bridge the gap between learning and implementation, transforming concepts into capabilities. The hands-on projects, guided exercises, and practical strategies in this chapter will help students, aspiring data scientists, or professionals sharpen their skills. By working through these examples, it will not only reinforce the understanding of data science but also build a strong portfolio of potential candidates that showcases their capabilities to future employers or collaborators.

We will start with a discussion about real-world data science projects, giving you a solid framework to tackle problems from start to finish. You will also find numerous exercises with detailed solutions to test and refine your skills. For those preparing to enter the job market, we will explore how to build a compelling portfolio and communicate your results effectively through storytelling and visual design. Finally, you will find numerous resources and communities that will support your continued growth in this fast-evolving field.

This chapter is your launchpad, where theory becomes practice, and practice becomes proficiency. Let us get started.

Structure

This chapter covers the following topics:

- Hands-on projects
- Guided exercises and solutions
- Building data science portfolio
- Presenting and communicating data science results
- Resources for continued learning

Objectives

In this chapter, you will gain practical experience by applying data science concepts and techniques to real-world projects through hands-on activities. You will work on various guided exercises designed to reinforce the problem-solving skills and deepen your understanding. You would learn how to build a compelling data science portfolio that effectively highlights your projects and expertise. Emphasis is also placed on mastering the art of communicating data science results clearly and persuasively using storytelling and visual communication best practices. Finally, you will be introduced to valuable resources and communities that can support your continued learning and growth in the ever-evolving field of data science.

Hands-on projects

One of the most effective ways to master data science concepts is through direct, hands-on experience. While theoretical understanding builds foundational knowledge, applying that knowledge to real-world problems helps solidify skills, build confidence, and prepare for professional work.

Real-world data science projects

Real-world data science projects expose learners to the full lifecycle of a data-driven solution from problem formulation and data collection to modeling, evaluation, and communication of results. These projects mimic scenarios encountered in industry, research, and policy, providing valuable experience with raw and unstructured data.

Some examples of real-world projects include:

- **Customer churn prediction**: Using customer data from a telecom or subscription-based service to predict which customers are likely to stop using the service.
- **Sentiment analysis on social media**: Analyzing tweets or product reviews to determine public sentiment toward a brand, product, or political issue.
- **Sales forecasting**: Using historical sales and economic data to forecast future sales for a retail chain or e-commerce platform.
- **Healthcare analytics**: Predicting patient readmission rates or identifying risk factors using anonymized hospital records.
- **Fraud detection**: Developing models to identify fraudulent transactions in banking or e-commerce data.

These projects are not just academic exercises; they are closely aligned with what data scientists do in industry. Working on such projects helps learners deal with real-world complexities such as missing data, feature engineering, model selection, and deployment constraints.

Step-by-step guidance

To ensure success in hands-on projects, a structured approach is essential. The following steps can be applied to most data science problems:

1. **Define the problem**:
   a. Clearly articulate the question you are trying to answer.
   b. Determine the project's scope and objectives.
   c. Identify relevant stakeholders (e.g., business users, technical teams).
2. **Collect and understand the data**:
   a. Locate appropriate datasets (e.g., open data platforms, APIs, or internal sources).
   b. **Explore the dataset**: understand its structure, types of variables, and data quality issues.
   c. Perform **exploratory data analysis** (**EDA**) to identify trends, outliers, and patterns.
3. **Preprocess and clean the data**:
   a. Handle missing values, inconsistent formats, and outliers.
   b. Encode categorical variables and normalize or scale numerical ones.
   c. Split the data into training and testing sets (and validation sets if needed).
4. **Feature engineering**:
   a. Create new variables that might enhance model performance.
   b. Select or reduce features using techniques such as **principal component analysis** (**PCA**) or feature importance ranking.
5. **Model building**:
   a. Choose appropriate algorithms (e.g., linear regression, decision trees, random forests, neural networks).
   b. Train models using the training data.
   c. Evaluate models using appropriate metrics (e.g., accuracy, precision, recall, (**root mean square error** (**RMSE**)).
6. **Interpretation and insight generation**:
   a. Understand the model thoroughly
   b. Use visualization tools (e.g., SHAP), feature importance plots) to explain model behavior.

7. **Communicate results**:

   a. Create visualizations and narratives to explain findings to non-technical audiences.

   b. Highlight actionable insights, not just technical outputs.

8. **Iterate and improve**:

   a. Revisit earlier steps based on feedback or model performance.

   b. Test alternative models or feature sets.

Hands-on projects not only reinforce learning, but they also make your skills visible and demonstrable. Whether you are preparing for a job interview, building a portfolio, or simply learning for personal growth, real-world data science projects with a structured workflow provide the experience and credibility you need to succeed in the field.

Guided exercises and solutions

While hands-on projects simulate the complexity of real-world work, guided exercises strengthen specific skills, such as data manipulation, statistical modeling, or machine learning evaluation. These exercises act as building blocks, enabling learners to incrementally build competence and confidence before tackling full-scale projects.

Practice problems

Practice problems help learners focus on core concepts and techniques in isolation, making them ideal for reinforcing theoretical knowledge with applied practice. These problems are typically designed around key data science domains:

- **Data manipulation**:

  Example: Given a dataset of sales transactions, calculate the total revenue by product category using pandas.

- **Data visualization**:

  Example: Create a boxplot to compare the distribution of salaries across departments using seaborn.

- **Probability and statistics**:

  Example: Given a dataset of coin flips, calculate the probability of getting at least seven heads in 10 flips.

- **Machine learning**:

  Example: Train a logistic regression model on a dataset to predict whether a customer will make a purchase.

- **Model evaluation**:

  Example: Compare the performance of two classification models using precision, recall, and F1 Score.

These exercises can be designed for different skill levels:

1. **Beginner**: Data cleaning, simple aggregations, plotting.
2. **Intermediate**: Feature engineering, training models, tuning hyperparameters.
3. **Advanced**: Model interpretability, deployment pipelines, time series forecasting.

Including a wide range of problem types and complexities ensures that learners are challenged appropriately and can identify areas that need more practice.

Detailed solutions

For the practical problems, it is important to have detailed, step-by-step solutions. These do more than just provide the correct answer. These solutions explain the why and how behind each step, helping learners build intuition and avoid common mistakes. A good solution should have the following:

- A good solution should:
  - Break down the problem.
  - Reframe the question in simpler terms to clarify what is being asked.
  - Identify the relevant data and tools needed.
  - Explain each step.
  - Describe what each line of code or formula is doing.
  - Justify the use of a particular method or algorithm.
  - Highlight best practices.
  - Demonstrate clean, readable code.
  - Include comments and modular code organization.
  - Explain performance or accuracy trade-offs when applicable.
  - Include visual aids were helpful.
  - Plots, diagrams, or tables can clarify complex ideas or patterns in the data.
  - Suggest follow-up activities.
- Encourage learners to tweak parameters, try alternative methods, or apply the solution to a new dataset.

Example problem: Given a dataset of customer reviews, identify the top 5 most frequently used words after removing stop words.

Step-by-step solution is as follows:

1. **Load and inspect data**: Use pandas to read the dataset and inspect the review column.
2. **Text cleaning**: Convert text to lowercase, remove punctuation, and tokenize.
3. **Remove Stop words**: Use **Natural Language Toolkit** (**NLTK**) list of English stop words to filter common non-informative words.
4. **Count word frequencies**: Use Python's collections. Counter or `pandas.Series.value_counts()`.
5. **Display results**: Return or plot the top five most common words.

Each step includes the code, comments, and a brief explanation of why that step is necessary.

Building data science portfolio

In a competitive and rapidly evolving field like data science, demonstrating your skills is just as important as learning them. A well-crafted data science portfolio depicts your capabilities, showcasing your technical expertise, problem-solving skills, and ability to communicate insights effectively. Whether you are seeking your first job, transitioning careers, or aiming to grow professionally, a portfolio is an essential part of your personal brand.

Importance of portfolio

The importance of a portfolio is as follows:

- **Demonstrates practical skills**: Employers often value demonstrated ability over academic credentials alone. A portfolio proves that you can:
  - Work with real-world data
  - Build and evaluate machine learning models
  - Perform analysis and draw meaningful conclusions
  - Create effective visualizations and narratives
- **Replaces experience for beginners**: If you are new to the field or do not yet have professional data science experience, your portfolio becomes your most powerful asset. It shows what you can do even if you have not done it in a formal job setting.
- **Sets you apart**: Many candidates list technical skills on their resumes, but fewer show those skills in action. A well-documented portfolio helps you stand out by providing tangible proof of your knowledge and creativity.

- **Serves as a talking point**: During interviews, projects in your portfolio provide ready-made topics to discuss. They allow you to demonstrate your thought process, explain decisions, and reflect on what you learned.

Showcasing projects effectively

A strong portfolio is a professional showcase of the work you have done in the field of data science. Here are key practices to help you present your work effectively:

- **Select quality over quantity**: Include the projects that you have performed that demonstrate depth and skills. Choose projects that span different areas: EDA, ML, NLP, time-series, etc. Prefer real-world or end-to-end projects over narrowly scoped exercises.
- **Tell a story with each project**: Each project should follow the following clear narrative arc:
  - **Problem statement**: What problem are you solving, and why does it matter?
  - **Data source**: Where did the data come from? What are its limitations?
  - **Methodology**: What steps did you take to explore, clean, and analyze the data?
  - **Modeling and evaluation**: What models did you use, and how did they perform?
  - **Insights and conclusions**: What did you learn? What recommendations can you make?
- **Focus on reproducibility**:
  - Clean, well-commented code is essential.
  - Organize your files clearly (e.g., **`data/`**, **`notebooks/`**, **`README.md`**).
  - Include instructions to replicate results if possible.
- **Host your work online**:
  - Make your work easy to access and share through the following platforms:
    - **GitHub**: The most common platform for hosting code and documentation.
    - **Personal website or portfolio blog**: A custom site allows for greater flexibility and professional branding.
    - **Kaggle**: Great for notebooks and participation in competitions or datasets.
    - **Medium or Substack**: Writing articles about your projects can boost visibility and help recruiters understand your thinking.

- **Use visuals and interactivity**: Visuals and interactivity in data science projects can be added in the following ways:
    - o In order to make your work look visually appealing, include charts, graphs, and dashboards.
    - o Consider tools like *Plotly*, *Tableau*, or *Streamlit* for interactive applications.
    - o Add screenshots or GIFs in your `README` or portfolio page to quickly convey results.
- **Reflect and iterate**: For each project, reflect on what went well, what was challenging, and what you would improve. This shows self-awareness and a growth mindset, which employers are looking for.
    - o Additionally, we can keep our portfolio updated to complete new work.
    - o We can add context to personal or academic projects, e.g., frame them as solutions to business problems.

A compelling portfolio helps us understand why it matters and how to communicate its value. With every project, one not only builds technical skills but also crafts a narrative that defines who one is as a data scientist.

Presenting and communicating data science projects

One of the most overlooked yet critical skills in data science is the ability to effectively communicate your findings. No matter how sophisticated your models are, their value is lost if stakeholders cannot understand or act on the results. Data storytelling and visual communication bridge the gap between technical work and decision-making, making insights accessible, memorable, and actionable.

Data storytelling techniques

Data storytelling is the art of combining data, narrative, and visuals to convey a clear and compelling message. Rather than simply presenting statistics or model outputs, storytelling transforms raw results into a journey with context, relevance, and impact.

Key elements of effective data storytelling:

- Clear purpose and audience awareness.
- Tailor your message to the audience's level of technical understanding.
- Define the *so what?* Why should the audience care?
- Focus on the decision or action the analysis should inform.

Narrative structure: Just like a good story, your data presentation should have the following structure:

- **Beginning**: Introduce the problem or question.
- **Middle**: Describe the methods and key findings.
- **End**: Deliver conclusions and actionable recommendations.

Contextualization: The data science project presentation must include the following:

- Always connect data to real-world meaning.
- Use analogies or comparisons to help non-technical stakeholders understand metrics or trends.

Highlight key insights: While presenting a data science project, the following should be considered:

- Avoid overwhelming the audience with every detail.
- Emphasize the most important findings and explain why they matter.
- Use data to support the story, not the other way around.
- Start with a hypothesis or question, not just a dataset.

Visual communication best practices

Visuals are a powerful tool to clarify complex ideas, reveal patterns, and support arguments. Poor visual design can be confusing or misleading. Following visual communication best practices ensures that your charts and dashboards are both informative and impactful, as follows:

- **Choose the right chart type**: The following types of charts may be used for visualization:
    - **Bar charts**: Comparing quantities across categories.
    - **Line charts**: Showing trends over time.
    - **Scatter plots**: Identifying relationships between variables.
    - **Box plots**: Showing distribution and outliers.
    - **Heatmaps**: Visualizing correlations or intensity.
- **Simplify and focus**: We can perform simplification in the following ways:
    - **Avoid clutter**: Remove unnecessary gridlines, 3D effects, or excessive labels.
    - Use minimalism to direct attention to key points.
    - Highlight important data points using color or annotations.

- **Use color intentionally**: Color may be used in the following ways:
  - Use color to differentiate categories or emphasize key insights.
  - Be mindful of colorblind accessibility (use color palettes like *ColorBrewer* or tools like *Viridis*).
  - Avoid using too many colors in one chart.
- **Label clearly**: Labels should be defined as follows:
  - All axes, legends, and titles should be clear and self-explanatory.
  - Add short, descriptive titles that explain the message of the chart and not just what it shows.
- **Tell one story per visual**: Each visual should convey a single insight or answer a specific question. Avoid trying to show too much at once.
- **Create interactive visuals**: Tools like *Tableau, Power BI,* or *Plotly* allow for interactive dashboards. Interactivity enables users to explore the data themselves. It is ideal for presentations or executive summaries.

Resources for continued learning

Data science is a fast-evolving field, with new tools, techniques, and applications emerging regularly. To stay current and competitive, it is essential to embrace a mindset of lifelong learning. Whether you are a beginner or an experienced practitioner, there are abundant resources, such as books, courses, platforms, and communities, that can support your ongoing development.

Recommended books, courses, and online resources

Books provide structured, in-depth learning and are a great way to master both foundational concepts and advanced topics. Here are some highly recommended titles:

- *An Introduction to Statistical Learning by Gareth James et al.*
- Beginner-friendly with R code examples; covers statistical modeling and machine learning basics.
- *Hands-On Machine Learning with Scikit-Learn, Keras, and TensorFlow* by *Aurélien Géron.*
- A practical guide using Python, great for building real-world ML models.
- *Data Science for Business* by *Foster Provost* and *Tom Fawcett* focuses on data science concepts from a business perspective. It is ideal for non-technical readers and practitioners alike.

- *Python for Data Analysis* by *Wes McKinney*. Written by the creator of pandas, it is essential for data wrangling and EDA in Python.
- *Storytelling with Data* by *Cole Nussbaumer Knaflic* is a must-read for mastering visual communication and data storytelling.

Online courses and platforms: Online courses offer flexibility and hands-on experience. Many platforms provide beginner to advanced tracks in data science:

- **Coursera**:
  - **Popular courses**: *IBM Data Science Professional Certificate, Johns Hopkins Data Science Specialization, Deep LeaedX*
  - Offers *MicroMasters* programs in data science from institutions like *MIT* and *UC San Diego.*
- **Udemy**: Affordable courses with lifetime access. Good for practical skills like Python, SQL, and machine learning.
- **DataCamp**: Interactive coding exercises focused on Python, R, and data skills. Great for practice-heavy learning.
- **Kaggle Learn**: Free mini courses on practical topics (e.g., pandas, SQL, machine learning, deep learning).
- **fast.ai**: Practical deep learning courses that emphasize getting results quickly, ideal for applied ML enthusiasts.

Other valuable online resources:

- **ArXiv.org**: Stay up to date with the latest ML and AI research papers.
- **Towards data science (Medium)**: Blogs, tutorials, and case studies from data science practitioners.
- **YouTube channels**: They comprise clear explanations of complex statistical concepts.

Joining data science communities and networks

Learning in isolation cannot bring you great success. Engaging with communities and professional networks provides motivation, collaboration, and exposure to real-world trends.

Online communities and forums include the following:

- **Kaggle**: Participate in competitions, explore datasets, and discuss solutions with peers.
- **Reddit**: Subreddits like *r/datascience, r/learnmachinelearning,* and *r/MLQuestions* offer vibrant discussions and learning opportunities.

- **Stack Overflow and cross validated (StackExchange)**: You can ask and answer technical questions. It is invaluable for debugging and conceptual clarity.
- **Data science Slack and Discord groups**: Join topic-based channels for mentorship, project feedback, and networking.

Professional networks include the following:

- **LinkedIn**: Follow influential data scientists, join relevant groups, and share your own projects to build your personal brand.
- **Meetup.com**: Find and attend local data science meetups, workshops, or hackathons, many of which are also virtual.
- **AI and data science conferences**: Conferences like *NeurIPS, KDD, Strata Data,* and *PyData* are excellent for learning and networking.
- **Mentorship and collaboration**: Find a mentor through data science bootcamps, LinkedIn, or community forums. Collaborate on open-source projects to gain team experience and contribute to real-world tools.

Conclusion

This chapter bridges the gap between foundational knowledge and real-world application in data science. It emphasizes the importance of experiential learning through hands-on projects that simulate real-world problems, providing step-by-step guidance to help readers build practical skills. Guided exercises with detailed solutions reinforce key concepts and offer opportunities for self-assessment and improvement.

A strong data science portfolio is presented as a critical asset for aspiring professionals, with strategies for effectively showcasing projects to potential employers or collaborators. Readers are also introduced to the art of presenting and communicating data science results, including storytelling techniques and best practices in visual communication that make insights both impactful and accessible.

Finally, the chapter outlines essential resources for continued learning, from recommended books and online courses to professional communities and networks. These resources encourage lifelong learning and engagement in the evolving field of data science.

By the end of this chapter, readers will be efficient not only with practical experience and a growing portfolio but also with the tools to communicate their work and continue progressing in their data science journey

Exercises

1. Choose a public dataset and outline a complete data science workflow for analyzing it (from data collection to model deployment).
2. Perform EDA on a dataset of your choice. What patterns or anomalies did you discover?
3. Build a predictive model using a real-world dataset. What metrics will you use to evaluate its performance, and why?
4. Document the steps you took in a recent data science project. How would you improve your workflow in the future?
5. Given a dataset with missing values, what techniques can you use to handle them? Apply one method and explain your choice.
6. A dataset contains class imbalance (e.g., 95% negative, 5% positive). What strategies can you use to build a fair and accurate model?
7. Create a data visualization that tells a compelling story. What tools did you use, and how did you decide what to show?
8. You have a dataset with hundreds of features. Describe how you would perform feature selection and dimensionality reduction.
9. List three types of projects that would make your data science portfolio stand out. Why did you choose them?
10. How would you tailor your portfolio to apply for a data science role in healthcare vs. e-commerce?
11. What platforms can you use to showcase your portfolio? Compare at least two in terms of audience and visibility.
12. Choose a project you've completed. Rewrite the results section as if explaining it to a non-technical audience.
13. What are the key components of a good data story? Create a basic outline using a dataset of your choice.
14. Identify a poorly designed chart online. Redesign it using visual best practices and explain your choices.
15. How can you use color, typography, and layout to make your visualizations more effective and accessible?
16. Identify three active online data science communities. What value do they offer, and how can you participate?

Index

C

D

E

F

G

R

S

T

U

V

W